ALTERNATE
ROUTES TO
TEACHING

ALTERNATE
ROUTES TO
TEACHING

C. Emily Feistritzer

National Center for Education Information
National Center for Alternative Certification

Charlene K. Haar

PEARSON

Merrill
Prentice Hall

Upper Saddle River, New Jersey
Columbus, Ohio

Library of Congress Cataloging-in-Publication Data

Feistritzer, C. Emily.
  Alternate routes to teaching / C. Emily Feistritzer, Charlene K. Haar.
    p.   cm.
  Includes bibliographical references and index.
  ISBN-13: 978-0-13-175041-8 (pbk.)
  ISBN-10: 0-13-175041-0 (pbk.)
    1. Teachers—Training of—United States.   2. Career changes—United States.
3. Alternative education—United States.   I. Haar, Charlene K.   II. Title.
  LB1715.F386 2008
  370.71'1—dc22

                                                                    2007001265

Vice President and Executive Publisher: Jeffery W. Johnston
Senior Editor: Darcy Betts Prybella
Development Editor: Amy Nelson
Production Editor: Kris Roach
Production Coordination: Thistle Hill Publishing Services, LLC
Design Coordinator: Diane C. Lorenzo
Cover Designer: Jason Moore
Cover Image: SuperStock
Production Manager: Susan Hannahs
Director of Marketing: David Gesell
Marketing Coordinator: Brian Mounts

This book was set in New Baskerville by Integra Software Services. It was printed
and bound by R.R. Donnelley & Sons Company. The cover was printed by
R.R. Donnelley & Sons Company.

Pearson Education Ltd.   Pearson Education Australia Pty. Limited
Pearson Education Singapore Pte. Ltd.   Pearson Education North Asia Ltd.
Pearson Education Canada, Ltd.   Pearson Educación de Mexico, S.A. de C.V.
Pearson Education–Japan   Pearson Education Malaysia Pte. Ltd.

10 9 8 7 6 5 4 3 2 1
ISBN-13: 978-0-13-175041-8
ISBN-10:   0-13-175041-0

PREFACE

Teacher education has been the subject of countless books and articles, the majority of which have dealt with aspects of teacher preparation through undergraduate and graduate college programs. Such programs still play a role in teacher preparation; however, significant new developments have occurred within the last 25 years. For example, in Texas, the nontraditional routes to teaching surpassed the traditional college-based teacher preparation route in 2004–2005.

For the first time, this book brings together a broad picture of alternate routes: pathways to teaching that appeal to those from many walks of life who want to teach. In 2006, more than 50,000 individuals switched from successful careers or other ventures to teaching in classrooms across America. They accounted for one-third of all new teachers hired that year.

The good news about alternate routes is much more than just numbers, impressive as they are! People switching midcareer and others with a noneducation liberal arts degree bring expertise into K–12 classrooms where children's needs are the greatest, such as inner-city schools and rural areas; schools that need teachers of mathematics, the sciences, and foreign languages; and special education teachers who are benefiting from this new supply of teachers.

Alternate routes tap into the supply of potential teachers through sophisticated recruitment programs such as Teach For America, Troops to Teachers, Recruiting New Teachers, and The New Teacher Project. The activity and inquiries on the interactive website of teach-now.org is just one more piece of evidence of the widespread interest in teaching, once available only through institutions of higher education. These institutions now play an important collaborative role in teacher preparation through alternate routes, at the same time that state authorities approve faster, more efficient, less costly, and innovative alternate routes.

In addition to documenting how states are responding to the accountability and highly qualified teacher requirements of the *No Child Left Behind* act, this book traces the history and development of alternate routes, especially those exemplary routes through which thousands of new teachers are prepared each year. Children and parents are not likely to know where or how teachers are prepared; they are concerned about raising student achievement, however. So are we, and so are those teachers prepared through exemplary alternate routes as discussed throughout this book.

The Plan of This Book

Because each chapter begins with a question, the reader should know that the answer and answers to related questions are presented within each chapter.

Chapter 1. What Are Alternate Routes to Teacher Certification?
Chapter 2. How Did Alternate Routes Develop?
Chapter 3. How Did New National Programs and Federal Involvement Promote Alternate Route Participation?
Chapter 4. What Constitutes State Alternative Routes to Teacher Certification?
Chapter 5. How Do Providers Implement State Alternate Routes?
Chapter 6. Who Are Alternate Route Teachers?
Chapter 7. What Does the Research Say About Alternate Routes?
Chapter 8. Where Will Alternate Routes Go From Here?

Chapter 1 is an overview of alternate routes, including definitions of terms that are used throughout the book and an explanation of how responses to some ill-defined terms gave rise to alternate routes.

Chapter 2 includes brief historic highlights on how states replaced local school districts as teacher licensing agents. When *A Nation at Risk* (1983) shocked the country into looking at the condition of American education, critics held tight to the status quo because power and positions were at stake. Some state officials got creative by passing laws that permitted individuals to become licensed to teach. Although the development of the first alternate route generated considerable publicity and opposition, other alternate routes emerged slowly, even as university and college officials discussed possible changes to the traditional (college campus–based teacher preparation routes) ways of preparing teachers. Expansion of alternate routes provoked scrutiny from critics and proponents alike.

Critics no longer argue that alternate routes to teacher certification should be ignored or that they will disappear. The numbers are too telling. Even as most alternate routes now share many common characteristics, the states continue to authorize unique ways of meeting the demands, not only for teachers but also for qualified teachers in today's marketplace.

Chapter 3 explains how federal government programs and funds have impacted the development of alternate routes and alternate route programs. For example, in 1992, within the reauthorization of the Higher Education Act, Congress appropriated funds for teacher recruitment programs that resulted in the innovative Teach For America and Troops to Teachers programs. In subsequent reauthorizations, Congress targeted teacher quality issues, including quantifiable results from federal grants. States that accepted federal funds for the programs authorized through the Higher Education Act were expected to comply with disclosure requirements.

Compliance required accountability. Congress tightened accountability through reauthorization of the Elementary and Secondary Education Act, widely known as the *No Child Left Behind* act. At the same time, Congress again made available grant funds to states, funds that were to target improving the quality of teachers and to encourage the transitioning of adults in other careers into teaching. As alternate route options expanded, some common characteristics emerged.

Chapter 4 is a state-by-state look at alternate routes that now exist in all 50 states and the District of Columbia. Tables and graphs help the reader visualize the common and unique characteristics of alternate routes.

As the states with the oldest alternate routes, the routes in New Jersey, California, and Texas also produce the most teachers and are featured in the chapter. The development of routes has been steady, although states have approved most of the alternate routes since 2000.

Likewise, most of the growth of alternate route programs has occurred since 2000. Chapter 5 tells the story of this growth through tables and figures. Through an analysis of data template responses, the reader can visualize the characteristics of alternate route programs being implemented by various providers throughout the states and the District of Columbia.

Chapter 6 includes the profiles of alternate route teachers as compiled from survey results in 2004–2005 that the National Center for Education Information administered to teachers who had participated in an alternate route program between 1999 and 2004. Alternate route teachers tend to be more mature, more likely to be men, and to represent ethnic minorities more often than teachers prepared through traditional programs. Alternate route teachers teach subjects in geographical areas where the demand for teachers is greatest. The most important finding is that most would not have become teachers without the availability of an alternate route program that permitted them to earn while learning. Teachers prepared through alternate route programs report a high degree of satisfaction with the decision they made and the program they selected.

Chapter 7 includes a discussion and review of selected research studies that have reflected the condition of alternate routes from 1986 and some that are ongoing. In addition to looking closely at various components of alternate routes and alternate route programs, recent research has focused on specific training components that are particularly effective in raising student achievement. As research methodologies become more carefully designed, the findings will become more useful in training quality teachers—regardless of the route taken or where the training takes place.

Alternate routes to teacher certification is a success story with a turbulent past and a fascinating future, as discussed in Chapter 8. States are being prodded in part by federal requirements, some of which have brought about changes as reported by the states. With outcomes uncertain, the chapter details how the states intend to use alternative routes to meet their staffing needs as well as the highly qualified teacher provisions in the *No Child Left Behind* act.

To date, alternate routes have survived and even thrived. With continued innovations in teacher preparation, we expect that trend to continue.

ACKNOWLEDGMENTS

Part of the joy of writing a book as a culmination of a career in education is the opportunity to engage others in the project. We especially thank the reviewers of the manuscript for their careful consideration, thoughtful reactions, and helpful suggestions. They are Joan Baratz Snowden; Leo Klagholz; Michael J. Petrilli; and Michael J. Podgursky. As one who was not only there at the creation of the first widely publicized alternate route but involved in its implementation in New Jersey, Leo Klagholz provided exceptional insights into the history of alternate routes, for which we gratefully thank him. Joan Baratz Snowden did great and loyal work, paying particular attention to manuscript form as well as substance, and we thank her very much. Michael Podgursky knows the value of alternate routes through the experience of an economist, and his suggestions reflected that background. We appreciate his insights and thank him as well. Having recently come from a position with the U.S. Department of Education, Michael Petrilli provided useful assistance with both the manuscript content in general and specific details also; we appreciate his valuable help.

We received considerable assistance from Tom Snyder and William Hussar of the National Center for Education Statistics, and Mary Rollefson formerly with NCES. The importance of the data that NCES collects and maintains cannot be overestimated.

We'd also like to thank all of the state and local providers of alternate route programs for supplying data and information to NCEI over the years—you enabled the story of alternate routes to be told.

The success of a book is guided by the publisher, and we are extremely grateful for the enthusiastic support from officials at Pearson Education: Jeff Johnston, vice president and executive publisher of the Merrill/Prentice Hall imprint of Pearson; Debbie Stollenwerk, executive editor; Amy Nelson and Dan Richcreek, our development editors; and Kevin Johnson, without whom this book would not have been produced. Our thanks also to Angela Williams Urquhart and the staff at Thistle Hill Publishing Services. We could not have done this without all of you; sincere thanks from us to you.

We have made every attempt to reflect the development of alternate routes accurately and to document this growth through statistical evidence. Any shortcomings are our own.

C. Emily Feistritzer
Charlene K. Haar

BRIEF CONTENTS

Chapter 1   Introduction   1

Chapter 2   How Did Alternate Routes Develop?   27

Chapter 3   How Did New National Programs and Federal
Involvement Promote Alternate Route
Participation?   65

Chapter 4   What Constitutes State Alternative Routes to Teacher
Certification?   88

Chapter 5   How Do Providers Implement State Alternate
Routes?   109

Chapter 6   Who Are Alternate Route Teachers?   125

Chapter 7   What Does the Research Say About
Alternate Routes?   143

Chapter 8   Where Will Alternate Routes Go from Here?   152

Appendix   166

References   177

Index   185

CONTENTS

Chapter 1   Introduction   1

What Are Alternate Routes to Teacher
Certification?   2
Definitions   3
Alternate Routes and the National Center
for Education Information   3
Why Alternate Routes?   6
The Beginnings of Alternate Routes   6
Alternate Routes Respond to Market Demands   8
New Teacher Graduates   9
Are Bachelor Degree Recipients a Reliable Market for
Teachers?   9
What Happens to Education Degree
Graduates?   11
Alternate Routes Provide Market Efficiency   11
Teacher Demand   12
Projections of Teacher Shortages   12
Who Are "New Teachers"?   12
SASS Later Revised New Teacher Designations   13
The Alternate Route Market for Teaching   16
The Context for Alternate Routes: K–12 Education
in the United States   17
Profile of the U.S. Public K–12 Education System   18
Public School Districts   18
Public School Size and Student Enrollment   20
Public School Student Enrollment and Teachers   24
Distribution of Schools, Teachers, and Students   25
Teacher Vacancies (Demand)   26
The Role Alternate Routes Play   26

Chapter 2   How Did Alternate Routes Develop?   27

Historical Highlights of Teacher Certification   27
From Ecclesiastical to Civil Authority   27
State-Approved Teacher Education Programs   28

The Nation Reacts   29
Expansion of the Role of the Federal
Government   29
National Commission on Excellence in
Education   32

New Jersey Begins the Debate About Alternative
Routes   35
Redefining the Traditional College-Based
Route   36
Emergence of an "Alternate Route"   36
Selling the Alternate Route Concept   37
New Jersey Launches the Provisional Teacher
Program   38

California Authorizes Alternate Route   40

Texas Approves Alternate Route   41

Alternate Routes Provoke Scrutiny   43
Haberman Justifies Support for Alternate
Routes   43
Groups Call for Changes in Traditional Teacher
Preparation Programs   45
Connecticut Designed Its Alternate Route to
Upgrade the Profession   53
Alternate Routes Respond to Market
Needs   54
Some Critics Hoped Alternate Routes Would
Disappear Quickly   55
Proponent Credits Alternate Routes as
a Bold Plan   56
Alternative Certification: An Effort to Deregulate
Teacher Preparation   57

Variations Were Characteristic as Alternate Routes
Showed Steady Growth   58
Variations Occurred at All Levels   58

The NCEI Sorts Out Alternate Route Data   61
NCEI Produces a State-by-State Analysis
of Alternate Routes   61
NCEI Develops a Classification System for
Alternate Route   62

Chapter 3 How Did New National Programs and Federal Involvement Promote Alternate Route Participation? 65

New National Programs Boost Alternate Route Participation 65
    Teach For America 65
    Troops to Teachers 67

The Federal Government Boosts Alternate Routes 69

Congress Adds Disclosure Requirements to 1998 Reauthorization of HEA 70
    Title II: Teacher Quality 71
    New Report Card Data Requirements 72
    AACTE Responds to Disclosure Requirements 73

Teacher Quality Issues Include K–12 Education 74
    Congress Probes Teacher Quality Issues 74

Congress Reauthorizes *No Child Left Behind* Act 76
    Title I: New Teacher Quality Requirements 76
    Title II: Improving Teacher Quality 77

U.S. Secretary of Education Issues Annual Reports on Teacher Quality 80
    State Barriers Discourage Career Switchers 80
    Education Secretary Highlights Innovative Alternative Routes 80
    Secretary Commits Support for Alternate Routes 81
    Secretary Reports Dominance of Five States 82
    Secretary Offers a Clarification 83

Groups Weigh in on Teacher Preparation 84
    The Teacher Unions Set Criteria for Alternate Routes 84

Alternate Routes Today 85
    Newest Routes Have Unique Characteristics 85
    Most Routes Now Share Common Characteristics 87

Chapter 4 What Constitutes State Alternative Routes to Teacher Certification? 88

Alternative Routes, State by State 88
    State Alternate Routes Differ 89
    Regional Differences 92

Lessons Learned from Successful Alternate Routes 95

Profiles of Selected State Alternate Routes 95
    New Jersey 95
    California 98

Texas   102
Florida   103
New York   105
Kentucky   106

**Chapter 5   How Do Providers Implement State Alternate
Routes?   109**
Diverse Alternate Routes Require Flexible
Providers   109
State-Approved Providers Vary from State
to State   109
Providers Report to NCAC Through a Data
Template   110
Analyses of Selected NCAC Data Template Responses
from Alternate Route Program Providers   113
Analysis of Program Provider Data   113
Who Administers the Alternate Route Program?   114
Requirements and Program Features   114
The Bottom Line   124

Chapter 6   Who Are Alternate Route Teachers?   125
Profile of Alternate Route Teachers   125
NCEI Conducted a National Survey of Alternate
Route Teachers   126
Findings from *Profile of Alternate Route
Teachers*   127
Why Do Participants Choose an Alternate Route
Program?   131

**Chapter 7   What Does the Research Say About Alternate
Routes?   143**
Different Studies Yield Similar Results   143
Compilations of Research on Alternate Routes   144
AERA Conclusions Were Similar to Others'
Findings   147
SRI Finds Variations Within Training Pathways
and Importance of School Context   148
Two Significant Studies of Alternate Routes
Are Ongoing   148
Sharing Research   151
National Association for Alternative
Certification   151
National Center for Alternative Certification   151

Chapter 8 Where Will Alternate Routes Go from Here? 152

    Why Alternative Routes Work   152

    Going Forward   153

    Looking Ahead at Alternate Routes   154
        Federal Requirements for Highly Qualified Teachers
        Could Play a Significant Role   154
        Role of Community Colleges   162
        Reciprocity Issues   163
        Potential Teachers   164

    Conclusions   164

  Appendix   166

  References   177

  Index   185

Note: Every effort has been made to provide accurate and current Internet information in this book. However, the Internet and information on it are constantly changing, so it is inevitable that some of the Internet addresses listed in this textbook will change.

1

Introduction

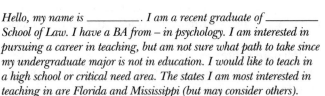

Hello, my name is _____. I am a recent graduate of _____
School of Law. I have a BA from – in psychology. I am interested in
pursuing a career in teaching, but am not sure what path to take since
my undergraduate major is not in education. I would like to teach in
a high school or critical need area. The states I am most interested in
teaching in are Florida and Mississippi (but may consider others).
If you could contact me with any information you may have to lead
me into the right path I would greatly appreciate it.
>   (E-mail received by the National Center for Alternative
>   Certification [NCAC], September 7, 2006)

Hello, I reside in [a large city with high demand for teachers]. . . .
I hold a 4-year bachelor's degree in industrial engineering. I am
considering a career in teaching math, but I was wondering if
there is a way to get certified or at least complete a portion of the
requirements before actually working in a classroom.
>   *Is there such a program?*
>   *Thanks for any information.*
>   (E-mail received by NCAC, September 15, 2006)

Hello, I am a man in my forties with three children. I have
a teaching certificate and cannot find a job. So much for a teacher
shortage. I am willing to move anywhere in the country to teach.
Can you help me find an alternate route in an area that needs
teachers?
>   (Phone call to NCAC, September 7, 2006)

Alternate routes to teaching target meeting the needs of thousands of such individuals who want to teach. Alternate routes are having a profound impact on the teaching profession, including changing who enters teaching, what individuals have to do to become a teacher, when they enter teaching, where they teach, and how they obtain certification to teach.

Individuals interested in becoming teachers, as well as educational leaders, researchers, and others, ask numerous questions such as these about alternative routes to teacher certification:

- What are alternative routes?
- How are they different from traditional routes?
- Is the teaching certificate that individuals who go through alternate routes get as good as, better than, or the same as the teaching certificate that individuals who go through college teacher education program routes get?
- Why do alternate routes exist?
- Why have the states created so many different routes to teacher certification?
- Who gets certified through alternative routes?
- Are individuals who enter teaching through alternate routes different from those who go through a traditional college teacher education program route?
- How have alternate routes responded to these demands:
  - Teachers in critical subject areas or specific shortage areas, such as inner cities?
  - Highly qualified teachers in every classroom in America?
  - Ensuring that prospective teachers have the knowledge and skills to be effective teachers?

This book answers these—and many other—questions pertaining to alternative pathways to teaching.

What Are Alternate Routes to Teacher Certification?

Alternate routes to teacher certification provide opportunities for school districts to hire talented individuals to teach who have subject-matter competency but who may not have studied education in college. In turn, schools provide these teachers with on-the-job training, mentoring, and support leading to certification.

Note that many seemingly different terms referring to *alternative routes*, in fact, mean the same thing. For example, numerous acronyms, such as

ATC, ACP, ARP, ARTC, ARC, AC, and AR, are used in the lexicon of alternative teacher certification. Regardless of the terminology or acronym, "alternative _____"—in the context of teacher certification—refers to creations by state licensing agencies that are alternatives to the traditional college, campus-based undergraduate teacher education program route culminating in a certificate (license) to teach. The most accurate term to describe what is now going on at the state level is "alternative *routes* to teacher certification."[1] These alternative routes are designed for individuals who already have at least a bachelor's degree—many of whom have experience in other careers—who want to teach the subjects in areas where there is a demand for teachers.

In 2006, all 50 states and the District of Columbia provided such alternative routes to teacher certification. These state certification routes are being implemented in approximately 485 program sites within the states, most accurately called "alternative teacher certification *programs*."

Definitions

Throughout this book, the terms *alternative* and *alternate* are used interchangeably, and distinctions are consistently made between route (the state's guidelines) and programs (the implementation of the routes by state-approved providers within the state). Some states call their initial authorization to teach a *license;* others call it a *certificate*. To date, each state is the only entity that can issue licenses or certificates to teach or grant licensing authority in the state in which one teaches. And, to teach in public schools in the United States, one has to have a license to teach in the state in which one is teaching. In this book, *license* and *certificate* are used interchangeably.

Alternate Routes and the National Center for Education Information

The National Center for Education Information (NCEI) has been tracking the alternative route to teacher certification movement since it began in New Jersey in 1983. C. Emily Feistritzer, principal author of this book, founded NCEI in 1979 to publish and furnish accurate, unbiased information on education. Since that time, NCEI has published 35 data-based

---

[1] The earlier and still frequently used term, *alternative teacher certification,* implied that individuals getting certified through alternative routes were issued an "alternative certificate" to the regular certificate individuals who go through traditional programs obtained. In most states, that is not the case. Completers of alternative routes are usually issued the same initial teaching certificate that completers of college-approved programs receive.

reports on education, most focused on teachers and teacher preparation and certification. Since 1990, NCEI has published annually *Alternative Teacher Certification: A State-by-State Analysis,* a compendium of data and information about alternate routes in each state. In 2003, with an unsolicited discretionary grant award from the U.S. Department of Education, NCEI established the National Center for Alternative Certification, a clearinghouse of data and information about alternative routes, which can be found at www.teach-now.org. Much of the data and information about alternate routes in *this* book builds on the studies and analyses of NCEI in this field.

NCEI Documents Proliferation of State Alternate Routes. When NCEI first began surveying states regarding alternative routes to teacher certification in 1983, eight states reported they had some type of alternative to the traditional college-based teacher education program route to teacher certification. By 2006, every state and the District of Columbia reported that it had at least one alternative route to certification for teachers. Additionally, many states have created multiple alternative routes to teacher certification (see Figure 1.1).

Figure 1.1   Number of Alternative Routes to Teacher Certification in Each State (2006)

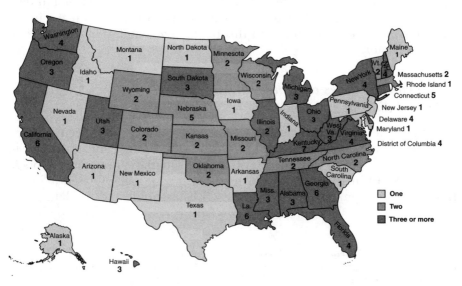

Source: Basic data submitted by state alternate route officials to the National Center for Education Information, 2006.

Alternate Route Programs Multiply. Not only have the number of state-established alternative *routes* to certification grown, the number of programs within states that implement these routes grew from 12 programs in 1983 to an estimated 485 alternate route *programs* throughout the country in 2006.

Participants in Alternate Route Programs Increase Dramatically. The number of individuals entering teaching through alternative routes rose from an estimated 285 in 1985 to about 50,000 in 2006. As shown in Figure 1.2, the increase in numbers of individuals in alternate route programs has been most dramatic since the late 1990s.

Figure 1.2 Number of Individuals Issued Teaching Certificates Through Alternate Routes (1985–2005)

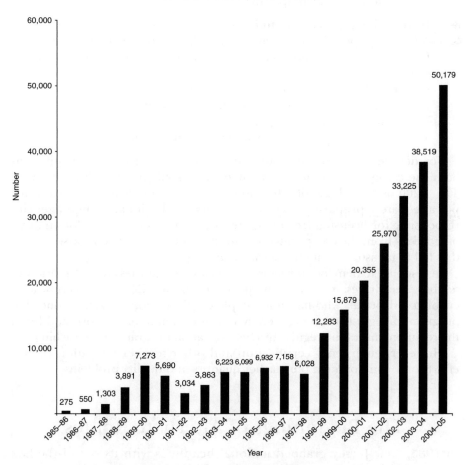

Source: National Center for Education Information, *Alternative Teacher Certification: A State-by-State Analysis 2006.*

In some states, alternative teacher certification programs produced 40% of new teachers hired in 2006. Data collected by NCEI indicate that as many as a third of the approximately 150,000 new teachers hired in 2006 came though alternative routes to teacher certification.

Why Alternate Routes?

Since the mid-1960s, reforming teacher education and certification has been the focus of solving both teacher quantity and quality issues. Having enough qualified teachers has been at the root of reform efforts concerning teachers.

Issues driving these reforms center around shortages of qualified teachers based on the following assumptions:

- Increased enrollments of students
- An aging population of teachers who will be retiring at faster rates
- High percentage of new teachers who leave within the first 3 years of teaching
- Undergraduates who train to teach and never do
- Increase in numbers of students with special needs
- Increasing diversity in the population
- Teachers teaching courses for which they are not qualified

For decades, teacher education and certification have been identified as both the cause and solution of many of the problems regarding teachers. The 1,200 or so colleges of education have taken the brunt of criticism for not adequately preparing qualified teachers. Additionally, state agencies responsible for licensing (certifying) teachers have been targets for an array of attacks—from the complicated certification processes to weak assessments that fail to measure competencies for teaching.

In response to demands for more teachers, state agencies created a variety of teaching certificates, including emergency certificates. Emergency certification enabled individuals who had not completed a traditional teacher education program to begin teaching (generally with no training or support) and finish the requirements of the regular teacher education program while teaching.

However, emergency certification and other teacher education reform efforts only compounded the teacher quantity and quality problems.

The Beginnings of Alternate Routes

In 1983, New Jersey grabbed national headlines with its out-of-the-box solution to the teacher quality problem. The state created an alternative route to teacher certification specifically to attract a new market for teaching—liberal arts graduates—and transition them into elementary and secondary teaching without going through a traditional college teacher education program. This solution to teacher quantity and quality demands began the alternative teacher certification movement, and the nation took notice.

The mid-1980s also brought a rash of news-breaking stories of projected huge shortages of teachers. The nation was going to need to hire 1 million, then 2 million, then 2.2 million *new* teachers "in the next decade." Legislators and policymakers charged forward to find ways to get more people into teaching. Some saw alternative routes to teacher certification as a solution to upcoming teacher shortages.

Licensing officials in some states were not enthusiastic about creating new routes to certification. So some state education licensing agencies began calling any and every certificate they had been issuing to people who had not completed the traditional college-approved teacher education program route "alternative teacher certification."

The term *alternative teacher certification* was used until the early 1990s to refer to a variety of ways to become licensed to teach. For those who wanted to become teachers, these ways included emergency certification as well as very sophisticated and well-designed programs for individuals who already had at least a bachelor's degree and considerable life experience.

Significant changes in alternative routes to teacher certification have occurred since the mid-1990s. As state licensing agencies became aware of each other's activities in the area of alternate routes and saw how their own state's "alternative" routes were being categorized, states made many changes:

- No state any longer calls its emergency certificates *alternative teaching certificates*.
- Most alternative routes to teacher certification established since 1995 have been created for the explicit purpose of attracting persons who already have at least a bachelor's degree and want to teach.
- The variation in alternate routes is largely attributable to who ultimately administers the program (e.g., college-administered programs generally require a lot more education coursework than do programs administered by school districts).
- Most states now issue the same initial teaching certificate to completers of their alternative routes as they issue to completers of traditional college teacher education programs.

In addition to the development of alternative routes at the state level, an evolving consensus of essential characteristics shows that most alternate routes share these characteristics:

- Designed specifically to recruit, prepare, and license individuals who already have at least a bachelor's degree—and often other careers

- Require rigorous screening processes, such as passing tests, interviews, and demonstrated mastery of subject matter content
- Provide on-the-job training
- Include coursework or equivalent experiences in professional education studies before and while teaching
- Involve work with mentor teachers and/or other support personnel
- Set high performance standards for completion of the programs

In 2004, the U.S. Department of Education highlighted six exemplary alternative route programs with these essential characteristics. "Innovations in Education: Alternative Routes to Teacher Certification" shared how these program elements have become part of the successful programs and offered suggestions and helpful guidance to others about the value of the "promising practices" (USDoE, 2004b, p. 6).

Alternate Routes Respond to Market Demands

A fundamental strength of alternate routes is their very raison d'être, which is to respond to market demands, including meeting the demands for these professionals:

- New teachers to replace teachers leaving the profession
- Qualified teachers in high-demand locations such as in inner cities and in subjects such as mathematics, the sciences, and special education
- Highly qualified teachers in every classroom in the nation as required by the federal *No Child Left Behind* act

There are growing numbers of alternative routes and alternate route programs. The fastest growing segment of alternate route programs are ones administered by institutions of higher education, but these programs are not your mother's teacher education program. Variations in the delivery range from college master of arts in teaching (MAT) programs to test-only options to teacher certification.

Alternative routes are just that—alternative routes. There is no one route, no one way, no best way. Alternative routes to teacher certification opened the floodgates, as it were, to a grand experiment in redefining the who, what, when, where, and how of becoming a teacher.

Alternate routes offer efficient and cost-effective means of producing the teachers the nation needs. What is often overlooked is that the success of alternate routes is attributable to their being responsive to the needs of different populations of individuals who are now choosing to teach, such as career changers and other experienced adults. Alternate route programs are created to recruit, train, and certify such individuals to teach where the demands for teachers are greatest.

Historically, the United States had relied almost exclusively on high school students going to college, majoring in education, and completing an undergraduate college teacher education program for its supply of new teachers (USDoE, 1993, p. 1). In fact, when the recruiting service called Recruiting New Teachers began in 1986, it was called Recruiting *Young* Teachers. Heavily funded with foundation and Ad Council support, a major advertising blitz was focused on getting high school students to go to college and become teachers (Dougherty, 1988, p. 1).

This population of prospective teachers also served as the source for making judgments about the quality of America's teachers. Beginning in the 1960s, Scholastic Aptitude Test (SAT) scores of high school students who indicated that they might major in education when they got to college were often cited as an indication of the poor quality of the teaching force (Ravitch, 1985, p. 90). While the undergraduate market still produces the majority of new teachers, data show this is changing.

New Teacher Graduates

Are Bachelor Degree Recipients a Reliable Market for Teachers?

Getting clarity about college graduates who are qualified to teach upon receiving their bachelor's degree and who go into teaching, as well as those who do not, is not easy.

The U.S. Department of Education's *Baccalaureate and Beyond Longitudinal Studies* tracks bachelor's degree recipients and are often cited for these data that are based on samples, so NCES does not report these findings in numbers of individuals but rather in percentages. As shown in Table 1.1 from *Baccalaureate and Beyond Longitudinal Studies,* 12.2% of baccalaureate degree recipients in 1999–2000 had taught as regular teachers "in a K–12 school at some point between receiving the 1999–2000 bachelor's degree and the 2001 interview" (USDoE, 2000/01, p. 5). Data from the NCES in its *Integrated Postsecondary Education Data System, "Completions Survey"* (IPEDS-C) show that degree-granting institutions conferred 1,237,875 bachelor's degrees in 1999–2000; furthermore, these data show that 108,034 of these bachelor's degrees were education degrees (USDoE, 2004a *Digest 2004,* Table 250).

Table 1.1 Percentage Distribution of 1992–1993 and 1999–2000 Bachelor's Degree Recipients by K–12 Teaching Status, by Selected Undergraduate Academic Characteristics (1994 and 2001)

Selected characteristics	Total	Taught					Had not taught	
		Total	Certified	Prepared, but not certified	Neither certified nor prepared	Total or	Certified prepared	Neither certified nor prepared
1994								
Total	10.1	6.5		1.1	2.4	89.9	4.9	85.0
Undergraduate field of study								
Business and management	1.7	0.4		#	1.3	98.3	0.7	97.6
Education	47.5	37.8		6.5	3.3	52.5	24.0	28.6
Humanities	10.8	4.7		1.1	5.1	89.2	4.3	84.9
Mathematics, computer science, natural sciences	6.2	3.2		0.9	2.1	93.8	2.1	91.7
Social sciences	4.5	1.6		0.2	2.8	95.5	2.9	92.7
Other	2.8	0.8		0.1	1.9	97.2	2.1	95.1
2001								
Total	12.2	8.5		1.2	2.6	87.8	2.9	84.9
Undergraduate field of study								
Business and management	1.2	0.6		0.1	0.6	98.8	0.8	98.0
Education	66.5	56.4		5.9	4.2	33.5	13.0	20.5
Humanities	16.8	9.8		2.0	5.1	83.2	2.9	80.3
Mathematics, computer science, natural sciences	5.5	3.3		0.6	1.7	94.5	1.8	92.7
Social science	9.1	4.7		0.6	3.8	90.9	2.6	88.3
Other	4.4	2.5		0.4	1.5	95.6	1.9	93.7

Rounds to zero.

10

Given that NCES data show that 1,237,875 bachelor's degrees were awarded by degree-granting insititutions in 1999–2000, one could estimate that 151,000 new graduates were teaching *at some point* within a year of receiving their baccalaureate degree.

Also, using the percentages shown in Table 1.1 for 2001, one could estimate that, of the 151,000 who received a bachelor's degree in 1999–2000 and were teaching in 2001, 21% were neither certified nor had prepared to teach as part of their undergraduate program (2.6% of BA recipients = 32,185). It is conceivable that some of these individuals were becoming certified to teach through alternate route programs. Further more, of the BA recipients who *were* certified and/or had prepared to teach as part of their undergraduate program, 23% were not teaching within a year of graduating.

Table 1.1 also shows statistics for 1992–1993 bachelor's degree recipients—within 1 year, 10.1% were teaching. Furthermore, a follow-up survey in 1997 of 1992–1993 baccalaureate degree recipients indicated that 13% of those graduates had taught by 1997. However, the B&B follow-up report also stated that "8 percent expected to teach full-time in three years and 7 percent expected to teach in the longer term. Thus, it appears that many graduates who teach soon after college do not expect to spend much time teaching, let alone make it a career" (USDoE, 2000, p. x).

What Happens to Education Degree Graduates?

More than a third (35%) of education bachelor's degree recipients in 1999–2000 were not teaching the following year. Furthermore, the data indicate that a fourth (25%) of education bachelor's degree recipients in 1999–2000 had not even prepared to teach and/or were not certified to teach. Fewer than half (47.5 %) of graduates with education degrees in 1992–1993 were teaching in 1994. So much for using college undergraduate education degree recipients to predict the supply of new teachers.

Alternate Routes Provide Market Efficiency

Alternative routes to teacher certification programs, in contrast, accept only individuals who not only already have a bachelor's degree but come into a program because *they want to teach*. In most alternate route programs, the participants fill particular existing teacher vacancies.

Alternative routes exist to recruit, train, and certify baccalaureate degree holders to meet the demand for specific teachers to teach specific subjects at specific grade levels in specific schools.

Teacher Demand

To see better how alternate routes to teaching fit into the whole picture of K–12 education, it is critical to understand the teacher demand and supply issue over time as well. Considerable concerns about projected dire shortages of teachers in the United States marked much of the discussion and many decisions concerning teachers from the mid-1980s well into the 1990s. The national shortages never materialized. This is not to say that the demand to fill teacher vacancies with qualified teachers was not a serious problem in some areas in some states. But it is important to put teacher supply and demand in perspective. Clarifying what "new hires to teaching" actually meant changed the discussions about teacher shortages and provided a more accurate base on which to make realistic decisions about teacher demand.

Projections of Teacher Shortages

From the early 1980s through the 1990s, much publicity was generated around projections that the nation would have to hire more than 2 million new teachers "in the next decade"—or, put another way, 200,000 to 210,000 new teachers per year would need to be hired to meet demand. Based on NCES supply and demand estimates as discussed in *The Making of a Teacher: A Report on Teacher Education and Certification*, data also showed that by 1992–1993, the supply of new teacher graduates would meet only two thirds of the demand for new teachers (Feistritzer, 1984, p. 7).

Such reports resulted in a Chicken Little "the sky is falling" phenomenon that encompassed the highest levels of federal government to the smallest schools across America. By the mid-1990s, the U.S. Department of Education had clarified the matter by defining what it meant by "new teachers."

Who Are "New Teachers"?

It was not until Mary Rollefson and others at NCES analyzed NCES data concerning who new teachers were that the true picture of teacher demand emerged.

In *Teacher Supply in the United States: Sources of Newly Hired Teachers in Public and Private Schools*, published in 1993, Rollefson stated, "The supply model (of past projections of teacher supply and demand by the NCES, 1985) was designed to project the numbers of *new teacher graduates* [emphasis added], and did not account for other possible sources of teacher supply" (USDoE, 1993, p. 1).

The report went on to state,

Even in the 1960s, when 67 percent of new teacher hires were new teacher graduates (as reported in NEA, 1987), this model did not fully account for teacher supply sources, and by the 1970s and 1980s when enrollments in teacher education programs had declined, shrinking that supply source to 17 percent of new hires (as reported in NEA, 1987), it was clearly inadequate. (USDoE, 1993, p. 1)

NCES stopped making its projections of teacher supply based on the assumptions of teacher graduates and created a new survey, the *Schools and Staffing Survey (SASS)*, "to provide better measures of teacher supply and demand conditions" (USDoE, 1993, p. 2).

The First *SASS* Defines New Teachers.   An analysis of the first *SASS* results in 1987–1988 showed that only about 27% of "new teachers" hired at the *school building level* were "newly minted" college graduates "which the nation has traditionally depended upon to meet the demand for new teachers" (USDoE, 1993, p. iii).

The primary source of new hires turned out to be former teachers—41% in public schools. Teachers who transferred from another school or from a private school or from another state accounted for 19% of new hires. Delayed entrants were defined as "first-year teachers, who, rather than coming straight from college into teaching, engaged in other activities between completion of their degrees and their first teaching jobs" (p. iii). This "older . . . and more diverse" group accounted for 14% of newly hired teachers in 1987–1988. Rollefson further noted differences between the two sources of first-time teachers hired: "If we hold to the standard of a major or minor with certification to qualify to teach, the data suggested that many [of delayed entrants] may benefit from alternative teacher training programs" (1993, p. 25).

SASS Later Revised New Teacher Designations

Rollefson and Broughman at the NCES continued these analyses through the 1993–1994 *SASS* and made further revisions in the definitions of newly hired teachers. New teachers were then defined by the following two categories and four types:

1. *First-time teachers* were either *newly prepared teachers* who were attending college or had earned their highest degree in the previous year or *delayed entrants* who had engaged in other activities in the year or years between graduating from college or receiving their highest degree and becoming teachers (USDoE, 1995, p. 2).
2. *Experienced teachers* who had been teaching in another school the year before (*transfers*) or teachers who had not been teaching in an elementary or secondary school the year before, but who had taught in the past (*re-entrants*) (USDoE, 1995, p. 2).

Counting all of the types of these "newly hired teachers" at the *public school building level* in 1993–1994, the nation did indeed hire more than 200,000 "new" teachers, as projected. In fact, it hired 381,000 in 1993–1994. However, only 140,000 of them were first-time teachers; of those, 80,000 were new graduates (at either the undergraduate or graduate level). At the school building level, the nation had been hiring 200,000 "new to school building level" teachers for decades.

Sources of Teacher Supply Redefined.   In preparation for writing this book, the authors requested from the NCES a special analysis (from *SASS* data) of who was teaching in K–12 schools across the nation by sources of teachers.

Continuing Teachers.   Table 1.2 shows that the bulk of teachers hired every year were continuing teachers (86%, 86%, 87%, 83%, and 84% of all teachers hired) from selected years of *SASS* data, including data from 2003–2004, the latest year for which *SASS* data are available.

Transfers at the Start of the Year.   After accounting for continuing teachers, the next highest source of "new hires" at the school building level are teachers transferring from one school to another, one district to another, one state to another, from private schools, to public schools or from public schools to private schools, or from colleges to K–12 teaching, as shown in Figure 1.3.

New Entrants.   The next category, representing from 5% to 8% of the total teacher workforce, of new hires is "new entrants"—teachers in the survey year who were not teaching the year before the survey was conducted. This group includes recent graduates, delayed entrants, and returning teachers.

The number of new entrants to teaching increased 65% in the decade between 1993–1994 and 2003–2004. Figures 1.3 and 1.4 show, however, that most of this growth is due to reentering or returning teachers.

Recent Graduates Who Teach.   As shown in Table 1.2 and Figures 1.3 and 1.4, the number of individuals who were hired to teach just having graduated from a college or university at the undergraduate or graduate level (45,000 in 1987–1988 to 85,000 in 2003–2004) is much smaller than the 200,000 projected figure for "new teachers" needed and constitutes only 2% to 3% of all teachers hired in each of those years.

Delayed Entrants to Teaching.   The other category of new, never taught before, first-time teachers—called "delayed entrants" in Table 1.2 and Figures 1.3 and 1.4—are individuals who had been doing something else

Table 1.2 *Number and Percentage Distribution of Public and Private K–12 Teachers by Their Workforce Categories and Employment Background: 1987–1988, 1990–1991, 1993–1994, 1999–2000, and 2003–2004*

Workforce categories and employment background	1987–1988 Number	%	1990–1991 Number	%	1993–1994 Number	%	1999–2000 Number	%	2003–2004 Number	%
Total workforce at the start of the year	**2,630,000**	**100**	**2,916,000**	**100**	**2,940,000**	**100**	**3,451,000**	**100**	**3,718,000**	**100**
Continuing teachers	2,261,000	86	2,518,000	86	2,558,000	87	2,874,000	83	3,106,000	84
New hires	370,000	14	398,000	14	381,000	13	577,000	17	612,000	16
Transfers at the start of the year	229,000	9	227,000	8	196,000	7	294,000	9	306,000	8
New entrants	141,000	5	171,000	6	185,000	6	283,000	8	305,000	8
Returning teachers	61,000	2	49,000	2	46,000	2	130,000	4	155,000	4
Delayed entrants	35,000	1	51,000	2	60,000	2	67,000	2	64,000	2
Recent graduates	45,000	2	71,000	2	80,000	3	86,000	3	85,000	2

Note: All numbers are estimates with confidence intervals varying from ± 2,200 to ± 72,000. Detail may not sum to totals because of rounding.

Source: U.S. Department of Education, National Center for Education Statistics, Schools and Staffing Survey (SASS), "Public Teacher Questionnaire" and "Private Teacher Questionnaire," 1987–1988; "Public Teacher Questionnaire" and "Private Teacher Questionnaire," 1990–1991; "Public Teacher Questionnaire" and "Private Teacher Questionnaire," 1993–1994; "Public Teacher Questionnaire," "Charter Teacher Questionnaire," and "Private Teacher Questionnaire," 1999–2000; "Public Teacher Questionnaire," and "Private Teacher Questionnaire," 2003–2004.

Figure 1.3   Percentage of K–12 Teachers Hired, by Source, by Year

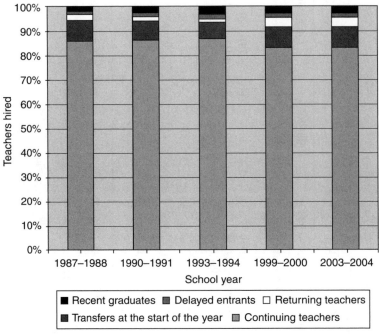

Source: Based on data from U.S. Department of Education, National Center for Education Statistics, "Public Teacher Questionnaire" and "Private Teacher Questionnaire," 1987–1988, 1990–1991, 1993–1994, 1999–2000, and 2003–2004.

other than teaching and/or going to school and obtaining a degree before being hired to teach. That group is slightly smaller than the recent graduates and constitutes about 2% of all teachers in each of the five *SASS* school years.

The Alternate Route Market for Teaching

The "delayed entrants" category of new teachers is most likely being served by alternative routes to teacher certification. These are individuals who, for a variety of reasons, got a baccalaureate or higher degree, then chose to engage in activities or jobs not related to teaching for varying lengths of time, and then decided to teach. Most of this population had no preparation to teach prior to the decision to become a teacher. Most alternate route programs are designed to attract this population of potential teachers.

Another likely alternate route participant group of "new entrants" to teaching are the "returning teachers." Many of these individuals need to upgrade their credentials, and alternate routes are satisfying that need.

*Figure 1.4   Number of New Entrants to Teaching at K–12 Schools,
by Source, by year*

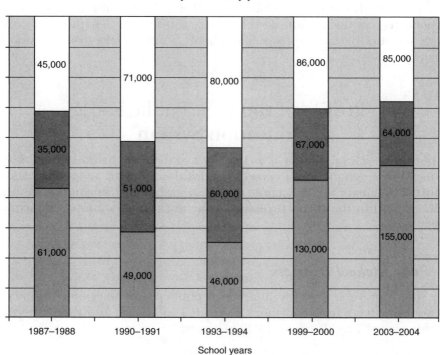

School years

☐ Recent graduates   ■ Delayed entrants   ■ Returning teachers

Source: Based on data from U.S. Department of Education, National Center for Education
Statistics, "Public Teacher Questionnaire" and "Private Teacher Questionnaire," 1987–1988,
1990–1991, 1993–1994, 1999–2000, and 2003–2004.

The Context for Alternate Routes:
K–12 Education in the United States

To understand better how alternative routes to teaching evolved and
why they have become so important in American education requires
knowledge of how education is structured in the United States. This section is devoted exclusively to this topic. All of the statistics used are from
the U.S. Department of Education's National Center for Education
Statistics (NCES).

NCES data show that an estimated 3.7 million teachers taught 54.7 million
elementary and secondary students in public and private schools across the

nation in the fall of 2005. Of total enrollment, 6.3 million students were in private schools, and of the total number of teachers, 400,000 taught in private schools (USDoE, 2005b, *Digest,* Table 1). Because not all private schools require that their teachers be state certified, this chapter deals only with statistics pertaining to public schools, where teacher certification is mandatory.

Profile of the U.S. Public K–12 Education System

The public school system is primarily a state responsibility. The state education agency (SEA) oversees the local education agencies (LEAs), most of which are regular school districts that have direct control over the schools within the district, including hiring teachers and other school personnel.

Public School Districts

As shown in Table 1.3, the number of public elementary and secondary school districts varies enormously—from 1 in Hawaii and the District of Columbia to 67 in Florida to 1,040 in Texas.

Table 1.3 Number of Regular Public Elementary and Secondary School Districts, by State (2003–2004)

	Regular school districts, including supervisory union components
United States	**14,383**
Alabama	130
Alaska	53
Arizona	313
Arkansas	309
California	989
Colorado	178
Connecticut	166
Delaware	19

District of Columbia	1
Florida	67
Georgia	180
Hawaii	1
Idaho	114
Illinois	887
Indiana	294
Iowa	370
Kansas	302
Kentucky	176
Louisiana	68
Maine	283
Maryland	24
Massachusetts	350
Michigan	553
Minnesota	348
Mississippi	152
Missouri	524
Montana	438
Nebraska	518
Nevada	17
New Hampshire	178
New Jersey	598
New Mexico	89
New York	726
North Carolina	117
North Dakota	213
Ohio	613
Oklahoma	541
Oregon	199
Pennsylvania	501
Rhode Island	38
South Carolina	89
South Dakota	172
Tennessee	136
Texas	1,040
Utah	40
Vermont	299
Virginia	134
Washington	296
West Virginia	55
Wisconsin	437
Wyoming	48

Source: U.S. Department of Education, National Center for Education Statistics, Common Core of Data (CCD), "Local Education Agency Universe Survey," 2003–2004.

School District Size and Student Enrollment. The sizes of school districts and where students are enrolled vary greatly and bear directly on teacher demand. As shown in Table 1.4, NCES data indicate there were 14,383 regular public school districts in 2003–2004. *Fewer than 2% of school districts enrolled a third of all the students enrolled in the United States.* These are the 256 school districts that enroll 25,000 or more students. When the next category of school districts by size is added—those that enroll between 10,000 and 24,999—587 additional school districts enter the count, taking the number of school districts that enroll 10,000 or more students to 843. These 843 school districts represent just *6% of all school districts and enroll more than half (52.1%) of all the public elementary and secondary students.*

At the other end of the spectrum, as also shown in Table 1.4, more than a fifth (2,994) of all school districts enroll between 1 and 299 students each and account for less than 1% of all students enrolled. *Nearly half of all school districts (6,703, or 46.6%) enroll fewer than 1,000 students each, and they collectively account for only 5.5% of total public elementary and secondary school enrollment across the nation.*

Because these local school districts are responsible for hiring and placing teachers, it is obvious that the needs and demands for teachers in a metropolitan school district with a diverse population that includes several hundred schools, each of which likely enrolls anywhere from fewer than 100 students to more than 3,000, are different from a school district that has a handful of small schools in a rural predominantly white community.

Alternate routes, again, by their very nature, address such disparities. Alternate routes are created to meet specific needs for specific teachers in specific areas.

Public School Size and Student Enrollment

As shown in Table 1.5, the NCES data indicate that *more than 1 in 10 (11.02%) of all schools and nearly 17% of secondary schools enroll fewer than 100 students each.* Furthermore, *more than a third (35.89%) of public secondary schools enroll fewer than 300 students each.* These statistics are crucial in any discussion about out-of-field teaching or having a teacher with a major or minor teaching every class in every school in the country. In these small schools, generally there is no more than one physics class, one chemistry class, and one biology class per day. The chances that a teacher with a major or minor in each of these sciences will be teaching each of those three classes per day in each of these schools are slim to none.

Many alternative routes to teacher certification meet the needs for highly qualified teachers in these and other high-demand subjects, such as special education, in small schools by targeting programs that ensure that teachers have—or obtain—content and pedagogical mastery in the subjects they are teaching. Alternate routes that utilize technology and distance learning opportunities are likely to appeal to the needs of small schools.

Table 1.4 Number of Regular Public School Districts, by Enrollment Size of District: Selected Years, 1990–1991 Through 2003–2004

| Enrollment size of district | Number of districts | | | | | | | | | | | | 2003–2004 | | |
1	2	3	4	5	6	7	8	9	10	11	12	Number of districts 13	Percent of districts 14	Percent of students 15
	1990–91	1993–94	1994–95	1995–96	1996–97	1997–98	1998–99	1999–2000	2000–01	2001–02	2002–03	13	14	15
Total	**15,358**	**14,881**	**14,772**	**14,766**	**14,841**	**14,805**	**14,891**	**14,928**	**14,859**	**14,559**	**14,465**	**14,383**	**100.0**	**100.0**
25,000 or more	190	206	207	216	226	230	236	238	240	243	248	256	1.8	33.4
10,000 to 24,999	489	525	542	553	569	572	574	579	581	573	587	594	4.1	19.0
5,000 to 9,999	937	973	996	1,013	1,024	1,038	1,026	1,036	1,036	1,067	1,062	1,058	7.4	15.4
2,500 to 4,999	1,940	2,008	2,013	2,027	2,069	2,079	2,062	2,068	2,060	2,031	2,033	2,031	14.1	15.0
1,000 to 2,499	3,542	3,570	3,579	3,554	3,536	3,524	3,496	3,457	3,448	3,429	3,411	3,421	23.8	11.7
600 to 999	1,799	1,785	1,777	1,777	1,772	1,775	1,790	1,814	1,776	1,744	1,745	1,728	12.0	2.8
300 to 599	2,275	2,162	2,113	2,104	2,066	2,044	2,066	2,081	2,107	2,015	1,987	1,981	13.8	1.8
1 to 299	3,816	3,294	3,173	3,123	3,160	3,165	3,245	3,298	3,265	3,127	3,117	2,994	20.8	0.9
Size not reported	370	358	372	399	419	378	396	357	346	330	275	320	2.2	†

† Not applicable.

Note: Size not reported includes school districts reporting enrollment of zero. Detail may not sum to totals because of rounding.

Source: U.S. Department of Education, National Center for Education Statistics, The NCES Common Core of Data (CCD), "Local Education Agency Universe Survey," 1990–1991 through 2003–2004. (This table 85 was prepared August 2005.)

Table 1.5 Number and Percentage Distribution of Public Elementary and Secondary Schools and Enrollment, by Type and Enrollment Size of School: 2003–2004

Enrollment size of school	Number and percentage distribution of schools, by type						Enrollment and percentage distribution, by type of school\1\					
	Total\2\	Elementary\3\	Secondary\4\		Combined elementary secondary\5\	Other\2\	Total\2\	Elementary\3\	Secondary\4\		Combined elementary secondary\5\	Other\2\
			All schools	Regular schools\6\					All schools	Regular schools\6\		
1	2	3	4	5	6	7	8	9	10	11	12	13
Number of schools..........	95,726	65,758	22,782	18,810	5,437	1,749	48,353,523	31,204,774	15,751,624	15,279,073	1,310,435	86,690
Percent\7\.......	100.00	100.00	100.00	100.00	100.00	100.00	100.00	100.00	100.00	100.00	100.00	100.00
Under 100	11.02	6.14	16.75	9.00	45.32	55.72	0.96	0.63	1.07	0.63	6.35	16.30
100 to 199	9.67	8.60	11.04	10.24	16.21	22.88	2.77	2.74	2.23	1.85	8.73	22.31
200 to 299	11.59	12.95	8.10	8.21	9.34	9.31	5.62	6.90	2.79	2.51	8.48	16.32
300 to 399	13.45	15.83	7.95	8.64	7.24	4.74	9.04	11.64	3.83	3.68	9.33	11.61
400 to 499	13.18	16.16	6.31	6.90	5.17	3.27	11.35	15.21	3.92	3.80	8.62	10.11
500 to 599	10.79	13.12	5.62	6.25	3.69	1.47	11.33	15.07	4.27	4.21	7.50	5.64

600 to 699	8.04	9.36	5.34	6.07	3.34	0.82	9.98	12.71	4.78	4.81	8.04	3.56
700 to 799	5.55	6.14	4.68	5.30	2.22	0.65	7.95	9.61	4.84	4.85	6.17	3.37
800 to 999	6.76	6.86	7.46	8.58	3.10	0.49	11.52	12.74	9.26	9.42	10.25	3.04
1,000 to 1,499 . .	6.09	4.18	12.73	14.58	2.73	0.33	13.96	10.23	21.55	21.83	12.31	2.88
1,500 to 1,999	2.16	0.52	7.39	8.54	1.01	0.16	7.11	1.82	17.67	18.07	6.44	2.20
2,000 to 2,999	1.38	0.13	5.42	6.28	0.33	0.16	6.25	0.61	17.73	18.19	2.87	2.65
3,000 or more	0.31	0.01	1.22	1.41	0.31	0.00	2.16	0.08	6.05	6.16	4.90	0.00
Average enrollment\7\ . . .	521	476	722	816	269	142	521	476	722	816	269	142

\1\Totals differ from those reported in other tables because this table represents data reported by schools rather than by states or school districts. Percentage distribution and average enrollment calculations exclude data for schools not reporting enrollment.

\2\Includes special education, alternative, and other schools not classified by grade span.

\3\Includes schools beginning with grade 6 or below and with no grade higher than 8.

\4\Includes schools with no grade lower than 7.

\5\Includes schools beginning with grade 6 or below and ending with grade 9 or above.

\6\Excludes special education schools, vocational schools, and alternative schools.

\7\Data are for schools reporting their enrollment size.

Note: Detail may not sum to totals because of rounding.

Source: U.S. Department of Education, National Center for Education Statistics, The NCES Common Core of Data (CCD), "Public Elementary/Secondary School Universe Survey," 2003–2004. (This table 92 was prepared July 2005 for Digest of Education Statistics 2005.)

Public School Student Enrollment and Teachers

As is the case of school district size and enrollment disparities, so is the case of school size, enrollment, and numbers of teachers in each state—from 12 states that enroll fewer than 250,000 students to 14 that enroll more than 1 million, as shown in Table 1.6.

Table 1.6 Teachers and Enrollment in Public Elementary and Secondary Schools, by State, Ranked by Number of Teachers (Fall 2003)

Rank	State	Teachers		Enrollment		% of All Teachers	Cumulative % of All Teachers
	United States	3,048,549	\2\	48,540,725	\2\		
1	California	304,311	\2\	6,413,862	\2\	10.0%	
2	Texas	289,481		4,331,751		9.5%	
3	New York	216,116		2,864,775		4.8%	
4	Florida	144,955		2,587,628		4.8%	
5	Illinois	127,669		2,100,961		4.2%	33.2%
6	Ohio	121,735		1,845,428		4.0%	
7	Pennsylvania	119,889		1,821,146		3.9%	
8	New Jersey	109,077		1,380,753		3.6%	44.7%
9	Georgia	97,150		1,522,611		3.2%	
10	Michigan.	97,014		1,757,604		3.2%	51.0%
11	Virginia.	90,573		1,192,092		3.0%	
12	North Carolina. . . .	89,988		1,360,209		3.0%	
13	Massachusetts	72,062		980,459		2.4%	
14	Missouri	65,169		905,941		2.1%	
15	Indiana	59,924		1,011,130		2.0%	63.4%
16	Tennessee	59,584	\2\	936,681	\2\	2.0%	
17	Wisconsin	58,216		880,031		1.9%	
18	Alabama	58,070		731,220		1.9%	
19	Maryland	55,140		869,113		1.8%	
20	Washington.	52,824		1,021,349		1.7%	
21	Minnesota	51,611		842,854		1.7%	
22	Louisiana	50,495		727,709		1.7%	
23	Arizona	47,507		1,012,068		1.6%	
24	South Carolina	45,830		699,198		1.5%	
25	Colorado.	44,904		757,693		1.5%	
26	Connecticut	42,370		577,203		1.4%	82.0%
27	Kentucky	41,201		663,885		1.4%	
28	Oklahoma.	39,253		626,160		1.3%	
29	Iowa	34,791		481,226		1.1%	
30	Mississippi	32,591		493,540		1.1%	
31	Kansas	32,589		470,490		1.1%	

32	Arkansas	30,876	454,523	1.0%
33	Oregon	26,732	551,273	0.9%
34	Utah	22,147	495,981	0.7%
35	New Mexico	21,569	323,066	0.7%
36	Nebraska.	20,921	285,542	0.7%
37	Nevada	20,234	385,401	0.7%
38	West Virginia	20,020	281,215	0.7%
39	Maine	17,621	202,084	0.6%
40	New Hampshire . . .	15,112	207,417	0.5%
41	Idaho	14,049	252,120	0.5%
42	Rhode Island	11,918	159,375	0.4%
43	Hawaii	11,129	183,609	0.4%
44	Montana	10,301	148,356	0.3%
45	South Dakota	9,245	125,537	0.3%
46	Vermont	8,749	99,103	0.3%
47	North Dakota	8,037	102,233	0.3%
48	Alaska	7,808	133,933	0.3%
49	Delaware.	7,749	117,668	0.3%
50	Wyoming	6,567	87,462	0.2%
51	District of Columbia . . .	5,676	78,057	0.2%

\2\Includes imputations for underreporting of prekindergarten teachers/enrollment.

Source: U.S. Department of Education, National Center for Education Statistics, The NCES Common Core of Data (CCD), "State Nonfiscal Survey of Public Elementary/Secondary Education," 2003–2004.

Four states—California, Florida, New York, and Texas—each enroll more than 2.5 million elementary and secondary students and account for a third (33.3%) of all the students enrolled in public elementary and secondary schools in the nation, as shown in Table 1.6. These four states are among the most aggressive in developing and using targeted alternate routes to meet their specific needs for specific teachers in specific areas.

As can also be seen in Table 1.6, half (51%) of all teachers are employed by 10 states (California, Florida, Georgia, Illinois, Michigan, New Jersey, New York, Ohio, Pennsylvania, and Texas). California, New Jersey, and Texas alone account for nearly a fourth (23%) of all teachers employed. These three states report that at least a third of their new hires to teaching have come through alternative routes.

Distribution of Schools, Teachers, and Students

Approximately a fourth of the schools, teachers, and students are in central cities; about half are in the urban fringe/large towns; and slightly more than a fourth of the schools and a fifth of the teachers and students are in rural/small town areas (USDoE, 2006c–313, p.13). Where schools are located in various communities, as well as how many students are enrolled in schools, has direct bearing on the demand for teachers.

Teacher Vacancies (Demand)

The 2003–2004 *SASS* data (2006–313) also show that the demand for teachers, as indicated by vacancies in schools and subjects, is greatest:

- In schools
  - At the secondary level
  - In central cities and urban fringe/large towns
  - With enrollments of 750 or more students
- In subjects of
  - Special education
  - English/language arts
  - Mathematics
  - Sciences
  - Foreign languages

All of these statistics are important in understanding the context in which teachers are hired and will need to be hired.

The Role Alternate Routes Play

Alternate route programs, by their very nature, are established to meet specific needs for specific teachers in specific subject areas in specific schools. The targeted nature of alternate routes is the reason they are proliferating at a rapid rate, why thousands of people who would not otherwise have done so are choosing to become teachers.

The remainder of this book discusses in detail the history and evolution of alternate routes, what they are and how they are being implemented throughout the country, who participates in them, and why and what the future portends for the alternate route movement in American education.

2

How Did Alternate Routes Develop?

A brief look back in time sets the stage for a discussion of how alternate routes began and why alternate routes meet the needs that the nation identified as critical to the future of America.

Historical Highlights of Teacher Certification

From Ecclesiastical to Civil Authority

In the United States, each state sets the standards for teaching and is the authority for licensing teachers, a practice that developed in the late 19th century. Long before then in colonial America, one or more local ministers were often responsible for approving the aspiring teacher for the classroom or one-room schoolhouse. But over the course of the 19th century, the authority for licensing teachers passed from ecclesiastical to civil authorities (Angus, 2001, p. 4).

At first, the civil authorities were local officials who issued a certificate to teach on the basis of the prospective teacher's moral character and performance on an oral or written examination. At that time, the examination covered knowledge of the subject matter that the teacher would be teaching, in part to be sure that the individual knew at least as much as the older children in the classroom or school.

In the late 19th century, state education officials sought and gained more control over the country's schools. The changes affected examinations and licensing as well. By 1843, state superintendents were issuing some certificates that varied by region and subject matter; other certificates were valid statewide (Angus, 2001, p. 5). In addition to subject matter, the examinations also included knowledge of pedagogy—training in how to teach.

From the early 19th century to the mid-1940s, teacher education was the domain of normal schools, educational institutions developed specifically for training teachers in established teaching standards or norms. Some early normal schools provided only a 2-year post–eighth-grade education to prepare teachers to teach in the primary grades in common (public) schools. Upon completion of the training, a state official or the trustees of these institutions issued certificates to teach to the graduates of these programs (Angus, 2001, p. 5).

As more and more students completed elementary schooling, opportunities and the demand for secondary public education increased. Consequently, the demand for more and better qualified teachers grew in cities and towns across America.

In response, many normal schools evolved into 4-year teacher colleges. Liberal arts colleges and universities eventually incorporated teacher education into their curriculum. A liberal arts education is intended to provide general knowledge and develop an individual's intellectual capacities, rather than to develop skills for a specific job such as teaching. Within the broader liberal arts program, an individual could still focus on or major in education, however, and thousands did so in the nation's institutions of higher education that offered a baccalaureate degree in education.

State-Approved Teacher Education Programs

By the 1950s, the "approved program" in teacher education was taking hold across the country (Angus, 2001, p. 23). Historically, a state department of education approved a teacher education program at a college or university within the state. University faculty in the institutions determined the program requirements. Upon successful completion of an approved program and a recommendation by the institution, the state issued a license to teach. Most approved programs for preparing teachers were at the undergraduate level, although some institutions eventually added graduate degrees, some of which were intended to professionalize teaching.

State control had proceeded rapidly. State departments of education increased their authority over admission requirements into institutions of higher education, content of teacher preparation programs and examinations, and all facets of licensing.

For critics of the teacher education system, neither additional training nor advanced degrees would sort out "the hodgepodge of programs which are in the main a travesty upon professional education" (National Commission on Teacher Education and Professional Standards, 1961, pp. 34–35). Attempts to do so, however, gave rise to the creation of the "professional standards movement." In addition, several organizations formed new groups intended to affect the standards of teacher education, govern accreditation, and determine the "essential" elements of teacher education programs and licensing (Angus, 2001, p. 26).

In 1952, the American Association of Colleges for Teacher Education (AACTE),[1] the Teacher Education and Professional Standards (TEPS),[2] and the National Association of State Directors of Teacher Education and Certification (NASDTEC)[3] formed the National Council for Accreditation of Teacher Education (NCATE) (Angus, 2001, pp. 22–24, 40). NCATE assumed responsibility for the accreditation of teacher education programs in institutions of higher education, including, more recently, some alternate route programs.

Organizations, institutions of higher education, and state departments of education were not the only entities interested in guiding teacher education programs. Along with the changes that were occurring within the states, international concerns caused the federal government to assess its role, if any, in education.

The Nation Reacts

Expansion of the Role of the Federal Government

Prior to 1958, federal involvement in education had been limited mostly to the school lunch programs; however, as a reaction to the 1957 Sputnik launch by the Soviet Union, the federal government enacted the National Defense Education Act (NDEA). The NDEA provided assistance to state and local school systems for strengthening instruction in science, mathematics, modern foreign languages, and other critical subjects and areas deemed necessary for national defense.

Great Society Programs Affected Education from Top to Bottom.
Although not tied to national defense, president Lyndon B. Johnson, the teacher who became president, built his comprehensive education program around the theme of building the Great Society. Of the federal laws passed from 1963 through 1968, 20 were federal programs for education and related activities. The legislation included the Vocational Education Act, support for expanded vocational education and training; the Higher Education Facilities Act, grant and loan program to upgrade classrooms, libraries, and laboratories in undergraduate and graduate institutions; the Civil Rights Act, support for

---

[1] In 1948, AACTE was created from a merger of the National Association of Colleges and Departments of Education, the National Association of Teacher Education Institution in Metropolitan Districts, and the American Association of Teachers Colleges, a department of the National Education Association (NEA).

[2] In 1946, the National Education Association (NEA) created TEPS, intended to be an independent voice for the classroom teacher in issues of professional standards and certification.

[3] NASDTEC has published the certification requirements for each state since 1984.

institutions of higher education and school districts to provide in-service programs for assisting instructional staff in dealing with problems caused by desegregation of schools; the Economic Opportunity Act, authorized grants for college work-study programs for students from low-income families and other work-training programs; the Elementary and Secondary Education Act, grants intended to aid elementary and secondary schools with pupils from low-income families; and the Higher Education Act (USDoE, 2002b, pp. 411–412).

The Civil Rights Act.　As part of the Civil Rights Act of 1964, Section 402, Congress directed the U.S. commissioner of education to "conduct a survey. . . within two years of the enactment of this title, concerning the lack of availability of equal educational opportunities for individuals, by reason of race, color, religion, or national origin." To comply with the directive, the assistant commissioner for educational statistics selected James S. Coleman, a Johns Hopkins University sociologist, and Ernest Q. Campbell, a sociology researcher from Vanderbilt University.

Coleman and Campbell (1966) produced what some still say was among the most extensive and best known studies of American education. To meet the congressional directive, the authors collected data from 570,000 students, 60,000 teachers, and 4,000 elementary and secondary schools across the country. Entitled *Equality of Educational Opportunity* (better known as the Coleman Report), the authors concluded that school might not be society's great equalizer after all. Black children started school trailing behind their white counterparts and essentially never caught up—even when their schools were as well equipped as those with predominantly white enrollments.

The authors found that few school-related "inputs" seemed to matter much. "Outputs," or improving student achievement, however, were influenced by teachers' verbal ability, teachers' level of education, and teachers' years of experience. When teachers exhibited those characteristics, black students benefited more than white students, although none of the effects was large. Subsequent analyses of the Coleman Report data suggest that Coleman's methodology was seriously flawed. Coleman conducted his analysis on data that had been aggregated to the school level. Researchers now understand that aggregating data in this way can distort findings (USDoE, 2003, p. 41).

Using test data to measure educational disparities and what children actually learned was a revolutionary innovation used in the Coleman Report. Researchers have revived and perfected this approach in subsequent studies to measure the effects of teacher qualities that add value to student achievement among all racial groups.

The Higher Education Act.　The Higher Education Act (HEA) of 1965 provided grants to strengthen developing institutions and teacher training programs. In addition, the HEA authorized federally insured student loans, provided for graduate teacher training fellowships, and established a national Teacher Corps with a $37.5 million budget (Steffensen, 1994, p. 128).

The Teacher Corps, whose initial purpose was to help solve the teacher shortages in the 1960s by providing job opportunities for returning Peace Corps[4] volunteers, was a domestic Peace Corps–like program. Teams consisting of an experienced teacher and several young college graduates were sent in to strengthen local school programs. The interns were not required to have a bachelor's degree in education, only an interest in teaching. Teacher Corps internships lasted approximately 2 to 3 years.

As individuals accepted the incentives and the teacher shortage began to subside, the program was reconstituted to encourage Teacher Corps members to teach in schools located in low-income neighborhoods (Earley & Schneider, 1996). Schools employed the teacher candidates, who simultaneously completed courses to earn a baccalaureate degree and to satisfy licensure requirements or, if available, the interns worked on a graduate degree in education. As a result, a shift occurred in where teacher education took place; Teacher Corps members received their training in schools and local school districts, not in colleges of education (Cohen-Vogel, 2005, p. 28).

> The legacy for Teacher Corps includes the contribution it made to encourage collaboration between schools and higher education institutions, well in advance of what is now regarded to be a hallmark of good teacher education. Teacher Corps can also be credited with stimulating higher education institutions to consider the desirability of offering multiple options for students who want to become teacher candidates. (Scannell, 1994, p. 5)

The federal program also provided incentive funding to higher education institutions to broaden teacher education programs. In the 1970s, when the teacher shortage turned into a teacher surplus, the Teacher Corps focus turned to the professional development of practicing teachers (Earley & Schneider, 1996).

Education Professions Development Act and Changes in Higher Education.   In 1967, President Johnson signed the Education Professions Development Act (PL 90–35), which extended the Teacher Corps program through 1970 and added programs to improve teacher training. To expand recruitment, the program included federal funds for teacher and administrator fellowships

---

[4] In late 1961, Congress authorized the Peace Corps, a program that President John F. Kennedy had created by executive order. The Peace Corps appealed to youth dedicated to the service of humanity and symbolized America's determination to assist with projects in noncommunist countries. The first volunteers served as teachers in the African nation of Ghana.

and training complexes that evolved into the Teacher Centers Program. Funding, however, was reduced in the mid-1970s. After the establishment of the U.S. Department of Education as a cabinet-level agency in 1980, both the Teacher Centers and Teacher Corps ceased to exist as federal programs.

But the egalitarian compensatory programs in education funded by the federal government faltered, noted Diane Ravitch (2003) when she reflected on the educational crises of the late 1970s: "A heap of public discontent about schooling had been accumulating since the sixties . . . when numerous accounts reported that schools had abandoned most academic requirements, replacing them with frivolous, fluffy electives, like cooking for singles" (p. 35). Scores on the Scholastic Aptitude Test (SAT), especially on the verbal portion, had fallen steadily since 1963. To determine reasons for the decline in scores, the College Board created a panel, headed by former secretary of labor Willard Wirtz (Ravitch, 1985, p. 60). The Wirtz panel affirmed in its 1997 report what citizens groups had also concluded about elementary and secondary education:

- An expansion of electives accompanied a decline in enrollments in basic academic courses.
- Standards within the schools had clearly fallen: An 'A' or 'B' means a good deal less than it used to.
- Promotion from grade to grade had become almost automatic.
- Homework had apparently been cut in half.
- Textbooks were written below grade level and included more pictures and graphics.
- Less critical reading was required.
- Careful writing had apparently gone out of style. (Ravitch, 1985, pp. 61–62)

Similar criticisms were levied against institutions of higher education. In *The Troubled Crusade,* Ravitch (1983) wrote that "One national survey found that the 'number of institutions requiring English, a foreign language, and mathematics as part of everyone's general education declined appreciably from 1967 to 1974—from 90 percent of the institutions surveyed to 72 percent for English, from 72 to 53 percent for foreign language, and from 33 to 20 percent for mathematics' " (p. 225). The quality of education at all levels became a problematic issue that would remain the subject of books, debates, and reform actions for decades.

National Commission on Excellence in Education

On August 21, 1981, U.S. Secretary of Education Terrell H. Bell created the National Commission on Excellence in Education as a result of the secretary's concern about "the widespread perception that something is seriously remiss in our educational system" (NCEE, 1983). The commission included several prominent educators: Chairman David P. Gardner, president of the University of Utah and president-elect of the University of California; Nobel laureate Glenn T. Seaborg of the University of California; Gerald Holton, professor of the history of science, Harvard University; and A. Bartlett Giamatti, president of Yale University. Secretary Bell directed the commission to examine the quality of education in the United States and to make a report to the nation.

A Nation at Risk.   On April 26, 1983, the commission delivered *A Nation at Risk: The Imperative for Education Reform,* a shocking report and "the most important education reform document of the twentieth century" (Ravitch, 2003, p. 33). "Our Nation is at risk," the report stated. "The educational foundations of our society are presently being eroded by a rising tide of mediocrity that threatens our very future as a Nation and a people" (NCEE, 1983).

Even some critics did not deny that a crisis existed in education, but they attributed the crisis to demographic and economic shifts more than to evidence of educational decline. The American Federation of Teachers (AFT) embraced the report and its findings, but the National Education Association (NEA) argued that the public schools were products of a new environment. Waves of immigrants mostly from Mexico, other nations, and several Asian countries helped create the new environment that challenged teachers who needed more support and more money (Spring, 2002, p. 127).

Some critics attributed the decline in test scores in part to the broadened school-age population taking the tests. Nevertheless, those critical of the decline on test scores and favoring the reforms proposed by *A Nation at Risk* were labeled "anti-public school" (Keegan, 2003, p. 30). Wayne Urban and Jennings Wagoner (2000) wrote that some critics "saw *A Nation at Risk* as another instance of public school bashing by an administration that seemed to exhibit contempt for nearly all public enterprises" (p. 353).

Joel Spring broadened the criticism. Spring (2002) claimed that "*A Nation at Risk* blamed public schools for America's difficulties in competing world markets," and that "the allegedly poor academic quality of American public schools was seen as the cause of lower rates of productivity than those of Japan and West Germany" (p. 206). At the time in the early 1980s, "the American economy was in recession, while the economies of Japan and several other Asian nations were booming," wrote Ravitch (2003, p. 35) in a retrospective of *A Nation at Risk* in *Education Next.*

Regaining academic requirements that had virtually been eliminated in the two decades leading up to 1983 were significant challenges addressed in *A Nation at Risk.* The commission organized its findings within four broad topics: content, expectations, time, and teaching. Along with its 24-count indictment of American primary and secondary education, *A Nation at Risk* included four major recommendations that demanded higher standards of performance:

- High-school graduation requirements should be strengthened so that all students acquire a solid foundation in five "*new* basics": English, mathematics, science, social studies, and computer science.
- Schools and colleges should adopt higher and measurable standards for academic performance.
- The amount of time students devote to learning should be significantly increased.
- The teaching profession should be strengthened by raising standards for training, entry, and professional growth. (NCEE, 1983)

A Nation at Risk suggested that the quality of teacher candidates and teacher education programs also contributed to the risks threatening the superiority of the United States. Along with recommending higher standards for teacher preparation programs, *A Nation at Risk* suggested establishing special means for staffing teacher shortages by utilizing recent graduates, retired scientists, and others with appropriate subject matter expertise (p. 4).

Alternate routes allowed liberal arts graduates—a new supply of potential teachers—to earn certification while teaching, the first of which was being designed in New Jersey at the same time that the Reagan administration's National Commission on Excellence in Education was writing its report. The commission released its *Nation at Risk* report first; the New Jersey alternate route announcement was held for release until the following September to coincide with the opening of school. After New Jersey announced its proposal, the federal administration began citing it as an exemplary local program that was consistent with its commission's recommendations concerning teacher quality. When the Reagan administration followed up *A Nation at Risk* by sponsoring a national Forum on Excellence in Education (Indianapolis, December 1983), New Jersey was invited to present its plan, and President Ronald Reagan personally touted it in the remarks he delivered at the Forum when he said,

> In New Jersey, Governor Tom Kean has a proposal that deserves wide support. Under his plan, the New Jersey board of education would allow successful mathematicians, scientists, linguists, and journalists to pass a competency test in their subjects and then go into classrooms as paid teaching interns. If they performed well, they would be issued permanent teaching certificates at the end of a year." (Reagan, 1983)

The resultant national publicity generated interest in other states, and Texas and California joined New Jersey in developing proposals. All three states implemented programs around the same time, but New Jersey officials had begun the process first, well before serious concerns about the quality of the teaching force spread from state to state. In 1983, James B. Hunt, Jr., then governor of North Carolina as well as chairman of the Education Commission of the States (ECS), "pushed other governors and corporate CEOs to address the problem" of major deficiencies revealed in the testing of public school students. Hunt's suggestion resulted in the creation of a high-level Task Force on Education for Economic Growth, "warmly received by the National Governors Association (NGA)" (Hunt, 2003, p. 24).

Hunt wrote that "nearly every leader of the NGA, Republicans and Democrats alike, made education, standards, and economic competitiveness" a theme in his state, just as President George H. W. Bush did as he convened the nation's first education summit[5] (Hunt, 2003, p. 26). One governor who focused on excellence in teaching or "what accomplished teachers need to know and be able to do" was Thomas H. Kean, Republican governor of New Jersey from 1982 to 1990 (Hunt, 2003, p. 26).

New Jersey Begins the Debate About Alternative Routes

Already in 1978 and a few years before Kean was elected governor, the New Jersey legislature had created the Commission to Study Teacher Preparation Programs in New Jersey Colleges "because of dissatisfaction with the quality and scope of the programs for the education of teachers . . . and the requirements for licensing." In its review of undergraduate preparation programs, the commission found that teacher preparation programs produced poorly educated graduates. In some instances, students were allowed to graduate as elementary teachers without any courses in science, mathematics, or history (Klagholz, 2000, p. 1).

Also, commission officials pointed to the low SAT scores of New Jersey high school graduates who indicated education as their intended major. Even though high numbers of these teacher candidates were deficient in basic skills as entering college freshmen, apparently most completed their teacher preparation programs. According to findings of the commission, the most valuable aspect of their preparation was "practice teaching," performed in school classrooms under the guidance of a school-based mentor teacher, not campus-based courses (Klagholz, 2000, p. 2).

---

[5] In 1989, President George H. W. Bush convened the nation's first education summit in Charlottesville, Virginia, which formulated six national education goals for America. In 1994, President Bill Clinton signed the Goals 2000: Educate America Act, consisting of eight national education reform goals set for achievement by 2000.

Redefining the Traditional College-Based Route

As the authority over college degree programs, the New Jersey State Board of Higher Education expanded on the commission's recommendations and required that all undergraduate education programs include the following:

- Approximately 60 credits of "pure" liberal education courses, distributed among relevant disciplines;
- A liberal arts or science major comprised of courses taken by liberal arts majors in the same field; and
- Progressively intensive practice teaching experiences. (Klagholz, 2000, p. 2)

New Jersey's public colleges were also to cease awarding undergraduate degrees in the field of education, except if education were the secondary emphasis in a dual major. As a result of these reforms, the traditional college-based route to teacher preparation was redefined so that all candidates were required to major in the liberal arts. In addition, prospective teachers were to participate in practice teaching with the help of a mentor. So, rather than relying on textbooks and lectures, teaching skills were to be acquired mainly through actual classroom practice by teacher candidates mentored by practicing teachers (Klagholz, 2000, p. 1).

Even after the New Jersey State Board of Higher Education issued the new regulations, harsh criticism of certification mandates and of education courses in general were still unresolved. Therefore, the New Jersey Department of Education began to study which, if any, education courses to include in teacher preparation in the traditional college-based program. Not unexpectedly, some existing education courses were deemed superfluous and were eliminated. The how-to-teach courses, however, were deemed education courses to which each new teacher ought to be exposed.

Emergence of an "Alternate Route"

During the review of the preparation programs and the investigation of options, the proposal for an "alternate route" to certification emerged. Through a review of rejected certification applications, the education department discovered that "many individuals with outstanding academic qualifications and pertinent experience were being barred from employment [as teachers] for lack of seemingly trivial courses" (Klagholz, 2000, p. 4). Consequently, the New Jersey Department of Education concluded that "there is a need to provide an alternate route to certification, . . . and thereby open the doors of the teaching profession to talented persons from all collegiate fields of study" (Klagholz, 2000, p. 4). For those who had majored in the liberal arts, a local school district could provide an internship.

Thomas H. Kean, Republican governor of New Jersey from 1982 to 1990, was an enthusiastic supporter of the proposed change. So were

Saul Cooperman, a member of Kean's cabinet and New Jersey commissioner of education, and Leo Klagholz, director of teacher preparation and certification in the state's Department of Education. Governor Kean made a rare gubernatorial appearance before the state board to introduce detailed presentations by Cooperman and Klagholz, all of whom formally proposed the plan to the New Jersey State Board of Education, which had legal authority to approve or reject the proposal.

Selling the Alternate Route Concept

Before asking the state board of education to adopt an alternate route to teacher certification, Governor Kean announced the formation of the Panel on the Preparation of Teachers in December 1983. Ernest L. Boyer, then president of the Carnegie Foundation for the Advancement of Teaching, headed the panel.[6] Governor Kean charged the panel of education researchers with reaching a consensus on what beginning teachers—both college-based and alternate route interns—would need to know. Simultaneously, a second panel of New Jersey educators and citizens would determine the details of an alternate route internship (Cooperman & Klagholz, 1985, p. 693).

The tactics were both offensive and defensive. Cooperman quickly found that winning support for alternative certification would be hard work. He and his deputy commissioners spoke extensively on the issue as part of a special Teacher Certification Speakers Bureau. Leo Klagholz, an architect of the New Jersey Provisional Teacher Program and director of Teacher Preparation and Certification in the state's Department of Education, assisted in garnering support for the proposal. The New Jersey Education Department sent out mass mailings of "Dear Friend" letters urging groups and individuals to write in support of the plan to legislators and the State Board of Education (Van Tassel, 1983).

Pros and Cons.   Groups supporting and opposing the plan formed quickly. The New Jersey School Boards Association, the New Jersey Principals and Supervisors Association, the state's Board of Higher Education, and the New Jersey Association of School Business Officials generally favored the ideas

---

[6] In addition to Ernest L. Boyer, the panel included David Berliner, professor of educational psychology at the University of Arizona, Tucson; Frank Brown, dean of education at the University of North Carolina, Chapel Hill; Edgar Epps, professor of urban education at the University of Chicago; Emily Feistritzer, director of the National Center for Education Information, Washington, D.C.; Jay Gottlieb, professor of educational psychology at New York University, New York City; Lawrence Lezotte, director of the Center for School Improvement, Michigan State University, East Lansing; Archie Lapointe, executive director of the Center for the Assessment of Educational Progress, Educational Testing Service, Princeton, New Jersey; Kathryn Maddox, director of the Multi-Institutional Teacher Education Center, Kanawha County Schools, Charleston, West Virginia; and Barak Rosenshine, professor of education, University of Illinois, Urbana.

outlined in the plan. However, the faculty senate at Trenton State College opposed an endorsement by its president and issued a stinging indictment of the proposal.

Opposition to the proposed changes in the certification requirements was swift and predictable. A coalition of 15 groups, including the 117,000-member New Jersey Education Association (NJEA) and the New Jersey Federation of Teachers, were led by the New Jersey Association of Colleges for Teacher Education. Its national office, the American Association of Colleges for Teacher Education (AACTE), whose membership included many of the colleges of education in the country, contributed information, personnel, and money to block the proposal (Van Tassel, 1983).

Vigorous arguments, pro and con, were offered to the alternate route plan. Opponents insisted that all prospective teachers needed "a body of knowledge . . . before teaching" and successful clinical experience before getting paid for responsibilities in a classroom. Support however, grew for the proposal. Even the media jumped into the fray with the *Star Ledger* of Newark, the state's largest newspaper, actively promoting the "alternate route" plan (Klagholz, 2000, p. 7).

After 3 months of work, the Boyer panel released its recommendations (Boyer, 1984). The suggestions were intended to improve the consistency of college teacher-training programs and to establish an on-the-job training program for qualified college graduates who wanted to teach. The Boyer panel ultimately recommended that all new teachers be instructed in curriculum and evaluation, student learning and development, and the classroom and the school. The panel's findings, popularly called the Boyer Topics, were eventually incorporated as reforms into the college-based teacher preparation program as well as into the New Jersey districtwide internship plan (Van Tassel, 1984).

With the alternate route plan in place, New Jersey was set to become the first state to grant permanent licenses to prospective teachers who had earned degrees in other fields, bypassed colleges of education, and received on-the-job training in the classroom (Klagholz, 2000). To respond to the key concerns of plan opponents, the state education department worked out elaborate agreements with the various interest groups. Even the title given to teachers employed through the program was changed from "interns" to "provisional teachers." By the start of the new program, only college teacher education groups remained opposed (Klagholz, 2000, p. 10).

New Jersey Launches the Provisional Teacher Program

In September 1985, New Jersey launched the Provisional Teacher Program with the dual purpose of enhancing the quantity and quality of teaching candidates. Candidates were required to have a bachelor's degree, a liberal arts major, and proof of passing subject area tests. Once employed, the candidate was instructed in the Boyer Topics as they completed a mentor-guided internship supplemented by study of core professional knowledge. "The only differences [between the alternate and traditional routes] involved the timing and sequence in which candidates completed the requirements" (Klagholz, 2000, p. 10).

In an article written for the *Phi Delta Kappan,* Cooperman and Klagholz (1985) also enthusiastically reported that "perhaps most importantly, the alternate route to certification will do away with the 40-year tradition of emergency certification in New Jersey" (p. 691). Amid predictions of teacher shortages, many states allowed school districts to hire individuals on temporary or emergency certificates, only to face required college-based courses later. State teacher certification offices generally issued the emergency certificates at the request of local school districts. School districts often made little effort to recruit and hire fully qualified and available teachers, resorting to emergency certificates. In other instances, school districts assigned teachers to teach courses out of the area for which they were trained. Rural school districts with few students enrolled were particularly vulnerable to the lack of qualified teachers for advanced classes, although city school districts were not without shortages in certain areas as well. Although the adoption of the Provisional Teacher Program eliminated this situation in New Jersey, many other states continued to issue emergency certificates, sometimes overlooking requirements and concerns about teacher quality issues.

In *Growing Better Teachers in the Garden State: New Jersey's Alternate Route to Teacher Certification,* Klagholz (2000) wrote,

> Ultimately, the state's new certification regulations established parallel requirements for the alternative and traditional routes, yet the former remains a true alternative: only 200 clock hours [the equivalent of 12 credit hours in most universities] of formal instruction in teaching methods are required.
>
> New Jersey's alternative certification program has markedly expanded the quality, diversity, and size of the state's teacher candidate pool. By 1998–99, 457 school districts had utilized the program. Applicants had higher scores on teacher licensing tests than traditionally prepared teachers and attrition rates for alternatively certified teachers were lower than those of their traditionally trained counterparts. The Provisional Teacher Program also became the dominant source of minority teachers for both urban and suburban schools. (p. vii)

Implementing an alternate route to certification in New Jersey did not stop the controversies over how much value there was in formal education courses either in New Jersey or elsewhere. Opponents such as the American Association of Colleges for Teacher Education (AACTE) continued to stress the need for a professional base. They argued that prospective teachers need to be equipped with essential knowledge and skills imparted through education courses in a school of education prior to teaching. AACTE (1985) stated its position this way: "AACTE opposes state actions that are described as alternative routes to certification but which deny the importance of professional understanding and skills" (p. 24). Including education courses as part of the training through alternate routes varied from state to state, as did the required time to be spent on education courses.

The Provisional Teacher Program differed somewhat from the newly designed teacher preparation programs in one significant way: Traditional teacher education candidates for certification in New Jersey was capped at 30 credits, and such training was required to include practical teaching experiences in the sophomore and junior years of undergraduate study, plus a full semester of student teaching in the senior year. Within some flexibility, this left only about 12 credits of education courses with the cap—an amount that, by design, was equivalent to the 200 clock hours of noncredit study in the alternative program. The appendix has additional information about the New Jersey Provisional Teacher Program.

California Authorizes Alternate Route

California reported that it had first created its university intern (alternative) route by statute in 1967. California does not offer education degrees, and its university intern program was created to provide an internship in schools before a full certificate was issued.

In 1983, without the fanfare or publicity generated in New Jersey, the California legislature authorized its teacher trainee program to address the high level of emergency certificates issued and the continuing shortage of teachers in certain secondary subject areas. In 1984–1985, with 160 trainees, the Los Angeles Unified School District (LAUSD) implemented its Teacher Trainee Program (Adelman, 1986, p. 100). The Teacher Trainee Program was designed to offer a second career for individuals with degrees in shortage fields and to provide a quality program for alternative certification.

LAUSD identified teacher shortage areas in the subjects of mathematics, science, English, and secondary social studies. Most were subject area shortages identified by officials in *A Nation at Risk*. Charles Kerchner, professor of education at the Claremont California Graduate School, noted that approximately 500 mathematics or science teachers were employed on emergency credentials in the state's eight largest school districts in 1983.

The California Commission on Teacher Credentialing administered the Teacher Trainee Program after legislative approval in 1983. Successful program completion required district collaboration with a university. University involvement included instruction in nine areas of professional knowledge and teaching specialty knowledge, supervision of the trainee by a teacher mentor, and a plan for assessing the trainee to ensure that a mentor would provide the necessary help (Oliver & McKibbin, 1985).

When it began, the Teacher Trainee Program prepared candidates only for secondary teaching who wanted to teach in LAUSD, a concern raised by the California Commission on Teacher Credentialing in 1987. Some in the

LAUSD program, however, saw this district specific learning and training as a strength of the program (Stoddart, 1990, p. 106).

In 1987, when LAUSD had student populations that were more than 50% minority, the legislature expanded the Teacher Trainee Program to include preparation for bilingual and elementary teachers. Little wonder. A few years before that, Kerchner wrote that bilingual education presents a persistent problem and the need for bilingual teachers is likely to grow for some time. By 1984, California had projected a shortage of between 8,600 and 11,600 bilingual teachers for that year (Kerchner, 1984, p. 293).

The California laws stipulated that these routes could be 1 or 2 years long, and, at a minimum, were required to meet the same procedural and performance standards as other teacher preparation programs in California. California's governor and legislature provided funding in 1993, so that

1. Districts and colleges and universities could develop or enhance existing programs to help districts meet their immediate need for teachers.
2. Persons could be brought into teaching who might not otherwise become a teacher and the teaching workforce could be further diversified.
3. The support and instructional segments of preparation programs that allow teachers to simultaneously be employed as a teacher while matriculating through a teacher preparation program could be strengthened. (McKibbin, 2001, pp. 138–139)

In 2002, recognizing the value of its intern programs in attracting and credentialing individuals in areas of need, state lawmakers included preparation for special education teachers through its district intern program. California's internship programs produced a third of the 24,000 new teachers hired in the state in 2004–2005 (CCTC). The appendix includes a description of California's Intern Programs in the Supplemental Information—California.

California has used alternative routes to increase the production of teachers in geographic and subject areas where demand is greatest. Alternative routes also facilitate the process of getting emergency certified teachers fully certified. In addition, alternative routes have expanded and diversified the teaching force by recruiting significant numbers of men and minorities into teaching.

Texas Approves Alternate Route

In 1984, while the media was focused on reporting the controversies surrounding New Jersey's creation of its alternate route to certification program, the Texas state legislature, faced with projections of dire shortages of teachers, voted to provide an alternate route to certification to alleviate shortages.

In the 1985–1986 school year, the state approved the alternate route training program proposed by the Houston Independent School District (HISD), making HISD the first school district in Texas to receive state approval (Cornett, 1990a, p. 60). The HISD enrolled 276 interns in the program the first year (Cornett, 1990, p. 70). By 1989–1990, 166 districts (15% of the state's total) and 1,215 interns had participated in the alternative route program in Texas (Cornett, 1990a p. 70).

Key among the concerns in Texas was a critical shortage of credentialed teachers, especially a lack of black and Hispanic teachers among graduates from colleges and universities (Dill, 1994). Even so, "Widespread debate continued to surround sweeping legislative reform measures in Texas, including discussion of the 18-hour limit or 'cap' on professional education course work," according to Dill and Stafford (1996, p. 49). Nevertheless, Texas House Bill 72 outlined a pathway for baccalaureate-degree holders to become teachers. Proponents cited that "an alternative mode of learning [was actually] more than the equivalent to 18 credit hours while learning and doing simultaneously" (p. 85).

Because regional service centers and independent school districts in Texas could develop alternative teacher certification programs, proponents believed program development would be collaborative for individuals who were "distinctly different" from the typical undergraduate teacher education major (Dill & Stafford, 1996, p. 85). "It has become apparent that the higher education model favors the young and the advantaged and holds inherent bias against a demographically representative teaching force" (p. 85). Those in Texas who supported alternate routes saw the Texas legislation as a bold lesson from which educators nationwide could draw insight.

Chapter 21, Educators, Section 21.049 is the current Texas law, which states:

> ALTERNATIVE CERTIFICATION. (a) To provide a continuing additional source of qualified educators, the board shall propose rules providing for educator certification programs as an alternative to traditional educator preparation programs. The rules may not provide that a person may be certified under this section only if there is a demonstrated shortage of educators in a school district or subject area. (b) The board may not require a person employed as a teacher in an alternative education program under Section 37.008 or a juvenile justice alternative education program under Section 37.011 for at least three years to complete an alternative educator certification program adopted under this section before taking the appropriate certification examination. (Texas Statutes, 2006)

To implement the law, the Texas State Board of Education rules established a district-based program whereby districts could hire teachers based on demonstrated staffing needs in K–12 schools. To meet the needs, school districts used the competency approach. Upon completion of appropriate training, teachers demonstrated they had met the requisite skills and knowledge to meet certification requirements.

Even as the district-based model grew, Texas approved additional providers to deliver alternative training. In addition to the district-based model, Texas permitted the higher education model, which included coursework and supervised in-school training while the intern was a first-year teacher. A third model, the educational service center model, relied on field-based experiences with supervision by a mentor teacher and included a requirement of some coursework.

In 1986, soon after school districts began to implement the district-based models, the Texas commissioner of education and the commissioner of higher education challenged the colleges of education to collaborate in alternative certification programs. After initiating a district/higher education cooperative effort through the alternative program, the University of Texas-Pan American at Brownsville quickly doubled its enrollment in the college of education.

Even with the new teacher preparation options, Texas could not keep up with the demand for qualified teachers. Additional information about the Texas alternate route is included in Chapter 4 and in the appendix.

Alternate Routes Provoke Scrutiny

Haberman Justifies Support for Alternate Routes

The Summer 1986 issue of *Action in Teacher Education* was devoted to articles about alternative teacher certification, one of which included statistics about traditional and alternate preparation routes. Martin Haberman, professor of curriculum and instruction, School of Education, University of Wisconsin—Milwaukee, served as the guest editor of the issue and contributed an article as well. In his comments as the editor, Haberman (1986) called "naive" those who would dismiss the alternative certification movement (p. iii).

That alternative certification might be a "movement" was anathema to Robert A. Roth, a past president of the Association of Teacher Educators.[7] Roth (1986) declared that these "non-traditional routes to enter into the teaching profession pose a serious threat to teaching as a profession" (p. 4). "Furthermore, such programs should be eliminated once the emergency situation no longer exists" (p. 5).

---

[7] The Association of Teacher Educators was founded in 1920 and devoted solely to the improvement of teacher education for both school-based and campus-based educators. In 1986, ATE members included individuals from over 650 colleges and universities, 500 major school systems, and the majority of the states' departments of education.

Haberman disagreed. The use of emergency teachers, along with misassignment (out-of-teaching field assignment) and alternative certification, represent a trend moving teacher education out of the universities and returning major responsibility for it back to the public school districts, wrote Haberman (1986) in "Alternative Teacher Certification Programs" (p. 15). Haberman (1986) applauded the change and used what happened in Texas in 1985 as an example. In Texas, for just the year 1985,

> 5,892 Emergency Licenses were issued and the number of teachers practicing out-of-field was estimated to be even higher. The universities (and there are 61 institutions educating teachers in that state) prepared 8,500. Of this 8,500, 34 percent or 2,870 did not enter the field. The net result for Texas for 1985 was that approximately 5,630 teachers were prepared in regular programs and took jobs in schools which, in turn, hired more than 12,000 other individuals as emergencies or out-of-field teachers. In two subject areas, math and science, 1,233 were professionally prepared in universities but 598 unlicensed teachers and an unknown number (undoubtedly greater) were hired as out-of-field teachers (p. 14).

Like others, Haberman (1986) asked questions. "What good does it do to improve the quality of teacher education programs offered in universities if more than double their number are untrained people hired directly by school districts?" (p. 14). Why indeed?

For proponents, alternative certification was viewed as an answer to endemic shortages of qualified urban teachers. Proponents believed alternative certification was a better way of dealing with teacher shortages than by using emergency credentials, which had few, if any, stipulations for training or supervision or required standards. Most alternative certification programs required some professional coursework and on-site training and supervision, choices "highly preferable to simply using emergency or misassigned personnel," Haberman (1986, p. 15) wrote in his critique.

Haberman wrote passionately about several reasons why alternative teacher certification programs would flourish even as the programs were just gaining ground. First and foremost, Haberman (1986) believed in the importance of the "return to the nineteenth-century pattern of the *school district bearing primary responsibility for the preparation of its teachers*" (emphasis in the original) (p. 16).

Along with the calls for improving schools, Haberman predicted that although most people may want better schools, they are wary of the costs inevitably associated with improving them. Furthermore, Haberman reasoned, as the costs of university-prepared teachers increases, the demand for more teachers to work in urban areas will increase as well. Urban teachers, however, will be prepared through alternate routes—on site where the need is the greatest. He wrote, "the graduates of our teacher education programs do not self-elect to pursue teaching careers in urban school districts"; school districts should initiate their own alternative certification programs (Haberman, 1986, p. 17). And so some districts did, even as some groups were recommending reforms in other areas.

Groups Call for Changes in Traditional Teacher Preparation Programs

The Holmes Group. Nationwide discussions in the mid-1980s created an atmosphere ripe for the deans of 38 leading schools of education to call for radical changes in the training and employment of public school teachers (Holmes Group, 1986, 1990, 1995). Eventually, nearly 100 research universities across the United States became part of the national consortium. As a national entity, "the Holmes Group was not an outside group recommending changes to education, but was rather a group of insiders committing to a new agenda" (Fullan et al., 1998, p. 54).

The Holmes Group, named for Henry W. Holmes, dean of the Harvard University Graduate School of Education from 1920 to 1940, was the first to propose restructuring job responsibilities and linking the problems in teaching to the quality of liberal arts instruction. Its reform agenda, reiterated in its three reports, included higher standards, extended programs of teacher preparation, closer ties with arts and sciences, and professional development schools (Fullan et al., 1998, p. 56).

In 1985, the institutions of teacher education recognized that the quality of the teaching force was critical to education reform and that maintaining the profession was essential. Judith E. Lanier, then dean of the College of Education at Michigan State University, was chair when the Holmes Group released its first report in 1986 and recommended abolishing the undergraduate degree in education, tough new tests for prospective teachers, and a three-tier hierarchy of teachers.

The report also urged states to allow liberal arts graduates to be "instructors" at the bottom of a layered structure. Teachers at the two higher levels—named "professional" and "career professional"—would closely supervise the instructors. These instructors also would receive extensive graduate training in pedagogy. At the end of 5 years, the instructors would either have to leave or begin graduate work in educational theory and methodology, the report suggested. Every state already required the two subjects as prerequisites for certification. Lanier acknowledged the expense of the plan, but she argued that additional staff costs for the supervision would be offset by the lower pay for instructors and greater use of paraprofessionals.

Not surprisingly, various universities had implemented different training programs, including extending the traditional 4-year baccalaureate level as recommended by the Holmes Group (Carnegie Forum, 1986; Clifford & Guthrie, 1988; Goodlad, 1990). At least early on, this strategy did not show much success. In a national survey of institutions with graduate programs in education, 90% provided a 4-year baccalaureate in elementary education, 89% in secondary education, and 67% in special education. Clearly, "the four-year program remains the primary route to teacher certification while the extended program is intended for students who decide late in their educational experience to pursue a teaching career" (Wong & Osguthorpe, 1993, p. 64). Wong and Osguthorpe concluded their report by writing "there is no research to indicate that the teaching profession itself will rise in stature following the implementation of extended programs" (p. 69).

The concept of the professional development school (PDS) was a descendant of the laboratory schools of the early 20th century whereby the new teacher learned to plan and teach alongside more experienced teachers. All worked collaboratively with university- and school-based faculty. Although a commitment to establish professional development schools was a requirement for membership in the Holmes Group (Holmes Group, 1986, p. 66), by 1990, "most PDSs were operated . . . on a basis not significantly different from that of other schools" (Fullan et al., 1998, p. 49).

Despite the framework calling for more rigorous teacher preparation—either in a professional development school setting or in university classrooms—many states were introducing policies that allegedly deemphasized professional preparation for teachers. In fact, the 1980s "were characterized by a growing public agenda for educational improvement that appeared to be simple, feasible and cost-effective, involving testing teachers at entry and exit points, limiting the number of hours of pedagogical training, and establishing alternative routes for new sources of candidates" (Fullan et al., 1998, p. 66).

In *The Rise and Stall of Teacher Education Reform*, Michael Fullan and colleagues (1998) concluded that the "efforts that began with enthusiasm in the first half of that decade [1985–1995], faltered with discouragement and confusion in the 1990s" as the Holmes Group faded away (p. 15). Even the involvement of influential insider institutions of higher education did little to affect the status quo, except perhaps to become more watchful of the growth of alternate route programs.

The Carnegie Forum.   In May 1986, the Carnegie Forum on Education and the Economy released its report, *A Nation Prepared: Teachers for the 21st Century, The Report of the Task Force on Teaching as a Profession*. The previous year, the Carnegie Corporation of New York had created the Carnegie Forum on Education and the Economy (CFEE). CFEE was intended to "draw America's attention to the link between economic growth and the skills and abilities of the people who contribute to that growth, and to help develop education policies to meet the economic challenges ahead" (p. iii).

David A. Hamburg, the Carnegie Forum's chairman, appointed a task force[8] that included New Jersey governor Thomas H. Kean, whose state had implemented the first highly publicized alternate route to teacher certification, and Judith E. Lanier, who had spearheaded the Holmes Group and was chair when its first report was issued in 1986. Lewis M. Branscomb, a research physicist and head of the Education Relations Board of IBM, served as the chairman of the task force. In the Carnegie Forum (1986) report, Branscomb listed the four purposes that had motivated the task force:

1. to remind Americans, yet again, of the economic challenges pressing us on all sides;
2. to assert the primacy of education as the foundation of economic growth, equal opportunity and a shared national vision;
3. to reaffirm that the teaching profession is the best hope for establishing new standards of excellence as the hallmark of American education; and
4. to point out that a remarkable window of opportunity lies before us in the next decade to reform education, an opportunity that may not present itself again until well into the next century. (p. 7)

The Carnegie Forum (1986) report included numerous charts and graphs, several of which were intended to support its contention that "we can anticipate a steep increase in the annual rate new teachers must be hired: from 115,000 new teachers in 1981 to 215,000 in 1992, by conservative estimates" (p. 31). The Carnegie Forum predicted that "between 1986 and 1992, 1.3 million new teachers will be hired" (p. 31).

That present and future teachers should be "professionals" was a critical point emphasized throughout the Carnegie Forum Task Force Report (1986), which stated,

> Professional work is characterized by the assumption that the job of the professional is to bring special expertise and judgment to bear on the work at hand. Because their expertise and judgment is respected and they alone are presumed to have it, professionals enjoy a high degree of autonomy in carrying out their work. They define the standards used to evaluate the quality of work done, they decide what standards are used to judge the qualifications of professionals in their field, and they have a major voice in deciding what program of preparation is appropriate for professionals in their field. (p. 36)

---

[8] Lewis M. Branscomb, International Business Machines Corporation (IBM); Alan K. Campbell, ARA Services; Mary Hatwood Futrell, NEA; John W. Gardner, writer; Fred M. Hechinger, New York Times Company Foundation; Bill Honig, California superintendent of public instruction; James B. Hunt, attorney; Vera Katz, speaker of the Oregon House of Representatives; Thomas H. Kean, governor of New Jersey; Judith E. Lanier, dean, College of Education, Michigan State University; Arturo Madrid, Tomas Rivera Center; Shirley M. Malcom, American Association for the Advancement of Science; and Albert Shanker, AFT.

The Carnegie Forum framework to "attract to teaching highly qualified people who would otherwise take up other professional careers" included some elements for the profession as a whole and some elements that required teachers to agree to higher standards for themselves and real accountability for student performance. These were the major elements of the Carnegie Forum Task Report (1986) framework:

- Create a National Board for Professional Teaching Standards, organized with a regional and state membership structure, to establish high standards for what teachers need to know and be able to do, and to certify teachers who meet that standard.
- Restructure schools to provide a professional environment for teachers, freeing them to decide how best to meet state and local goals for children while holding them accountable for student progress.
- Restructure the teaching force, and introduce a new category of Lead Teachers with the proven ability to provide active leadership in the redesign of the schools and in helping their colleagues to uphold high standards of learning and teaching.
- Require a bachelor's degree in the arts and sciences as a prerequisite for the professional study of teaching.
- Develop a new professional curriculum in graduate schools of education leading to a Master in Teaching degree, based on systematic knowledge of teaching and including internships and residencies in the schools.
- Mobilize the nation's resources to prepare minority youngsters for teaching careers.
- Relate incentives for teachers to school-wide student performance, and provide schools with the technology, services and staff essential to teacher productivity.
- Make teachers' salaries and career opportunities competitive with those in other professions. (pp. 55–56)

Interestingly, only Mary Hatwood Futrell, then president of the National Education Association (NEA), issued a "Statement of Support with Reservations." Among the six issues she noted, this was the sixth. Futrell wrote, "I believe the report presumptuous in advocating a singular model of teacher preparation—a graduate-level program—at a time when those who teach teachers are debating numerous ways to improve professional training. Further, no mention is made of the need for increased funding to teacher training programs" (p. 118).

Despite the lengthy discussions, the Carnegie Task Force Report (1986) did not press institutions of higher education to become more aggressive in the reforms outlined in the report. In fact, the only area of action determined by the task force was its intention to "convene a group immediately to plan for the National Board for Professional Teaching Standards (NBPTS)" (p. 111), a project that resulted in the establishment of NBPTS in 1987.

American Association of Colleges for Teacher Education.   By 1986, the American Association of Colleges for Teacher Education (AACTE) acknowledged that "teacher shortages and public discussion about the quality of teacher education have been a catalyst for the implementation in several states of alternative routes to certification for teachers." AACTE responded with its own definition of alternative certification (ERIC Digest, 1986):

> Typically, these state requirements include specific numbers of undergraduate credit hours from institutions of higher education in subject matter (such as math and English), in professional studies (such as child development and teaching methods), and in student teaching. Universities and colleges "certify" that their graduates have met these minimum credit hour standards as part of the state teacher licensure process. In some states, certificates are issued at graduation; in others, certificates are issues [sic] after a probationary teaching period. *Alternative teacher certification* [emphasis added] may be defined, then, as any significant departure from this traditional undergraduate route through teacher education programs in universities and colleges" and can vary according to the particular state's definition. (p. 3)

As the national membership organization of some of the institutions of higher education with traditional teacher preparation programs, AACTE went on record opposing the "trend moving teacher education out of the universities and returning major responsibility for it back to the public school districts" that Haberman had championed in his writings.

The previous year, AACTE had issued a position statement on alternative certification advocating that alternative teacher preparation programs (1) use selective admission standards, (2) employ a curriculum that provides the knowledge and skills needed by beginning teachers, (3) incorporate a supervised internship, and (4) assure competency in the subject field and in professional studies through use of an examination.

In its definition of alternative teacher certification, AACTE acknowledged that states might define alternative teacher certification in unique ways, just as others were devising their own definitions and assessing alternate routes.

U.S. Department of Education.   An influential report made its debut in 1986. The U.S. Department of Education supported the research of Nancy Adelman with assistance from Joan Michie and Joanne Bogart. The report was "intended for federal policymakers" and department staff to assess the following:

- The effects of federal actions on state and local alternative route operations,
- Methods for improving intergovernmental relations regarding alternate routes, and
- The effectiveness of federal programs in serving national priority groups. (p. 5)

This early national study has become the basis for much of the subsequent research on alternate routes. At the time, Adelman (1986) reported that "at least 18 states" allowed "alternate routes to a teaching certificate"; she described 12 alternative certification programs and eight retraining programs (p. 7). In addition to the state-approved alternative certification programs, Adelman (1986) acknowledged the "long-range proposals to restructure the teaching profession" as suggested by the Holmes group and the Carnegie Forum on Education and the Economy (p. 7). She correctly noted, however, that although the Holmes and Carnegie initiatives would likely "take some time," "alternative certification and retraining programs are already serving more immediate state and local school staffing needs" (p. 7).

Adelman Defines Alternative Certification Programs. In *An Exploratory Study of Teacher Alternative Certification and Retraining Programs,* Adelman (1986) defined alternative certification programs as "those teacher preparation programs that enroll noncertified individuals with at least a bachelor's degree, offering shortcuts, special assistance, or unique curricula leading to eligibility for a standard teaching credential" (p. 16). The study came about "because of concerns about the supply and quality of American teachers [especially] special types of teacher training programs that have been developed by states, localities, and institutions of higher education" called alternative certification programs (p. 7).

Adelman Studies 20 Alternative Certification Programs in 1986. Of the 20 programs studied, 12 related to alternative certification programs,[9] and 8 were retraining programs for subject-matter shortage areas. The retraining programs focused exclusively on offering veteran teachers new opportunities to retrain to become science and math teachers. Retraining programs are not reviewed here.

Adelman wrote that the sample used was some [unspecified] proportion of the total number [of alternate routes] in existence, but that "the size of the universe remains unknown" (p. 17). The study focused on programs that had "graduated" at least one cycle of participants by the summer of 1986 when the author collected the information.

---

[9] The 12 programs were Arizona Partners Project, George Mason University Career Switcher Program, Harvard University Math and Science Program, Houston Alternative Certification Program, Los Angeles Unified School District Trainee Program, University of Maryland Alternative Certification Program, University of Massachusetts Math/English/Science Technology Project, Memphis State University Lyndhurst Program, New Jersey Provisional Teacher Program, University of New Mexico/Santa Fe Public Schools Intern Program, Pennsylvania Teacher Intern Program, and University of Southern Maine Teachers for Secondary Schools Program.

The analyses and findings were based on a literature review and descriptions of the 20 programs. Within the report, Adelman provided the details of each program and descriptions of the components using the following outline:

I. Name of program
    A. Program Goals and Expectations
    B. Recruitment, Application, and Selection
    C. The Program
       1. Overview
       2. Formal Instruction
       3. Field Experience
       4. Supervision
       5. Evaluation of Participants
       6. Post-program Placement
       7. Program Evaluation
    D. Financing of the Program and Program Participants

Adelman included an annotated bibliography with the study. In it, she identified 60 studies, whose research findings assisted her in this study. Most of the literature reviewed focused on preparation programs, the need for mathematics and science teachers, teacher quality, state reforms, and certification issues.

Only two titles in the Adelman bibliography referred specifically to alternative certification, an indication of the paucity of early research on the subject. In one reference used by Adelman (1986), J.S. Hazlett wrote in *Contemporary Education*, "teacher education should be reformed rather than disregarded. Attention must be given to the profession itself before the discipline can be modified. Areas for improvement include salaries, working conditions, and teacher control over curriculum. Efforts at establishing alternative certification plans should be directed at improving current education programs" (p. 149).

The other title referenced was produced by the Southern Regional Education Board (SREB) in 1984. The paper covered "Alternative certification for teachers: 1984 state actions" and listed the legislative efforts in alternative certification among states within the Board's jurisdiction (p. 155). Also in 1984, SREB published a paper on state initiatives for developing alternative certification routes aimed at liberal arts graduates (p. 155).

To provide the context for why the alternative certification programs were developed, the literature review covered the following:

- Documentation of the extent of teacher shortages
- Recent state changes in teacher preparation and certification requirements
- Professional standards for mathematics and science teachers
- Assessment of teacher performance

Although the programs varied as to administrative control—combinations of a state educational agency (SEA), local educational agency (LEA), and institution of higher education (IHE)—the authors wrote that this diversity provided enough similarities to allow comparisons. The researchers noted some unique traits such as the involvement of business and industry.

Of the 20 programs, Adelman found various combinations with regard to the amount of formal coursework required, the length of the internship or student teaching period, provisions for financial and psychological support, and sources of funding. Adelman also reviewed the characteristics of the participants and the program components. All of the alternative certification programs met three of the four criteria suggested by the AACTE. Not all programs (or the states in which they were located) required a qualifying or competency examination for certification.

Of all 20 programs reviewed, including the New Jersey Provisional Teacher Program and the Houston Alternative Certification Program, all were administered in part by IHEs, most often in collaboration with an SEA and/or an LEA. Adelman (1986) identified only the Los Angeles Unified School District Teacher Trainee Program as administered by an LEA, without the involvement of an IHE (pp. 14–15).

Adelman and her assistants conducted telephone interviews with 76 individuals in 10 of the programs. Program administrators provided the names of program participants. Adelman "deliberately selected participants who had been placed in schools or school districts with several other trainees on the theory that the interviewees therefore would be able to compare and contrast their own experiences in the program with those of other participants whom they saw frequently" (p. 85). In turn, program participants named two supervisors who could evaluate their performance.

The supervisor identified a "regular teacher" to gauge the "attitude of traditionally prepared staff toward new strategies for professional training" (p. 86). Adelman noted that "regular teachers were particularly elusive" (p. 86).

Adelman Finds High Skills and Proficiency in Alternate Route Program Participants. Adelman reported the findings pursuant to the questions the study had addressed. Findings related to alternative certification were as follows:

- *Characteristics and Career Goals of Participants.* Alternative certification programs appear to be attracting well-educated individuals with a sincere interest in teaching. Participants' previous job experiences are diverse, but the majority of this sample had engaged in some type of instructional activity at some point prior to entering an alternative certification program. Participants' most common reason for enrolling in an alternative certification program is a personal commitment to go into teaching at some time (p. 8).

- *Characteristics and Success of Programs.* Alternative certification programs feature more field experience and more intense supervision in the field. Formal coursework is a compressed version of traditional teacher education. Full-time teaching responsibilities and attending formal instruction after work is highly stressful. Alternate route candidates had the most difficulty with classroom management skills, not unlike traditionally trained beginning teachers (p. 9).
- *Evaluations and Perceptions.* Alternative certification programs produce subject area–proficient teachers who are also rated highly on instructional skills (when compared to traditionally prepared beginning teachers). All alternatively certified teachers interviewed intended to teach. Supervisors described hostile or cynical reactions to the programs from some of their colleagues.

The Adelman report identified 7 of the 12 alternative certification programs that included salaries paid to the program participants during the time that the interns had full responsibility in a classroom. Such salaried opportunities, however, were not without criticism.

Connecticut Designed Its Alternate Route to Upgrade the Profession

Such criticism did not apply to Connecticut, where the state legislature had established the Connecticut Education Enhancement Act in 1986. As part of a comprehensive reform package, Connecticut's alternate route to teacher certification was designed to upgrade the profession and to ultimately raise teacher salaries (Bliss, 1990, p. 35). Not only did starting salaries for teachers with a BA degree increase, the median starting salary doubled within 7 years, benefiting all teachers in Connecticut regardless of their preparation route.

As a result, keen competition for public school teaching positions occurred in Connecticut. Salary increases made teaching a desirable career, and even when its supply of outstanding teachers exceeded the demand, the pool of qualified applicants to the alternate route did not diminish (Bliss, 1990, p. 45). "Burgeoning competition for a dwindling number of jobs," wrote Bliss, made teaching in Connecticut an attractive and valued profession (p. 46). Those who are not hired become part of the state's teacher reserve pool, "an important component of future supply and demand in Connecticut with massive retirements expected throughout this decade" (p. 47).

In *Alternate Certification in Connecticut: Reshaping the Profession,* a 1990 evaluation of the Connecticut Alternate Route to Certification, the author wrote,

With a three-year record of accomplishment, alternate certification in Connecticut has enjoyed enormous popularity with program participants as well as school personnel who work with alternate route teachers. The continued high employment rate in a fiercely competitive market is a key indicator of the program's contribution to the profession.

The danger with the type of positive data reported throughout this article, however, is that it can be used out of context. That Connecticut Alternate Route teachers are performing at least as well as teachers from standard programs should not be used as a general endorsement of the alternate route concept in states which take a different approach. (Bliss, 1990, p. 52)

Bliss reiterated the components of Connecticut's rigorous program and intensive training, including 2 years of mentoring from a state-trained mentor and a district-appointed supervisor (p. 52).

Alternate Routes Respond to Market Needs

Flexibility of Local School Needs. Proponents elsewhere suggested that alternative certification programs were market sensitive because they could be tailored to address teacher shortages. Where shortages in subjects such as mathematics, science, and special education were acute problems, alternative certification programs could be designed to train individuals for those specific positions. (McKibbin & Ray, 1994, p. 205). This flexibility was an advantage to the school district as well as to the alternate route program.

Favorable to Ethnic Minorities. Furthermore, it was confirmed that black teacher candidates were more likely to pass a classroom evaluation (instead of an examination), as was available in the Virginia Beginning Teacher Assistance Program, an alternate route to licensure program (Smith, 1988, p. 186).

To address the teacher quality issue within their teacher preparation programs, some institutions of higher education began to require entrance examinations and educational requirements to raise the standards for candidates to university-based teacher education programs. As testing requirements became more commonplace, criticism mounted against the requirements. An article that appeared in the *Journal of Negro Education* in 1988 pointed out the effects of competency testing on ethnic minority teachers and prospective teachers. "In every state where data are available," the author wrote, "disproportionate numbers of minority candidates are failing admission and teacher certification tests" (Smith, 1988, p. 180). The declining number of minority teachers prepared through traditional teacher education programs and, consequently, the declining proportion of ethnic minorities in the teaching force was a national concern that those favoring alternate routes did not overlook.

Despite assertions of negative impact, several studies confirmed that alternative certification had increased the numbers of minorities and men entering teaching (Dill, 1994; Feistritzer, 2005a; Natriello & Zumwalt, 1992, 1993).

One of the strongest arguments for alternate routes to teaching was that the routes created opportunities for tapping into new pools of prospective teachers, especially in subject-matter shortage areas (Darling-Hammond, 1990, p. 140). Another pro–alternate route argument cited the success in recruiting particular types of teachers, including minorities and men. Because alternate routes target individuals to meet the specific needs of the schools in which there are teacher vacancies, alternate routes in some states have more success in placing teachers where they are needed than teacher preparation programs that do not target specific populations for high-need subjects and high-need locations (Lutz & Hutton, 1989, p. 242).

Some Critics Hoped Alternate Routes Would Disappear Quickly

In writing an article for the U.S. Department of Education, Linda Darling-Hammond (1990) covered the concerns that others were expressing about the proliferation of alternate routes. Darling-Hammond is an outspoken advocate of traditional teacher preparation programs. She wrote, "it seems an appropriate time to review the status of this policy idea [alternate routes] in light of knowledge about teaching and teacher effectiveness, and to assess the outcomes of alternative certification programs for teacher supply and quality" (p. 123).

As Darling-Hammond (1990) compared the variations among alternate routes, she noted, "some initiatives consist primarily of new recruitment strategies for full teacher certification, while others really create an 'alternative certificate' which diverges substantially from the regular certification process in terms of both the standards and methods for teacher preparation and entry" (p. 124).

Of the significant differences between fast-track routes and lengthier teacher preparation programs, according to Darling-Hammond, are the differing beliefs about what it is that teachers need to know to be effective. Fast-track (alternate) routes assume that with brief preliminary training teachers will learn on the job, including critical pedagogical skills. Inconsistent supervision, however, results in less than effective clinical training and on-the-job experiences. Darling-Hammond (1990) cited several studies that concluded, "fully prepared and certified teachers are generally more highly rated and more successful with students than teachers without full preparation" (p. 130).

Like other proponents of traditional teacher education programs, Darling-Hammond regarded fully prepared as those individuals whose teacher preparation had been through a traditional program. "Fully prepared" meant that a teacher's knowledge of the subject matter to be taught made a difference in teaching up to some level of basic competence, however, teachers also needed to know about learners and the learning process.

Properly presented professional education courses (pedagogy) can affect teacher performance in the classroom, especially in developing higher order skills and problem solving tasks. And finally, Darling-Hammond provided references to substantiate the importance of high-quality induction support for beginning teachers.

Because the creation of alternate routes was not yet 10 years old at the time of the article, considerable variations existed among those routes that had been implemented. Darling-Hammond suggested that states and policymakers consider establishing high standards in all aspects of alternate route programs if states adopted such routes. Alternate routes to teaching did create a new pool of prospective teachers and even attracted more minority teachers. Nevertheless, Darling-Hammond (1990) concluded,

> [S]tate policies will need to include investments in continuing improvements to teacher salaries, working conditions, and other factors influencing the attractiveness of teaching, along with subsidies for teacher preparation and incentives for the continuing improvement of teacher education. If alternate routes are successful in the short term at suggesting some viable, high-quality options for preparing teachers for the more challenging demands of 21st century schools, their success should be measured in the long term by their disappearance, and the incorporation of their best-tested features into a reconstituted teacher education and certification structure." (p. 149)

Proponent Credits Alternate Routes as a Bold Plan

In opposition to critics and opponents, Chester E. Finn, Jr.,[10] voiced support for the continuation and growth of alternate routes. In 1991, Finn wrote,

> Perhaps the boldest way to attract and keep more able and better qualified people in school teaching is to redefine the pool of prospective instructors. . . . Do not confine entry into teaching to recent graduates of traditional preparation programs. Instead, invite midcareer people (and young college graduates with degrees in academic fields) to try it, providing them with enough on-the-job supervision, mentoring, and pointers on classroom craftsmanship to create a reasonable chance that they will succeed. Retain those who do well; urge those who don't to seek other lines of work. (pp.194–195)

Finn was also not shy about commenting about those who resisted the idea of alternative routes to teacher certification. Finn (1991) wrote, "Yet—as one might expect—the idea is resisted by colleges of education, whose monopoly it menaces; by state license givers, who previously needed only to scrutinize

---

[10] Chester E. Finn, Jr., served as assistant secretary for research and improvement and counselor to the secretary of the U.S. Department of Education from 1985 to 1988. He is now president of the Thomas B. Fordham Foundation, a nonprofit organization that supports research, publications, and action projects of national significance in elementary/ secondary education reform.

a candidate's transcript and test scores, not to worry about their classroom effectiveness; and by teacher unions, who fear its ominous implication that if any one can become a teacher, what's the value of specialized professional expertise? (p. 195).

Alternative Certification: An Effort to Deregulate Teacher Preparation

When he was a professor in the college of education at the University of Arizona, Tucson, Gary D. Fenstermacher (1990) created a unique perspective for looking at alternative certification (p. 160). His views included the customary concepts of competition, opportunity, and supply and demand of the marketplace. Fenstermacher (1990) noted that deregulation and a revival of the market economy were also part of the political agenda in the last quarter of the 20th century. Some saw alternative certification as an extension of the deregulation effort because it provided a way to enter teaching by avoiding what some thought to be the monopoly controls of the teacher education colleges and universities (p. 161; Stoddart & Floden, 1995, pp. 2–3). No doubt some supporters of alternative certification became proponents to "break the lock that teacher education institutions appear to have on entry into the teaching profession" (Fenstermacher, 1990, p. 160).

As protectors of the status quo and the bargaining agent for some in higher education, the NEA responded to alternate routes. Alternate routes gave authority to school district officials to recommend teachers for certification, authority previously assumed by college and university faculty. In a resolution, first adopted in 1990 (amended in 2000), the NEA declared, "individuals interested in teaching as a career should attend institutions accredited by the National Council for Accreditation of Teacher Education[11] (NCATE)" (NEA, 2005, p. 245). This was precisely one of the "locks" that Fenstermacher (1990) had referred to in his writing (p. 160).

Dale Ballou and Mike Podgursky (2000) expounded on the relationship of the unions and NCATE (along with several other organizations) in *Conflicting Missions: Teachers Unions and Educational Reform:* "Regulations, control of licensing and accreditation of institutions that prepare professionals have long been used as a device to restrict entry to the profession, to reduce the amount of competition found, and to promote, and ultimately to hire" (p. 80). Furthermore, they wrote, "By available objective measures, there is virtually no relationship between NCATE accreditation and the quality of newly trained teachers" (p. 87). Yet the NEA has

---

[11] The National Education Association supports NCATE through various resources, including contributions. In 2005, NEA contributed more than $370,000 to NCATE.

promoted the notion that NEA affiliates should seek through bargaining that districts will only hire teachers who have come from programs accredited by NCATE.

Similar findings resulted from a study by Arthur Levine (2006), in which he found that "Accreditation by the National Council for the Accreditation of Teacher Education (NCATE) does not assure program quality. Of 100 graduate schools of education ranked by *U.S. News and World Report,* three of the top ten are accredited as compared to eight of the lowest ten" (p. 5).

As for costs, Ballou and Podgursky (2000) noted, "If NCATE accreditation were required of all teacher education programs, the costs of compliance could drive small programs in liberal arts colleges from the market" (p. 99).

Variations Were Characteristic as Alternate Routes Showed Steady Growth

Variations Occurred at All Levels

Researchers and educators acknowledged that the variations of alternate routes to teacher certification were as different from one another as they were from the widely divergent traditional routes (Darling-Hammond,[12] 1990, p. 124; Feistritzer, 1990; Kennedy, 1999; Zumwalt, 1991). Some (Ashton, 1991; Bliss, 1990) wrote about inconsistencies in policies and programs affecting teacher preparation for elementary and secondary teachers. Significant differences in standards also existed within subject-matter fields, with higher standards expected of those who were preparing to teach science or mathematics or elementary English. The analyses showed that "teacher preparation" was not a single phenomenon, and neither were the demands coming from the school districts (Feistritzer, 1999; Wilson et al., 2001, p. 5).

Even after being prepared to teach, several states issued a variety of licenses to teach depending on the criteria (if any) required to fill the vacancies. For example, some states issued a so-called eminence credential. This license, when issued to persons of great distinction and accomplishment in a particular field, permitted them to teach courses in the area of their expertise. This, too, complicated the study of alternate routes.

---

[12] Darling-Hammond considered an *alternate route* as a program that provided full preparation for standard certification but that did so in a "nontraditional" manner—that is, at the graduate school level, with flexible scheduling, and/or coursework targeted at special recruitment pools. Darling-Hammond concluded that *alternative certification* changed the rules by which certification was granted, by modifying or eliminating certain coursework or student teaching requirements, resulting in more limited preparation than required by standard certification.

Licensure Requirements.   Within the alternative certification routes, states created different licensure requirements, including temporary licenses, restricted licenses, and other variations (Feistritzer, 1999, p. 3). In 1990, a Congressional Research Service report indicated to Congress that there were at least four different ways to obtain an initial teaching license. One, through traditional teacher education, was also known as the approved programs approach. The second and third mechanisms were emergency credentials and alternative certification, respectively. The fourth way was direct application, wherein an applicant assembles a documentary record showing that all state requirements for a license have been met and submits this record directly to the state for review and issuance of a license.

A problem for alternate routes had been its association with emergency credentials or licenses. In 1991, when Karen Zumwalt was dean of education at Teachers College, Columbia University, she suggested that alternative certification programs were disguised emergency licensing programs (1991, p. 41). Often in desperation to fill a teacher vacancy, school officials issued emergency certificates to individuals who neither had teaching credentials nor were expected to acquire them. Disguised or not, almost all states acknowledged that the licensing authorities issued more emergency certificates in 1989 than were issued in 1985 (Feistritzer, 1990, pp. 13–16).

Neither emergency teacher certificates nor certificates issued to completers of alternate route programs eliminated all teacher vacancies, and there were still many questions about who was getting hired to teach and how. Recall, however, that New Jersey officials announced that the state's alternate route had eliminated emergency licenses in that state.

Program Names.   The issuing of various licenses, the variety among program components in alternative routes to teacher certification, the continued growth of alternative routes, and curiosity about those individuals opting to learn to teach through on-the-job training added to the confusion surrounding alternate routes. Perhaps most confusing of all was the practice of calling some programs alternate routes, a change in name only, a practice identified by Lynn M. Cornett (1990a) an official with the Southern Regional Education Board (SREB). Cornett reviewed the results of state policy changes after the recommendations of the SREB's Task Force on Higher Education and the Schools. Among its recommendations, the SREB Task Force suggested that states should modify certification requirements to permit graduates in mathematics and science who lack professional education preparation to teach at the secondary levels, with safeguards to ensure the quality of instruction.

Although all 15 SREB states reported alternative certification programs in place in 1990, not all existing programs met the author's definition of alternative certification programs: "state programs that alter licensure requirements through (a) completing a different set of standards (i.e., limiting the number of education courses required); and (b) meeting licensure requirements by demonstrating competency (i.e., passing tests for certification, on the job evaluations, and/or completing a supervised internship)" (Cornett, 1990b, p. 57).

Among the findings, Cornett (1990b) reported,

- SREB states that did not alter licensure requirements for alternative certification programs: Alabama, Louisiana, and Oklahoma
- SREB states that did alter licensure requirements for alternative certification programs: Arkansas, Florida, Georgia, Kentucky, Maryland, Mississippi, North Carolina, South Carolina, Tennessee, Texas, Virginia, and West Virginia
  - The 12 states (above) require tests and on-the-job performance assessment of all beginning teachers.
  - Entrance requirements are equal to or higher than those entering regular teacher education programs.
  - Additional supervision (mentors) is often required.
  - All are joint efforts of higher education institutions and schools.
- The alternative certification programs are attracting individuals who would not otherwise enter teaching:
  - *Older persons:* "In 1989, twice as many persons were prepared through alternative certification programs in SREB states as were prepared just two years before."
  - *Minorities:* "A larger portion of persons trained through alternative certification programs were minorities as compared to the traditional teacher education programs."
  - *Gender:* "A larger proportion of the candidates being prepared were male as compared to the traditional programs."
  - *Pass Rates:* "In Texas, alternative certification interns have higher pass rates on certification tests than do traditional education graduates. Minorities have markedly higher pass rates than minorities who are initially certified through regular channels." (p. 78)

Cornett took her conclusion of the findings to the next step: SREB states must begin to track teachers and their performance in the classroom to get conclusive answers on the effectiveness of different teacher preparation models.

Leo Klagholz recalls the challenges and pressures as the states considered alternate routes. As alternate route programs in pioneer states began to show some success, state certification directors elsewhere were caught between two kinds of pressure. On one hand, they were being asked by politicians, state board members, and citizen groups in their home states to propose alternate route programs of their own. On the other hand, their college teacher education constituents were opposing alternate routes and urging them to stand firmly against the new idea. Some certification directors themselves sincerely opposed the idea, but others sought only to weather the storm by placating the public with nominal alternate routes. Some dusted off and renamed existing mechanisms, like transcript review or the master of arts in teaching (MAT), claiming they had "alternate routes" all along. Others proposed true alternate routes but burdened them with so many restrictions that they had little impact. Still others proposed workable programs that were corrupted and rendered unworkable in the give-and-take of the public processes of state boards and legislatures.

The NCEI Sorts Out Alternate Route Data

Meanwhile, to sort out what was happening state by state, the National Center for Education Information (NCEI), established by Emily Feistritzer in 1979, began to collect information and data from the state directors of teacher education and certification at the time that New Jersey was establishing its alternative route.[13] In its polling of officials in the 50 states and the District of Columbia, NCEI asked officials to "Check the statement which describes your state's status concerning alternatives to approved college teacher preparation programs for certifying teachers":

- Considering alternatives
- Have proposed alternatives
- Implementing alternatives
- Not even considering alternatives

NCEI endeavored to find out more and to get answers to such questions as: What actually were alternative routes? Whom did they serve? What was required to get into an alternate route? What was required to get through one? What were the program components? Who operated alternate route programs?

As more state authorities began to permit alternate routes and approve alternate route programs, NCEI asked about the status of alternative teacher certification, types of certificates issued by each state, and the number of certificates issued in each year.

NCEI Produces a State-by-State Analysis of Alternate Routes

NCEI president Emily Feistritzer created a format to describe each of the programs in existence at the time and published the data in *Alternative Teacher Certification: A State-by-State Analysis* in 1990 and updated it annually.

The 31 states that reported they were implementing alternative teacher certification programs in 1990 revealed enormous variation in entry requirements, program requirements, certification requirements, and the length of

---

[13] Dr. C. Emily Feistritzer served on a task force that New Jersey officials convened in 1983 to help shape the new alternate route.

time required to complete the program. Furthermore, close scrutiny of the data revealed that very few states had actually designed a certification path specifically for the growing market of adults who already had at least a bachelor's degree, had little or no formal training in professional education courses, and who wanted to teach.

Of states that had designed alternative routes to certification, some routes were available only if there were a shortage of traditionally certified teachers. Other states designed alternative routes only for secondary teachers. Still other states allowed the institutions of higher education in their state to design alternatives to their college-approved teacher education programs. A few states used transcript analysis—that is, they made a determination concerning certification on the basis of a review of college transcripts and résumés of applicants. Several states had combinations of two or more of the above. One state required that an applicant to its alternative certification route have 5 years of prior teaching experience (Feistritzer, 1990, p. 9).

NCEI Develops a Classification System for Alternate Routes

In 1991, in an attempt to provide some order to the different alternate routes, as well as attempt to give some direction to the movement, NCEI developed a classification system. The system made distinctions among the routes, including the reason for establishing the route, who administered it, the entry requirements, and restrictions, if any (Feistritzer & Chester, 1991, pp. 17–24).

Class A.   Class A is reserved for those routes that meet the following criteria:
- The alternative teacher certification route has been designed for the explicit purpose of attracting talented individuals who already have at least a bachelor's degree in a field other than education into elementary and secondary school teaching.
- The alternate route is not restricted to shortages, secondary grade levels, or subject areas.
- The alternative route involves teaching with a trained mentor and formal instruction that deals with the theory and practice of teaching during the school year, and sometimes in the summer before and/or after.

Class B.   Class B is for teacher certification routes that have been designed specifically to bring talented individuals who already have at least a bachelor's degree into teaching. These routes involve specially designed mentoring and some formal instruction. However, they either restrict the route to shortages and/or secondary grade levels and/or subject areas.

Class C.   Class C routes entail review of academic and professional background, and transcript analysis. They involve individually designed inservice and course taking necessary to reach competencies required for certification, if applicable. The state and/or local school district have major responsibility for program design.

Class D.   Class D routes entail review of academic and professional background, and transcript analysis. They involve individually designed inservice and course taking necessary to reach competencies required for certification, if applicable. An institution of higher education has major responsibility for program design.

Class E.   These routes are postbaccalaureate programs based at an institution of higher education.

Class F.   Class F routes are basically emergency routes. The prospective teacher is issued some type of emergency certificate or waiver that allows the individual to teach, usually without any on-site support or supervision, while taking the traditional teacher education courses requisite for full certification.

Class G.   Class G routes are for persons who have few requirements left to fulfill before becoming certified through the traditional approved college teacher education program route (e.g., persons certified in one state moving to another or persons certified in one endorsement area seeking to become certified in another).

Class H.   Class H includes those routes that enable a person who has some "special" qualifications, such as a well-known author or Nobel Prize winner, to teach certain subjects.

Class I.   Class I is for states that reported they were not implementing alternatives to the approved college teacher education program route for licensing teachers. States, however, submitted other information for publication in *Alternative Teacher Certification: A State-by-State Analysis,* such as the number of IHEs offering approved teacher education programs and the numbers of new teachers produced and certificates issued. This class no longer exists.

Class J.   Class J programs are designed to eliminate emergency routes. They prepare individuals to meet basic requirements to become qualified to enter an alternate route. This class was added in 2000.

Class K.   Class K avenues to certification accommodate specific populations for teaching (e.g., Teach For America, Troops to Teachers, and college professors who want to teach in K–12 schools). This class was added in 2002.

This classification system became the standard for describing what the states called alternative routes to teacher certification. Of this and subsequent work by NCEI, Leo Klagholz (personal communication, 2006) said, "NCEI's role in this regard was important. NCEI's surveys and publications were important because they not only classified disparate state efforts; they ultimately influenced what states were doing and helped generate continuity. A sorting-out process was made necessary because alternate routes essentially emerged in individual states, not in response to any common set of national occurrences."

Since the late 1990s, more and more state alternative routes have been designed specifically for nontraditional populations of postbaccalaureate candidates, many of whom come from other careers (classes A and B).

There has also been an increase in state alternative routes administered by colleges and universities (classes D and E) and a decrease in the number administered by school districts (class C). The bulk of alternate routes in 2006 were class A through E routes.

Over the years, NCEI has continued to report and analyze developments in the field of alternative certification as reported by a state's contact responding to the annual NCEI questionnaire.

State data gathered for the report for the year in question include reporting on these factors:

- Additions, changes, or deletions from the prior year's alternate routes
- Numbers of teaching certificates issued to persons who completed an alternate route
- Racial, ethnicity, gender, and age characteristics of alternate route candidates
- An estimation of the primary activity of alternate route candidates prior to program entry
- The types of communities that alternate route participants teach in
- The employment (full time or part time) and cost of the alternative route
- The number of *newly hired* teachers by the state
- The numbers of total teachers employed by the state
- The numbers of persons in the state who completed an approved college teacher preparation program
- The numbers of emergency teaching licenses issued by the state
- The numbers of temporary/other teaching licenses issued by the state

The annual report includes a longitudinal sequence for each of the data sets since 1985–1986. In addition, *Alternative Teacher Certification: A State-by-State Analysis* includes a descriptive profile of each alternate route in each of the states and the District of Columbia. The appendix includes several examples of state alternate routes.

Amid the scrutiny from individuals, groups, and organizations who opposed or supported alternate routes, state officials proceeded to develop, expand, and approve alternate routes to meet the specific needs within their states. What started in New Jersey, California, and Texas had become a movement by 1990, with 31 states reporting they had some type of alternate route to teacher certification. In 2006, all 50 states and the District of Columbia reported having at least one alternate route to teacher certification.

3

❖

How Did New National Programs and Federal Involvement Promote Alternate Route Participation?

*A*lternative routes to certification were state programs, not federal programs. Alternate routes continued to grow by meeting the needs of local school districts. Armed with statistics of shortages and needs, proponents of alternative routes to teacher certification appealed to the supply of experienced individuals willing to commit to teaching in challenging subjects and locations.

New National Programs Boost Alternate Route Participation

Teach For America

By chance, Wendy Kopp, Princeton class of 1989, surmised that top-notch new college graduates might also feel a calling to teach. By design, Kopp turned her senior thesis into a "blueprint for revitalizing the teaching profession" with energetic idealists just out of college (Mabry, 1990). Teach For America (TFA) looked somewhat like the old Teacher Corps, but Kopp likened it more to the Peace Corps—selective, competitive, and prestigious—but funded by corporate donations and foundation grants, as well as federal funding.

Similar to the Peace Corps program of the 1960s, a 2-year commitment in TFA did not necessarily result in a new degree or in a teaching certificate.

After training by TFA staff and placement of TFA cohorts in schools, TFA corps members make a commitment to teach for 2 years in a high-need school.

Although the media, and even education researchers and analysts, often refer to TFA as an alternate route, it was not and is not an alternate route to teacher certification. Rather, it is a *recruitment and leadership program,* as its mission states:

> Teach For America is the national corps of outstanding recent college graduates of all academic majors who commit two years to teach in urban and rural public schools and become lifelong leaders in the effort to expand educational opportunity. Our mission is to build the movement to eliminate educational inequity by enlisting some of our nation's most promising future leaders in the effort. (TFA, 2005, p. 11)

No doubt, some of the identity confusion comes from the way in which TFA recruits are employed. According to the TFA Website, school districts hire TFA corps members through state-approved alternative certification programs. TFA corps members must meet specific requirements and demonstrate proficiency in the subject areas they will teach. These program requirements vary by region and by position, but in most cases corps members must pass subject-area tests before teaching and take ongoing coursework during the school year.

TFA staff work with school districts, states, and schools of education to ensure that corps members have access to coursework, test information, and preparation tools to meet these requirements. In many regions, TFA has established partnerships with graduate schools that enable corps members to obtain a master's degree in education. Although TFA connects corps members to these resources, ultimately corps members are responsible for ensuring they meet the required standards and cover the related costs. As beginning teachers, all TFA corps members receive the beginning salary and benefits of the school district in which they are teaching. As reported by TFA on www.teachforamerica.org/program/html, 39% of TFA alumni are teaching or are administrators in K–12 schools.

Since 1990, Teach For America (2005) reports that its "corps members have directly impacted the lives of 2 million students and form a growing force of civic leaders committed to ensuring that our nation lives up to its ideal of opportunity for all" (p. 11). TFA represents a significant new supply of individuals in the marketplace, who, for a limited time, meet the demands of high-need schools[1] but who may lack the formal education requirements

---

[1] High-need school means a school that (a) is located in an area in which the percentage of students from families with incomes below the poverty line is 30% or more; or (b) is located in an area with a high percentage of out-of-field teachers; is within the top quartile of elementary schools and secondary schools statewide, as ranked by the number of unfilled, available teacher positions at the schools; is located in an area in which there is a high teacher turnover rate; or is located in an area in which there is a high percentage of teachers who are not certified or licensed.

to teach unless TFA corps members complete their education requirements in the requisite 3-year period. True to its founder's intent, TFA has become increasingly selective and competitive, as these statistics from 2005 show:

> More than 17,000 individuals applied to join Teach For America in 2005, including 12 percent of the senior classes of Yale and Spelman, 11 percent of the graduating classes at Dartmouth and Amherst College, and 8 percent of Princeton and Harvard graduates. Applicants undergo a rigorous selection process; in 2005 Teach For America had a 17 percent acceptance rate. Upon joining the program, new corps members take part in intensive pre-service training, followed by a program of ongoing support throughout their first two years in the classroom. (TFA, 2005, p. 11)

In 2005, TFA reported that 3,500 first-and second-year corps members were teaching in over 1,000 schools in 22 regions across the country most profoundly impacted by the gap in educational outcomes (TFA, 2005, p. 11). This represents TFA corps member enrollment in alternate route programs in 17 states and the District of Columbia. Also, TFA reported in 2005 that "63 percent of our alumni (more than 10,000) are currently working full-time in education," although it provided no breakdown among those teaching, starting schools, becoming principals, or serving as district administrators (TFA, 2005, p. 11).

As part of its mission, TFA acknowledges, "In the long run, we build a force of leaders with the insight and conviction that comes from having taught in a low-income community, who work from inside education and from every other sector to effect the fundamental changes needed to ensure that all children have an equal chance in life" (TFA, 2005, p. 11). In addition, other TFA alumni are working to expand educational opportunity while pursuing careers in law, public policy, medicine, and business.

In a survey of 2,000 of its teacher corps members, TFA (2005) found that "Teacher quality and expectations of students outranked funding as both causes of and solutions to the [achievement] gap" (p. 1). TFA reported that "as corps members spend more time in the classroom the priority they place on funding gives way to other factors, such as school leadership" (p. 1). As a result, corps members expressed skepticism about increasing funding without addressing the allocation of resources" (p. 1).

What began as an entrepreneurial venture, TFA is now a public-private partnership with a 2005 operating budget of $38.5 million. Corporations, foundations, and individuals fund 70% of the budget; public source funds come from the federal AmeriCorps program (8%) and the school districts in which TFA works (www.teachforamerica.org).

Troops to Teachers

Another popular program that recruits highly qualified individuals into teaching is Troops to Teachers, originally conceived as a plan for retired military noncommissioned officers to teach in inner-city schools (Sawyer, 1993).

Because 96% of noncommissioned officers (NCOs) did not have a baccalaureate degree, however, Congress amended the law in 1993 to allow NCOs to obtain an undergraduate degree as well as be eligible for the Troops to Teachers benefits. Benefits included federal grant funds and subsidies while teaching.

"A drill sergeant, when you strip it of the myth, is really a teacher," said Robert H. MacDonald during a newspaper interview in 1993 about the program. At the time, MacDonald was director of the Military Career Transition Program at Old Dominion University in Norfolk, Virginia. After 4 years, the Virginia program had recruited 800 individuals for the program, and 151 retired military servicemen and women had completed the training and had been placed as teachers (Sawyer, 1993).

Troops to Teachers was authorized by the Congress of the United States in the Defense Authorization Bill introduced in 1993. Since 1994, the Defense Activity for Non-Traditional Education Support (DANTES) has collected data and provided daily program administration. Since 2000, the U.S. Department of Education has had program oversight and management (U.S. GAO, 2006, p. 2). Troops to Teachers provides referral assistance and placement services to military personnel interested in beginning a second career in public education as a teacher. DANTES helps applicants identify teacher certification requirements and programs leading to certification and employment opportunities.

Unlike TFA corps members, former military personnel may opt to enroll in a traditional teacher education undergraduate program or graduate program or an alternate route program. As a federally funded program, Troops to Teachers came under congressional review in 1998 when Congress considered reauthorization and funding of programs in the Higher Education Act of 1965.

Alternate routes were providing more choices for those interested in teaching. Recruitment programs added even more options to teaching as a career or as an opportunity to "build the movement to eliminate educational inequity."

In 2005, when NCEI conducted a survey for Troops to Teachers, Troops indicated they had used several routes to certification, as shown in Figure 3.1.

Fifty-eight percent entered teaching through a traditional teacher education program and 40% entered teaching through an alternate route program; 2% were not sure what kind of program they went through (Feistritzer, 2005c, p. 32).

In addition to contributing to the much needed supply of teachers, Troops teachers met significant other needs as well. For example, in their attitudes about students, 90% of Troops survey respondents favored requiring students to meet the rigorous requirements of mathematics, history, English, and science for all students. Troops teachers agreed with the survey statement: "Socio-economic background does not prevent students from performing at the highest levels of achievement" (p. 10). Troops teachers also reported that they highly value the skills and discipline that they gained through their military training and would advise others to consider assistance to teaching through Troops to Teachers (p. 20).

Figure 3.1   Programs Through Which Troops to Teachers Candidates Entered Teaching

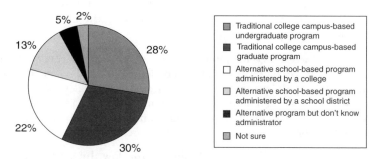

Source: National Center for Education Information, *Profile of Troops to Teachers,* 2005.

From 2002 through 2004, Troops to Teachers received about 3,500 registrations per year; it assisted about 1,200 participants to begin teaching as a new career. Not surprisingly, survey results showed that most Troops participants are men, and most teach at the high school level. In addition, many are persons of color: American Indian/Alaskan, Asian/Pacific Islander, black, Hispanic, and multiracial (p. 16). Troops teachers bring maturity and considerable life experience to the job of teaching the nation's youth. And Troops teachers have responded to the demand for teachers in inner cities.

Military veterans as well as other military personnel continue to represent a huge pool of individuals who could become teachers through an alternate route. According to military officials, since 2001, approximately 100,000 military individuals with at least a baccalaureate degree have retired from the military. In addition, some 140,000 National Guard and Reserve members have at least a bachelor's degree and 10 or more years of active duty. These qualifications make them eligible for assistance from Troops to Teachers to enroll in a teacher preparation program. As of 2005, nearly 8,000 former military personnel had entered K–12 teaching through this program (Feistritzer, 2005c, p. 39).

The Federal Government Boosts Alternate Routes

Alternative teacher certification got a boost at the national level in July 1992. It was then that President George H.W. Bush signed the 5-year reauthorization of the Higher Education Act of 1965, which by then had been under discussion for over a year in the U.S. Congress. For the first time, PL 102–325 authorized federal funding (President Bush requested $20 million) to assist implementation of state programs of alternative teacher certification.

Congress failed to fund the authorization. Nonetheless, recognition of the importance of alternative teacher certification by the president of the United States gave legitimacy to the movement that it had not enjoyed previously.

Specifically, subpart 2 of part D of Title V: Educator Recruitment, Retention, and Development established,

> this program of assistance for alternative routes to teacher certification or licensure, to improve the supply of qualified elementary and secondary school teachers and principals by assisting State programs to help talented professionals who have demonstrated high competence in a subject area and wish to pursue education careers to meet State certification licensing requirements, with special emphasis on minority group member participation.

At the time President Bush (1992) signed the law, he said, "In pursuing the reauthorization of the Higher Education Act of 1965, my administration was guided by three major principles:

1. Improving access to postsecondary education—especially for middle- and low-income students and families;
2. Enhancing accountability of all who play a role in postsecondary education programs; and
3. Promoting educational excellence. (p. 1).

President Bush (1992) also said that he was gratified that the reauthorization provided "for an alternative certification program by which States will develop new routes to teacher certification" (p. 1) and new academies for teachers and school leaders "to provide these educators with in-service training in academic and other educational areas" (p. 1).

Despite Congress's refusal to appropriate funds for part D of Title V for the 2 years requested, state legislatures were not deterred, nor were others who were concerned about providing opportunities and choices for those who wanted to teach.

Congress Adds Disclosure Requirements to 1998 Reauthorization of HEA

Political leaders continued to respond to public pressure to seek ways to assure accountability from those pursuing careers in education as well as those entities preparing teachers. Criticism of classroom teachers did not subside; rather, it began to expand to the faculty and administrators of teachers' colleges as well. In 1998, state politicians reacted, and so did members of Congress with the reauthorization of the Higher Education Act (HEA).

Because available student aid affects student decisions on whether to attend college, Congress directed its attention to updating the student financial aid components in the HEA of 1965. As noted earlier, the HEA of 1965 began as a vehicle to help needy college students attend institutions of higher education by establishing a system of federal grants and loans. Such decisions at the federal level impacted states as legislators set budgets for higher education and weighed possible expansion of programs and costs depending on changes in enrollment. As Congress began the debates for the 1998 reauthorization of the HEA, "There was an unusual amount of interest in how the federal government might leverage changes in teacher education" (Earley, 1998, p. 1). Some proposed changes included a program of federal funds that would support minority teacher recruitment; another proposed program linked an institution of higher education's eligibility for HEA funds to the pass rate of students on the state's teacher licensure examination (Earley, 1998, p. 1).

Congress considered various proposals; some could have been highly detrimental to traditional teacher preparation programs. "One such bill would have refashioned [one section of HEA] a program directed only to supporting alternative certification programs created and operated in lieu of education schools, colleges or departments" (1998, p. 1), according to an article by Penelope M. Earley, then a member of the government relations team at the American Association for Colleges of Teacher Education (AACTE). AACTE and other opponents of the bill pressured Congress to exclude the provisions of that bill and others before the final reauthorization bill was passed by both chambers in late September. On October 7, 1998, when President Clinton signed the reauthorization of the Higher Education Act of 1965, it contained new provisions and more funds for accountability and disclosure requirements for teacher education.

Title II: Teacher Quality

Title II of the 1998 HEA reauthorization incorporated provisions that related to teacher quality. Title II authorized separate grant programs focusing on

- Improving student achievement
- Improving teacher quality
- Holding institutions of higher education accountable for preparing well-qualified teachers
- Recruiting highly qualified teachers

Grant priority would be given to states that implemented initiatives to improve academic content and teaching skills of prospective educators in high-poverty urban and rural areas, initiatives that alternate routes most often incorporated into their programs. After the regulations were in place, the government began to award the competitive grants to states.

In fiscal year 2002, the U.S. Department of Education awarded grants to 21 states; the average continuation award for state grants was just over $1 million (USDoE, 2006a, p. 3). Among other provisions, grant funds could be used to create alternatives to traditional preparation for teaching. The act also permitted the expansion or improvement of alternative routes to state certification of teachers for highly qualified individuals, including

- Midcareer professionals from other occupations
- Paraprofessionals
- Former military personnel
- Recent college graduates with records of academic distinction

In 2005, Congress appropriated $68.3 million and in 2006, $59.8 million for the Teacher Quality enhancement grants through the Higher Education Act reauthorization. However, President George W. Bush's budget for 2007[2] did not include a request for continued funding (USDoE, 2006a, p. 17). The state recipients of the Teacher Quality enhancement grants do not identify how much, or if any, of the grant funds were used to enhance, improve, or implement alternate routes.

New Report Card Data Requirements

Title II in the HEA reauthorization of 1998 sets forth very specific accountability and reporting requirements for the states, institutions of higher education, and teacher preparation programs that receive federal grant funds through the reauthorized act. The state agencies report data through a state report card on the quality of teacher preparation in the state, including alternate route programs. At a minimum, as required by Section 207, the report card was to include the following stipulations:

(1) A description of the teacher certification and licensure assessments, and any other certification and licensure requirements, used by the State.

(2) The standards and criteria that prospective teachers must meet in order to attain initial teacher certification or licensure and to be certified or licensed to teach particular subjects or in particular grades within the State.

(3) A description of the extent to which the assessments and requirements described in paragraph (1) are aligned with the State's standards and assessments for students.

(4) The percentage of teaching candidates who passed each of the assessments used by the State for teacher certification and licensure, and the passing score on each assessment that determines whether a candidate has passed that assessment.

---

[2] President Bush requested a continuation of the Improving Teacher Quality State Grants, which are distributed through the Elementary and Secondary Education Act (*No Child Left Behind*). These grants have been funded since fiscal year 2002; Congress appropriated $2.9 billion in fiscal year 2006, the same amount requested by the president for 2007.

(5) The percentage of teaching candidates who passed each of the assessments used by the State for teacher certification and licensure, disaggregated and ranked, by the teacher preparation program in that State from which the teacher candidate received the candidate's most recent degree, which shall be made available widely and publicly.

(6) Information on the extent to which teachers in the State are given waivers of State certification or licensure requirements, including the proportion of such teachers distributed across high- and low-poverty school districts and across subject areas.

(7) A description of each State's alternative routes to teacher certification, if any, and the percentage of teachers certified through alternative certification routes that pass State teacher certification or licensure assessments.

(8) For each State, a description of proposed criteria for assessing the performance of teacher preparation programs within institutions of higher education in the State, including indicators of teacher candidate knowledge and skills.

(9) Information on the extent to which teachers or prospective teachers in each State are required to take examinations or other assessments of their subject matter knowledge in the area or areas in which the teachers provide instruction, the standards established for passing any such assessments, and the extent to which teachers or prospective teachers are required to receive a passing score on such assessments in order to teach in specific subject areas or grade levels.

The act further required that the U.S. secretary of education compile the data into a Report of the Secretary on the Quality of Teacher Preparation and to make that report widely available. Citizens can access and view the state reports and the secretary's report at www.title2.org.

AACTE Responds to Disclosure Requirements

Reacting to the reauthorization in an issue paper for AACTE, Penelope M. Earley (1998) cautioned,

> The data reporting requirement may have positive and negative consequences. States must report the number of certification waivers they grant each year and disaggregate the information by low- and high-income school districts. This may provide useful information to teacher educators and others regarding the actual supply and demand profile for teachers in the state. States also are charged with reporting pass rate data, by institution, on teaching candidates licensure examination scores. (p. 4)

Earley (1998) speculated that the data reporting requirements "reflects skepticism in the Congress about the quality of teacher education in the United States," adding, "but possibly to a greater extent it illustrates lawmakers' confusion about where the accountability for ensuring good teaching resides" (p. 4).

Teacher Quality Issues Include K–12 Education

The federal government did not give up searching for teacher quality solutions and continued to revise its previous education statutes. Such was the case in 1999 as Congress considered changes to the reauthorization of the Elementary and Secondary Education Act (ESEA) of 1965. Initially passed in 1965 as a compensatory program, Congress authorized grants for school programs intended to compensate for some disadvantages incurred by K–12 students from low-income families. Subsequently—every 5 or 6 years—Congress has reauthorized the law; however, Congress allocates funds annually.

"In his 1999 State of the Union address, President Clinton challenged Congress to tie ESEA spending—more than half of the $21 billion total federal investment in elementary and secondary education—to results on five key measures of state and local performance" wrote Andrew Rotherham (1999, p. 3). These were the five key measures:

1. Ending social promotion
2. Improving teacher quality
3. Reconstituting failing schools
4. Issuing school report cards
5. Enforcing discipline codes

For improving teacher quality, President Clinton proposed that states demonstrate that they were taking reasonable steps to curtail out-of-field teaching, implementing rigorous testing procedures for all teachers to improve teacher quality, and offering alternative paths (not simply emergency certification) to attract qualified people into the profession. The results would be indicated by improvements in student achievement (Rotherham, 1999, p. 15).

Congress Probes Teacher Quality Issues

To that end, on May 13, 1999, the U.S. House of Representatives Committee on Education and the Workforce convened a hearing as part of its deliberations during the process of reauthorization of ESEA. Information gathered through this and other hearings was intended to build on what had been accomplished in the reauthorization of the Higher Education Act, enacted in late 1998 and extended through fiscal year 2003.

Subcommittee chairman Howard P. "Buck" McKeon noted that the hearing was the "fourth in a series of hearings focused on issues related to teacher quality." Congressman McKeon said that previous hearings had revealed the strong correlation between teacher quality and student achievement and the potential positive impact of professional development on teaching ability. Also through the hearings, Congress was reviewing the current role of the federal government in providing assistance to states and localities to improve their teacher force.

Feistritzer Testifies About Quality Alternate Routes.   In her testimony in May 1999, C. Emily Feistritzer, NCEI president and founder, outlined the components of "really effective alternative routes" including strong academic coursework components and a field-based requirement (Serial No. 106–37, p. 5). "The best alternative programs are a collaborative effort among state departments of education that license teachers, colleges and universities that train teachers, and school districts that hire teachers" (p. 5), Feistritzer said. She cited the alternate route programs in California, Texas, and New Jersey as the "best and the most effective in recruiting, training, and placing teachers" (p. 12).

Despite the challenges, other states were quietly developing new alternate routes and expanding other successful alternate route programs.

California Official Testifies About Quality Assessment.   California was one of those states expanding its alternative route programs. Beverly Young, associate director for teacher education and K–12 programs at California State University, Long Beach, testified that from 1997 to 1999, state legislation had had a "major impact" on teacher preparation and development. For example, state legislation appropriated $67.8 million in funding that would "allow every eligible teacher in California" to participate in its Beginning Teacher Support and Assessment Program" (BTSA). A statewide program, BTSA is an integral piece of the teacher education and induction program, which requires program accountability as well as an assessment of all 21,000 new teachers in California each year on the basis of "rigorous standards for teaching performance" (Serial No. 106–37 1999, p. 11). These state requirements applied to alternative routes as well as to the traditional college-based routes to certification.

Kanstoroom Offers Changes to Improve Quality.   Agreeing that the emphasis should be at the state level, Marci Kanstoroom, then research director at the Thomas B. Fordham Foundation and Research Fellow, Manhattan Institute, Washington, D.C., submitted a policy manifesto directed at the teacher quality problem. Several prominent officials had signed the document, which called for setting high standards for school reform results and flexible means for achieving those results (Serial No. 106–37, 1999, p. 11). To boost the quality of teaching, Kanstoroom suggested that "The teaching profession should be deregulated; entry into it should be widened, and personnel decisions should be decentralized to the school level. Instead of requiring a long list of courses and degrees, we should test future teachers for their knowledge and skills" (Serial No. 106–37, 1999, p. 12).

Preparation through alternate routes was one way of widening the entry to teaching. Removing the restrictions or deregulating the process fit in with alternate route programs as well, provided that accountability was required throughout the process.

As for federal responsibility, Kanstoroom told committee members, "It is crucial, though, that you insist that everything supported with federal funds be judged by evidence that it yields higher pupil achievement" (Serial No. 106–37, 1999, p. 12).

Congress Reauthorizes *No Child Left Behind* Act

Three days after taking office in January 2001 as the 43rd U.S. president, George W. Bush announced his framework for education reform that he described as the "cornerstone of my administration." Less than a year later with overwhelming bipartisan support, Congress passed *No Child Left Behind*, the 21st-century iteration of the Elementary and Secondary Education Act of 1965. President Bush signed it into law on January 8, 2002. *No Child Left Behind* asks states to set standards for student performance and teacher quality. Secretary of Education Rod Paige said, "The law establishes accountability for results and improves the inclusiveness and fairness of American education" (USDoE, NCLB Guide, 2006e).

Title I: New Teacher Quality Requirements

The most extensive provisions of *No Child Left Behind* applied to Title I, the programs to compensate for the link between family poverty and low student achievement. In 2001, more than 90% of all school districts provided supplemental instruction for 12.5 million students through Title I (Moore, 2001, p. 53). For the school year starting in 2002, the Title I budget was over $11 billion (USDoE, 2006a, p. 3).

Perhaps the most dramatic policy shift of NCLB was the new requirement of Title I that *all* teachers of core academic subjects be "highly qualified"[3] no later than the end of the 2005–2006 school year (USDoE HQT Guidance, 2005c, p. 1). Title I funds *were not* to be used to hire new teachers in the core academic areas who did not meet the definition of highly qualified.

---

[3] NCLB defines a "highly qualified teacher" as a teacher holding, at a minimum, a bachelor's degree, full state certification (including certification and licensure obtained through alternative routes to certification), and the ability to demonstrate competency (passing state test, completing coursework, or advanced degree) in each subject he or she teaches. For a complete definition, see Section 9101(23) of the ESEA.

According to the NCLB Non-regulatory Guidance, "In exchange, agencies that receive funds are held accountable to the public for improvements in academic achievement (p. 21).

In all, *No Child Left Behind* included 10 separate titles,[4] each of which provided the framework for ways in which the federal government would provide grants for specific projects for K–12 schooling. Programs ranged from assistance to Alaska Native education to school facilities infrastructure improvement.

Title II: Improving Teacher Quality

Through Title II of ESEA (coincidentally the same title as in the Higher Education Act), the law also gave states and districts the flexibility to find innovative ways to improve teacher quality. Innovations cited in the law included alternative certification and merit pay and bonuses for people who teach in high-need subject areas such as math and science. These were major program changes. Federal grants gave state and local education agencies (SEAs and LEAs) the flexibility to select the strategies that best met their particular needs for improved teaching that would help raise student achievement in the core academic subjects.[5]

In return for the flexibility, LEAs were required to demonstrate annual progress in ensuring that all teachers teaching in core academic subjects within the state were highly qualified. Also within Title II of ESEA, the president's budget request included funds for the Troops to Teachers program and Teach For America and requested funds for new grants for teacher preparation (U.S. GAO, 2006, p. 11).

Transition to Teaching Grants Support Career Switchers into Teaching.
President Bush's 2001 budget request also included funds for Transition to Teaching. The Transition to Teaching program supported the recruitment and retention of highly qualified midcareer professionals, including qualified

---

[4] The titles in Public Law 107–110, the reauthorization of the Elementary and Secondary Education Act of 1965 (also known as the *No Child Left Behind* act) were Title I—Improving the Academic Achievement of the Disadvantaged; Title II—Preparing, Training, and Recruiting High Quality Teachers and Principals; Title III—Language Instruction for Limited English Proficient and Immigrant Students; Title IV—21st Century Schools; Title V—Promoting Informed Parental Choice and Innovative Programs; VI—Flexibility and Accountability; Title VII—Indian, Native Hawaiian, and Alaska Native Education; Title VIII—Impact Aid Program; Title IX—General Provisions; and Title X—Repeals, Redesignations, and Amendments to Other Statutes.

[5] As specified in ESEA, core academic subjects means English, reading or language arts, mathematics, science, foreign languages, civics and government, economics, arts, history, and geography [Section 9101(11)]. Although the statute includes the arts in the core academic subjects, it does not specify which of the arts are core academic subjects; therefore, states must make this determination.

paraprofessionals and recent college graduates who had not majored in education, to teach in high-need schools and districts. Some grant funds would support the development of new or enhanced alternative routes to certification.

Chapter B, Section 2311, sets forth the purposes of the Title II of ESEA:

(1) to establish a program to recruit and retain highly qualified mid-career professionals (including highly qualified paraprofessionals), and recent graduates of an institution of higher education, as teachers in high-need schools, including recruiting teachers through alternative routes to certification; and

(2) to encourage the development and expansion of alternative routes to certification under State-approved programs that enable individuals to be eligible for teacher certification within a reduced period of time, relying on the experience, expertise, and academic qualifications of an individual, or other factors in lieu of traditional course work in the field of education.

NCLB gave the U.S. secretary of education the authority to make grants on a competitive basis to eligible entities to develop state and local teacher corps or other programs to establish, expand, or enhance teacher recruitment and retention efforts. According to Chapter B, Section 2312, of Title II of ESEA,

[T]o be eligible to receive such a grant, an entity shall be a state educational agency; a high-need local educational agency; a for-profit or nonprofit organization that has a proven record of effectively recruiting and retaining highly qualified teachers, in a partnership with a high-need local educational agency or with a state educational agency; an institution of higher education, in a partnership with a high-need local educational agency or with a state educational agency; a regional consortium of state educational agencies; or a consortium of high-need local educational agencies.

Through a competitive process, in 2005 qualified applicants could apply for 5-year grants as part of the $44.9 million that Congress appropriated for Transition to Teaching programs.[6] Grantees were to develop and implement comprehensive approaches to train, place, and support teacher candidates they had recruited into their programs. The programs were required to meet relevant state certification or licensing requirements. Grantees then had to ensure that program participants were placed to teach in high-need schools and districts and support candidates to serve in these placements for at least 3 years (USDoE Website, www.ed.gov/programs/transitionteach/).

After the first 3 years, the U.S. Department of Education reported that it had distributed grants to 12 grantees from 2002 to 2005. Thelma Leenhouts, team leader for the Transition to Teaching grant program in the Office of

---

[6] Congress appropriated $31 million for the first year of the program in 2001.

Innovation and Improvement at the U.S. Department of Education, reported on the program at the 2006 NCAC Conference. Leenhouts reiterated the purposes of the Transition to Teaching program:

- To recruit and retain highly qualified mid-career professionals (including highly qualified paraprofessionals), and recent graduates of an institution of higher education, as teachers in high-need schools operated by high-need LEAs; and
- To encourage the development and expansion of alternative routes to certification under State-approved programs that enable individuals to be eligible for teacher certification within a reduced period of time. (p. 2)

Figure 3.2 shows the breakdown of the entities that received Transition to Teaching grants during the first 3-year period.

Although the U.S. Department of Education has not disaggregated the data to determine which of the grantees used (or developed) an alternate route, the American Institutes for Research released its preliminary evaluation of the Transition to Teaching Program in October 2005. The report consists of eight case studies, four of which are identified as alternative certification programs.

Figure 3.2   Transition to Teaching Grants Awarded (2002–2005)

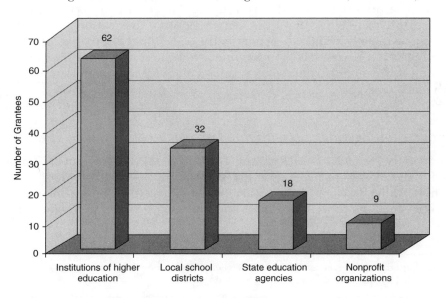

Source: Basic data from Thelma Leenhouts's PowerPoint on the Transition to Teaching Program at the National Center for Alternative Certification Conference, February 9, 2006. Accessed from www.teach-now.org/Leenhouts_TTT.ppt#327,10, Types_of_Applicants: Current_Grantees.

U.S. Secretary of Education Issues Annual Reports on Teacher Quality

State Barriers Discourage Career Switchers

As required by the Higher Education Act, the U.S. secretary of education, Rod Paige,[7] issued the first *Secretary's Annual Report on Teacher Quality* in June 2002. (USDoE, 2002b). State-submitted statistics disclosed that

> Many academically accomplished college graduates and mid-career profession-als with strong subject matter backgrounds are often dissuaded from entering teaching because the entry requirements are so rigid. At the same time, too many individuals earn certification even though their own content knowledge is weak. States' systems seem to maintain low standards and high barriers at the same time. (p. vii)

The first report acknowledged that because alternate routes are defined by each state, "there is little comparability of these routes across states" (p. 47). Even so, the report noted that several states had been ruled out of compliance with the Title II reporting requirements (p. 47). Some states had not reported the alternative route pass rates[8] separately from those teacher candidates prepared through regular routes to certification. Despite the problems, the U.S. Department of Education reported that approximately 175,000 teachers nationwide[9] held alternative certifi-cates, out of approximately 3.1 million teachers, accounting for 6% of the teaching force in 2001, numbers and percentages that have increased in later years.

Education Secretary Highlights Innovative Alternative Routes

The *Secretary's Second Annual Report on Teacher Quality* (USDoE, 2003), indi-cated that "states were making progress in raising academic standards for teachers while lowering unnecessary barriers" (p. 6). Along with other advancements, the report cited innovative alternative routes to teaching. It

---

[7] Roderick (Rod) Paige served as the 7th U.S. secretary of education from 2001 to 2005. He was succeeded by Margaret Spellings in January 2005.

[8] In their reports, institutions of higher education must include the pass rates of their graduates or program completers on required state teacher assessments as well as program information such as the number of students in their teacher preparation programs and the faculty-to-student ratio in supervised practice teaching.

[9] These data correspond with the data collected by NCEI and published in *Alternative Teacher Certification: A State-by-State Analysis 2001.*

reported that all but nine states (including the District of Columbia, Guam, and the Virgin Islands) had approved an alternative route to certification as of October 2002.[10]

The report dedicated six pages to innovative routes to teaching, most of which had been operating previously, and highlighted the American Board for Certification of Teacher Excellence (ABCTE). Secretary Paige recognized ABCTE as a new alternative pathway and a "distinctive alternate (Passport) certification to the teaching profession" (p. 26). As an alternative pathway, ABCTE "does not require would-be teachers to attend a school of education in order to apply for certification" (p. 26). Teaching candidates who hold a bachelor's degree will demonstrate mastery of their subject matter by passing a rigorous test of professional knowledge and complete a preservice program of professional development. A state would first need to recognize the ABCTE's Passport as valid before the candidate could teach in the state's public schools. According to the report, "The ultimate goal is to create a certificate that is recognized in all 50 states" (p. 27).

Secretary Commits Support for Alternate Routes

The third *Secretary's Report,* issued in 2004, covered a variety of issues related to teaching and teacher quality, including alternative routes to the classroom. A chapter was devoted to federal activities and federal funding programs that supported national teacher quality initiatives. Included were improving teacher quality state grants ($2.9 billion), teacher quality enhancement grants ($88.9 million), and transition to teaching grants ($45.3 million), grants that may impact alternate routes. In addition, the report noted that the "Department is committed to continuing to forge strong partnerships with

---

[10] Although most of the information from the Title II state reports matches that collected by NCEI, there are noticeable differences. The contacts for Title II reporting list several more master's in teaching (MAT) programs as alternative routes than do the contacts for NCEI. NCEI obtains its information about alternative routes to teacher certification from the offices in each state that directly administer alternative routes to teacher certification. In some cases, that is the overall teacher education and certification offices; in others, it is a special office within the state office of teacher education and certification; in others, it is a licensing commission or board in charge of teacher licensing. Who, at the state level, is "in charge of" alternative routes to teacher certification is as much a moving target as the routes themselves. In some states that have large numbers of individuals coming into teaching through alternative routes to teacher certification, namely, California, Texas, and Georgia, teacher licensing has been in the hands of state commissions or boards separate from the state department of education. Organizational changes could result in the responsibilities being transferred to the state departments. Another problem with state data has been the lack of uniform reporting and data collection procedures.

states, institutions and national organizations, such as the American Board for the Certification of Teacher Excellence [and] the National Center for Alternative Certification"[11] (USDoE, 2004c, p. 13).

Secretary Reports Dominance of Five States

In 2005, the *Secretary's Fourth Annual Report* was longer and more detailed than the previous reports. Alternative routes to certification resulted in 35,353 graduates, "close to 20 percent of new teacher graduates" (p. 5). In 2004, the top five states producing teachers through alternative certification were California, Georgia, New Jersey, New York, and Texas. Together, these five states produced 82% of all teachers prepared through alternative routes to teacher certification nationally[12] (p. 27).

Teacher distribution shortfalls persist in certain subject areas and grade levels, as well as in rural, urban, and outlying area locations. The number of teacher education programs designated as low performing decreased to 20, down from 25 in 2003.

Department of Education regulations of teacher quality required states to stop granting waivers of state certification requirements to teachers of core academic subjects by the close of the 2005–2006 school year. States grant waivers to teachers to alleviate staffing shortages in schools. A waiver may allow a teacher to teach while working to meet certification requirements, to teach a subject outside of the field in which he or she was trained, or even be used as a stopgap measure to fill classroom vacancies. Teachers on waivers do not meet the requirements for full certification. They generally hold some kind of provisional, emergency, or temporary license (p. 39).

For the 2004 data reporting cycle, the definition of a waiver was revised to align more closely with the NCLB provisions for highly qualified teachers. The Higher Education Act 2004 waiver reporting requirements were "modified to exclude both teachers participating in alternative routes who are considered fully certified for purposes of NCLB, and those teachers who are short- or long-term substitutes (as defined by the state)" (p. 39).

In her message to readers of the *Secretary's Fourth Annual Report,* Secretary of Education Margaret Spellings said, "Throughout America, teachers, school districts, local governments, states, public and private entities, and institutions of higher education are participating in a wide variety of initiatives that are leading the way to improving traditional and alternative teacher preparation

---

[11] The National Center for Alternative Certification (NCAC) was established in September 2003 by the National Center for Education Information (NCEI) with a U.S. Department of Education grant of $2.25 million. NCAC is the nation's first clearinghouse for alternative routes to teaching and can be accessed at www.teach-now.org.

[12] The data may not include the number of alternative route completers from states that do not have testing programs.

programs and keeping good teachers in the nation's classrooms. Many of these initiatives are identified in this report. However, despite the progress being made, much remains to be done" (p. iii).

Secretary Offers a Clarification

A change in the regulations was perhaps one reason for the "progress being made," especially the increased participation in alternate routes. In December 2002, and updated by the Non-Regulatory Guidance issued August 3, 2005, the U.S. Department of Education responded to this question: When can a teacher in an alternative route to certification/licensure program be considered "highly qualified"? The response is as follows:

> A teacher in an alternate route to certification program may be considered highly qualified if the teacher holds at least a bachelor's degree, has already demonstrated subject-matter competency in the core academic subject(s) the teacher will be teaching, and is participating in an alternate route to certification program in which the teacher:
>
> (1) receives, before and while teaching, high-quality professional development that is sustained, intensive, and classroom-focused in order to have a positive and lasting impact on classroom instruction;
>
> (2) participates in a program of intensive supervision that consists of structured guidance and regular ongoing support for teachers or in a teacher mentoring program;
>
> (3) assumes functions as a teacher for a period not to exceed three years; and
>
> (4) demonstrates satisfactory progress toward full certification as prescribed by the State. The State must ensure, through its certification and licensure process, that these provisions are met [Section 200.56(a)(2) of the *Title I*[13] regulations, December 2, 2002]. If the teacher does not complete the alternative certification program within the three-year period, the teacher is no longer considered to be highly qualified. (p. 5)

The regulations were intended to "give states the opportunity to create high-quality alternative certification programs, while guarding against the possibility that teachers currently on waivers were relabeled as 'alternative certification' teachers" (USDoE, *Secretary's Annual Report*, 2003, p. 6). During the 2001–2002 school year, seven states reported having more than 10% of their teachers on waivers (teaching with emergency, temporary, or provisional licenses) (USDoE, *Secretary's Annual Report*, 2003, p. 7).

Tabulations of the numbers of alternate routes, the supply and demand, the demographics of the individuals being licensed through alternate routes,

---

[13] Title 1, Part A, funds are required to develop and implement a plan to have all teachers of core academic subjects highly qualified no later than the end of the 2005–2006 school year, according to the U.S. Department of Education, Non-Regulatory Guidance of August 3, 2005.

where they were teaching, and what subjects they were teaching were included in *The Secretary's Annual Report* from state-reported data. Even with state standards in place, the tasks of assessing highly qualified teachers, the process of preparing and certifying highly qualified teachers, and what states were doing to produce highly qualified teachers were daunting.

Quality is difficult to quantify. Sometimes the quality or even the adequacy of the alternate route program was at issue, rather than the qualification of the individual teacher. It has only been recently that student achievement has been related to quality teaching, the technology of which is still being developed.

Groups Weigh in on Teacher Preparation

The Teacher Unions Set Criteria for Alternate Routes

In a 2003 publication, the National Education Association (NEA) made a distinction between "nontraditional routes to licensure, which prepare prospective teachers to receive a teaching license using the same rigorous standards as traditional programs, and alternative certification, which waives coursework or other requirements in order to expedite the entry of teachers into the classroom" (NEA, 2003, p. 20). While acknowledging that alternative certification programs are a growing trend, NEA suggested that these programs must be "evaluated thoroughly to be sure they are preparing teachers adequately for success in the classroom" (p. 20).

The American Federation of Teachers (AFT) comes close to actually supporting alternate routes, with caveats. For example, in 2004, when the AFT executive council adopted a resolution on alternate routes, it noted that the "AFT does not support inadequate or shortcut alternative route programs" (AFT, 2004).

The AFT adopted the criteria identified by NCEI, which classified alternate route programs to be of high quality if they have these characteristics:

- Been specifically designed to recruit, prepare, and license talented individuals who already have at least a bachelor's degree for the teaching profession
- Require candidates to pass a rigorous screening process, such as passing tests, interviews, and demonstrated mastery of content
- Are field-based
- Include coursework or equivalent experiences in professional education studies before and while teaching
- Require candidates to work closely with mentor teachers
- Require candidates to meet high performance standards for completion of the program (AFT, 2004)

In addition, the AFT wants "state departments of education and licensing bodies to only grant full certification to individuals who have participated in an on-going mentoring program for the entire period prior to receiving full state certification and achieved full certification as prescribed by the state within three years of entering the classroom" (AFT, 2004, p. 1). To meet its mentoring requirement, the union wants to "assist with the planning, development and implementation of the mentoring component," and the AFT wants to include the mentoring component in the collective bargaining agreement" (AFT, 2004, p. 1). Mentoring is frequently a component of high-quality alternative route programs, as is a preservice component.

Alternate Routes Today

Newest Routes Have Unique Characteristics

The American Board for Certification of Teacher Excellence (ABCTE).

ABCTE, an alternate route option that began in 2002, encompasses the Passport to Teaching program and the Master Teacher certificate. Each is a portable teacher credential, portable to the extent that a state recognizes the credential and permits the individual to teach. In 2006, six states recognized ABCTE's Passport to Teaching: Florida, Idaho, Mississippi, New Hampshire, Pennsylvania, and Utah.

The Passport to Teaching or Passport identifies qualified beginning teachers, and when it becomes available, the Master Teacher certification is intended to recognize accomplished teachers. Qualified individuals must pass two rigorous examinations and accept simultaneous mentoring support while teaching, if the state determines it is necessary. In some cases a state may require completion of additional coursework as well.

On behalf of Mathematica Policy Research, Inc., Steven Glazerman and Christina Tuttle are conducting *An Evaluation of American Board Teacher Certification: Progress and Plans.* The study of the ABCTE began in 2005 and is to be a 5-year evaluation of the certification programs—the Passport certification and the Master Teacher certificate. The first phase of the report was issued in May 2006.

After an initial grant of $5 million in 2001, in 2003, Congress awarded a 5-year $35 million grant to the ABCTE. ABCTE's challenge was to reduce the barriers to teaching by developing a streamlined process to certification. After its initial research and development of a set of examinations, ABCTE reported that the Passport is a "cost-effective route to earning a teaching credential based on subject-area mastery and professional teaching knowledge as demonstrated by meeting rigorous testing standards" (ABCTE, 2006, p. 1).

In part because candidates must produce a college transcript indicating receipt of a baccalaureate degree prior to completing the remaining requirements, ABCTE considers the Passport to Teaching an alternative route to teacher certification. Program completion includes passing two rigorous examinations. A minimum passing score (270 out of 500) is required on the 3-hour professional teacher knowledge test (multiple choice and essay). A minimum passing score (252 out of 500 for biology, but varies by subject) is required on the 4-hour subject-area knowledge test (p. 5).

Similar to other alternate routes, the ABCTE Passport process is quicker and more cost effective than the traditional college-based route to teacher certification. States, however, must approve the Passport to Teaching before Passport holders are certified to teach in any state.

Temporary Teacher Certificate in Texas.   In the spring of 2004, the Texas State Board for Educator Certification approved the Temporary Teacher Certificate to let school districts instantly certify college graduates as teachers to ease shortages in certain subject areas, such as math and science in grades 8 through 12.

The *Dallas Morning News* (Stutz, 2005, p. 1) reported that only two small districts have been authorized to offer the Temporary Teacher Certificate, although several districts had contacted the education agency's director of field services for educator certification about it. Before the state will issue the Temporary Teacher Certificate for 2 years, an individual must have a college degree in the needed subject area, pass a state competency test, and have a job offer from a school district. In addition, the district would be responsible for mentoring, supervising, and training the individual with the Temporary Teacher Certificate, resources that many districts may lack.

As of December 2005, an estimated 1,640 people had applied for the Temporary Teacher Certificate, but only one individual received a state certification. All others were denied a state certification because they did not meet one or more of the requirements.

California Teaching Foundations Examination.   California also allows individuals to test out of most of the pedagogical coursework. If other prerequisites such as subject matter and basic skills have been met and an individual passes the Teaching Foundations Examination, the candidate enters an Early Completion Intern Option. Then, after completing the California Teaching Performance Assessment with their students, the individual receives a preliminary credential to teach. Potentially, an individual could be fully credentialed in 6 months under this Early Completion Intern Option. The California Teaching Commission reports that fewer than 300 individuals in 4 years have entered teaching through the California Teaching Foundations Examination option.

Most Routes Now Share Common Characteristics

Despite the unique characteristics of the newest alternate routes, most alternate routes share these several common characteristics:

- They are specifically designed to recruit, prepare, and license talented individuals who already have at least a bachelor's degree—and often other careers—in fields other than education.
- They require rigorous screening processes, such as passing tests, interviews, and demonstrated mastery of content.
- They are field based.
- They permit coursework or equivalent experiences in professional education studies to be obtained before and while teaching.
- They require working with mentor teachers and/or other support personnel.
- They demand high performance standards for completion of the programs.

It is more than coincidence that alternate routes share many of the same characteristics, yet not all similarities can be attributed to design either. A number of connections among the various elements become quite obvious upon review. For example, Teach For America was founded at Princeton University in New Jersey, the state that first developed an alternate route program. At the time (1989), the New Jersey alternate route was in full swing and receiving extensive media coverage. The New Jersey Department of Education was sending recruiters out to Ivy League universities to describe the program to interested liberal arts students who might be enticed to become teachers and to help alleviate teacher shortages.

As a Texan, whose state had also voted to permit alternate routes to alleviate teacher shortages, George H. W. Bush supported the Troops to Teachers recruitment and placement program as a military veteran and during his administration as president. And when George H. W. Bush selected Rod Paige as the U.S. secretary of education, Paige too was a Texan familiar with alternate route programs. Paige had been superintendent of the Houston Independent School District, which had the first and one of the largest district-run alternate route programs in the nation.

Leo Klagholz (personal communication, 2006) who is intimately familiar with the events during the development of alternate routes, said, "Although alternative certification appeared in different locales at the grassroots level, its evolution was less piecemeal and coincidental than a purely sequential portrayal might suggest. All of the pieces developed in parallel with NCEI's efforts to connect the pieces."

4

What Constitutes
State Alternative Routes
to Teacher Certification?

State legislators and policymakers increasingly turned to alternate routes to teacher certification to help alleviate teacher quantity and quality problems. Lawmakers reacted to projected severe teacher shortages by creating ways to get more people into teaching in the areas where they were needed the most in the fastest ways possible. Those ways were characterized by two rather divergent phenomena. First, there was a flurry of activity in several states to rename existing teacher certification routes, such as emergency and other forms of temporary certificates, as alternate routes, practices that had been curtailed considerably over the years. Second, there was a focus in the states to develop new and different ways of recruiting nontraditional candidates for teaching by creating new pathways for certifying them to teach. Throughout the 1990s and to the present, lawmakers have focused on new and different alternative pathways to teaching as teacher quality and accountability issues have become critical to student achievement.

Alternative Routes, State by State

In 2006, 50 states and the District of Columbia reported they were implementing a total of 125 alternative routes to teacher certification. Some states list four or five alternate routes, yet use some of them sparingly or not at all. From year to year, routes are added and routes are dropped by states, as demands for teachers change.

Table 4.1   Number of State Alternate Routes by NCEI Classification (1991–2006)

Year	A	B	C	D	E	F	G	H	I	J	K	Total
1991	12	7	10	11	10	15	16	9	0	0	0	**90**
1992	12	7	13	12	10	16	13	11	0	0	0	**94**
1993–1994	14	7	13	14	11	17	15	10	0	0	0	**101**
1995	13	12	13	15	13	16	14	10	0	0	0	**106**
1996	14	13	13	15	14	16	14	9	0	0	0	**108**
1997	13	13	15	16	13	16	16	10	0	0	0	**112**
1998–1999	14	13	16	15	16	14	15	10	0	0	0	**113**
2000	9	15	16	17	15	16	15	14	0	2	0	**119**
2001	12	13	12	19	12	14	16	10	3	2	0	**113**
2002	16	16	14	21	17	13	16	13	0	2	1	**129**
2003	21	20	14	24	16	14	17	13	0	2	1	**142**
2004	14	17	3	23	17	0	19	9	0	0	16	**118**
2005	16	19	5	18	18	0	17	8	0	0	14	**115**
2006	20	18	6	20	21	0	18	8	0	0	14	**125**

Source: Basic data from National Center for Education Information, *Alternative Teacher Certification: A State-by-State Analysis* (selected year).

Table 4.1 shows the number of alternate routes by NCEI's classification system for 1991 to 2006. As you can see in the table, no state now considers emergency certificates or waivers (class F) *alternate routes.* The growth in alternate routes is in new routes designed specifically for nontraditional populations of postbaccalaureate candidates (classes A–E), many of whom come from other careers.

State Alternate Routes Differ

Table 4.2 shows the number of the different classifications of alternate routes each state reported being implemented in 2006. Descriptions of each of these routes, as presented in *Alternative Teacher Certification: A State-by-State Analysis*, points out important distinctions. Although all 50 states and the District of Columbia in 2006 indicated that they all had at least one alternative route to teacher certification, they all were not actually implementing programs created by the state as an alternate route. For example, in 2006,

- Four states—Alaska, Indiana, North Dakota, and Rhode Island—either did not have a state alternate route on the books and/or were not utilizing such an alternate route. Some states that receive federal Transition to Teaching (TTT) grants call their TTT programs alternate routes.
  - Alaska actually has created an alternate route to certification but, to date, has not used it.

Table 4.2   Number of Alternate Routes, by NCEI Classification, and by State (2006)

State	A	B	C	D	E	F	G	H	I	J	K	Total by State
Alabama		2			1							**3**
Alaska												**0**
Arizona				1								**1**
Arkansas		1										**1**
California	2			1			1	2				**6**
Colorado	2											**2**
Connecticut		1			1		2					**4**
Delaware		1			3							**4**
District of Columbia		1			2						1	**4**
Florida	2				1		1					**4**
Georgia	1			1	1			1			2	**6**
Hawaii		1			1		1					**3**
Idaho				1								**1**
Illinois				1	1							**2**
Indiana												**0**
Iowa				1								**1**
Kansas				1							1	**2**
Kentucky		1		1				1			4	**7**
Louisiana	1			1	4							**6**
Maine							1					**1**
Maryland	1											**1**
Massachusetts	2											**2**
Michigan					1		1				1	**3**
Minnesota	1	1										**2**
Mississippi		2			1							**3**
Missouri		1		1								**2**
Montana							1					**1**
Nebraska							3				1	**4**
Nevada							1					**1**
New Hampshire			2		1			1				**4**
New Jersey	1											**1**
New Mexico	1											**1**
New York	1				1		1				1	**4**
North Carolina			1				1					**2**
North Dakota												**0**
Ohio	1		2									**3**
Oklahoma				1								**1**
Oregon				2				1				**3**
Pennsylvania	1											**1**
Rhode Island												**0**
South Carolina		1										**1**

												TOTAL
South Dakota		1			1						1	**3**
Tennessee				2			1					**3**
Texas	1											**1**
Utah	2										1	**3**
Vermont			1				1					**2**
Virginia				2			2					**4**
Washington		2						1			1	**4**
West Virginia		1	1	1								**3**
Wisconsin		1	1									**2**
Wyoming				1			1					**2**
												0
TOTAL, by Class	**20**	**18**	**6**	**20**	**21**	**0**	**18**	**8**	**0**	**0**	**14**	**125**

Source: Basic data from National Center for Education Information, *Alternative Teacher Certification: A State-by-State Analysis* 2006.

- Indiana has never really had an alternate route; however, the state received TTT grants from 2001 to 2004 that it distributed to colleges of education in the state for postbaccalaureate programs. Indiana's 38 college teacher education programs are among the most prolific in the nation.
- North Dakota also had a federal TTT grant that it called an alternate route. However, until the Transitions grant, North Dakota reported to NCEI every year until 2006 that it was "not even considering" alternatives to approved college teacher preparation programs for certifying teachers.
- Rhode Island has been considering alternate routes for years but has never created one on the books. Rhode Island also has had a TTT grant, that the state calls an alternate route.
- Three states—Maine, Montana, and Nevada—reported they were implementing only alternate routes that accommodated individuals "who have few requirements left to fulfill before becoming certified through the approved college teacher education program route (e.g., persons certified in one state moving to another or persons certified in one endorsement area seeking to become certified in another," NCEI's class G).
- Nebraska reported it was implementing four (three class G and one class K) alternate routes to "accommodate specific populations for teaching, e.g., Teach For America, Troops to Teachers and college professors who want to teach in K–12 schools" (Feistritzer, 2006, p. 37).
- Fifteen states were implementing class A alternate routes that met the following criteria:
  - Designed for the explicit purpose of attracting talented individuals who already have at least a bachelor's degree in a field other than education into elementary and secondary school teaching;

- Not restricted to shortages, secondary grade levels, or subject areas;
- Teaching with a trained mentor, and formal instruction that deals with the theory and practice of teaching during the school year, and sometimes in the summer before and/or after.
- Fifteen states had implemented alternative teacher certification routes designed specifically to bring individuals who already have at least a bachelor's degree into teaching, with specially designed mentoring and some formal instruction. However, these class B routes are restricted to subject-area shortages and/or secondary grade levels.
- Fifteen states reported they had class E alternate routes that were post-baccalaureate programs based at an institution of higher education, all of which included teaching while learning. Of these 15 states, only Illinois and Michigan did not also have a class A or B alternate route.

These classes A through E were designed for the explicit purpose of transitioning postbaccalaureate candidates into teaching through on-the-job programs. An analysis of what states are describing as alternative routes to teacher certification is critical in getting an accurate picture of what is actually going on in the states with regard to alternative teacher ertification.

When all is said and done, it's safe to say that, in 2006, 42 states and the District of Columbia had gone back to the drawing board and designed 85 alternative routes to the traditional college-based teacher education program route. As shown in Figure 4.1, alternate routes classified as A, B, D, and E show continuous growth.

Additionally, 10 of those 42 states and the District of Columbia also have 14 class K alternate routes for special populations of individuals, such as Teach For America and Troops to Teachers. Seven of these 42 states have eight class H alternate routes for exceptional individuals such as Nobel Prize winners, although these routes are rarely used.

Regional Differences

An analysis of alternate routes to certification across the United States shows that although every state now reports that it has at least one alternative route to certification, the bulk of alternate routes being implemented and producing the most teachers are states in the western, eastern, and southern regions of the country. The Midwest and northern states have few alternate routes of notable size.

Of the eight states that employ more than 100,000 teachers each, five states—California, Florida, New Jersey, New York, and Texas—have aggressive alternate route programs that are producing growing proportions of new teachers in the states. In contrast, Illinois, Ohio, and Pennsylvania— states in mid-America—have not been particularly active in

*Figure 4.1   Number of State Alternate Routes
by NCEI Classes A–E, by Year*

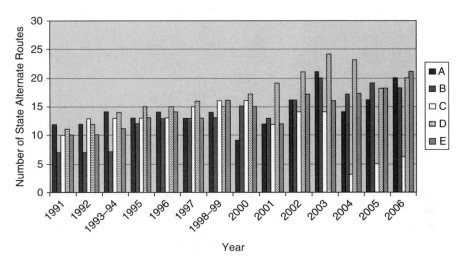

Year

Source: Data from National Center for Education Information, *Alternative Teacher Certification:
A State-by-State Analysis,* (selected years).

using alternative routes to certification. A possible link is the fact that states in mid-America account for a high proportion of the traditional colleges and universities that train teachers. Another likely explanation is declining enrollments of students in these regions of the country. *Projections of Education Statistics to 2015,* published by The National Center for Education Statistics (NCES) states, "the expected 6 percent national increase in public school enrollment between 2003 and 2015 plays out differently in most states" (NCES, 2006b, p. 6).

Elementary and secondary enrollment increases are projected for 32 states, as shown in Table 4.3. Decreases in enrollment are projected for 18 states and the District of Columbia, as shown in Table 4.4.

NCES further projects that, by region of the country, between 2003 and 2015, public elementary and secondary enrollment will change in these ways:

- *Increase* 13% in the South.
- *Increase* 8% in the West.
- *Decrease* 1% in the Midwest.
- *Decrease* 5% in the Northeast.

These projections will likely impact what individual states do in adding or subtracting certification routes to teaching.

Table 4.3 Projected Increases in Public Elementary and Secondary Enrollment, by State (2003–2015)

State	Percentage Increase	State	Percentage Increase
Nevada	35.7	Alaska	4.8
Arizona	31.8	Nebraska	4.1
Texas	22.6	Oregon	3.2
Georgia	19	California	2.9
Idaho	17.9	Minnesota	2.7
Utah	17.4	Oklahoma	2.7
Florida	16.9	Kentucky	2.6
North Carolina	14.7	Indiana	2.3
Colorado	12.7	Missouri	2.3
Delaware	11	New Jersey	2.1
Hawaii	10.6	Mississippi	1.2
Virginia	9.9	Iowa	1.2
Tennessee	8.1	Louisiana	1
Arkansas	6.4	Illinois	0.3
Maryland	5.3	Washington	0.2
South Carolina	4.9	Kansas	*

* Rounds to zero.

Source: U.S. Department of Education, NCES, The NCES Common Core of Data surveys and State Public Elementary and Secondary Enrollment Model.

Table 4.4 Projected Decreases in Public Elementary and Secondary Enrollment, by State: 2003–2015.

State	Percentage Increase	State	Percentage Increase
Vermont	−12.8	West Virginia	−3.8
North Dakota	−12.6	Wyoming	−3.8
District of Columbia	−8.7	Ohio	−3.6
New York	−7.9	New Hampshire	−3.6
Maine	−6.3	South Dakota	−1.3
Pennsylvania	−5.7	Montana	−1.2
Connecticut	−8	Alabama	−0.6
Rhode Island	−5.1	Wisconsin	−0.4
Massachusetts	−4.1	New Mexico	−0.3
Michigan	4		

Source: U.S. Department of Education, NCES, The NCES Common Core of Data Surveys and State Public Elementary and Secondary Enrollment Model.

Lessons Learned from Successful Alternate Routes

As states continue to add, delete, change, and modify alternative routes to certification of teachers to meet demands for an increase in supply of teachers of high quality, they would do well to heed lessons learned from states that have created and are implementing successful alternative routes.

The most prolific alternate routes in terms of production of new teachers are the oldest and most established in the states of California, New Jersey, and Texas. The alternative routes to teacher certification in these three states began in the mid-1980s, with some additions and modifications since then. The number of individuals certified through the alternative routes in these three states in 2005 accounted for nearly half of all teachers certified through alternate routes that year. New Jersey reported that about 40% of its new hires came through alternate routes. For Texas and California, about a third of their states' new hires came through alternate routes. In Texas, nontraditional routes to teaching now outpace traditional teacher education programs in production of new hires in the state.

Additional states where alternative routes to teacher certification are growing rapidly in producing more and more of the state's new teachers are Alabama, Florida, Georgia, Kentucky, Louisiana, South Carolina, and Virginia. As noted, many states have alternate routes specifically designed to attract nontraditional candidates to fill the demand for more and more qualified teachers.

Profiles of Selected State Alternate Routes

We first highlight the alternate routes of New Jersey, California, and Texas as exemplary alternate routes. All still thrive today and serve as models for other states in the development of their alternative routes. Figure 4.2 shows the growth of the number of teachers certified through alternate routes in California, New Jersey, and Texas from 1985–1986 through 2004–2005. Changes and alterations in the alternate routes in these three states have kept these routes viable, growing, and expanding.

New Jersey

Production of Teachers Through Alternate Routes in New Jersey.   New Jersey did not create its alternate route program to respond to a teacher shortage, as some other states had done. As a result of its Provisional Teacher Program, however, New Jersey did increase the pool of teachers, diversify the teaching force, and bring mature adults from other careers into teaching, benefits realized by other states.

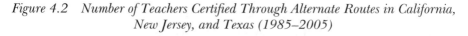

Figure 4.2   Number of Teachers Certified Through Alternate Routes in California, New Jersey, and Texas (1985–2005)

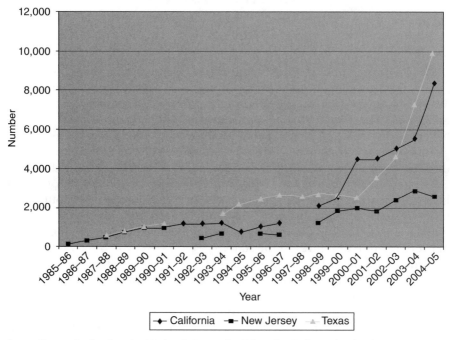

Source: Data submitted to the National Center for Education Information by the states, 2006.

In the first 5 years of New Jersey's alternate route program (1985–1989), the number of alternate route teachers increased from 121 to 422, as shown in Table 4.5.

Also, in the first 5 years, 246 school districts employed alternate route teachers. As the number of participants increased, by 1990, a fourth of new hires in the state were from the alternate route and were teaching in half of the state's school districts. Table 4.5, from the New Jersey Department of Education, shows that starting in 2001 and continuing through 2005, approximately 40% (3,000 teachers) of the new teachers hired each year had entered the profession through alternate routes.

Since the establishment of the New Jersey alternate route in 1984, school districts have hired nearly 24,000 teachers prepared through New Jersey's Provisional Teacher Program for Alternate Route Candidates.

Retention of Provisional Teacher Program Teachers.   New Jersey has not kept data about recipients of its certificates and therefore does not have longitudinal data about teachers who entered teaching through the

Table 4.5   Cumulative Employment of New Teachers in New Jersey, by Source (1985–2005)

Year	Traditional	Alternate	Total
2004–2005	4,435 (62%)	2,736 (38%)	7,171
2003–2004	3,918 (57%)	2,905 (43%)	6,823
2002–2003	4,084 (60%)	2,724 (40%)	6,808
2001–2002	4,934 (62%)	3,062 (38%)	7,996
2000–2001	5,230 (70%)	2,194 (30%)	7,424
1999–2000	4,508 (71%)	1,832 (29%)	6,340
1998–1999	4,050 (75%)	1,321 (25%)	5,371
1997–1998	3,865 (77%)	1,148 (23%)	5,013
1996–1997	2,907 (81%)	692 (19%)	3,599
1995–1996	2,484 (77%)	745 (23%)	3,229
1994–1995	2,276 (74%)	793 (26%)	3,069
1993–1994	1,054 (61%)	674 (39%)	1,728
1992–1993[*]	415 (57%)	611 (43%)	1,026
1991–1992 (Oct.–June)		115[†]	115
1990–1991 (Oct.–Sept.)		364[††]	364
1989–1990 (Oct.–Sept)		378	378
1988–1989 (Oct.–Sept.)		422	422
1987–1988 (Oct.–Sept.)		373	373
1986–1987 (Oct.–Sept.)		320	320
1985–1986 (Oct.–Sept.)		270	270
1985 (Sept.)		121	121
Total	**44,160**	**23,800**	**67,960**

[*]Requirement rescinded for traditional route teachers: November 1992
[†]Data represents October through June only. Percentage of alternate teachers hired for *entire academic year* is unavailable.
[††]Data collected for October through September in all years from September 1985 through September 1991. Percentage of alternate route teachers hired for an entire academic year is unavailable.
Source: New Jersey Department of Education, 2005.

alternative route and who have continued to teach. However, preliminary data from an evaluation of the alternate route program in New Jersey that is expected to be completed by summer 2007 show that 97% of alternate route respondents said they would be teaching the following year. More than half (55%) said they expected to be teaching more than 10 years. One in five (22%) were undecided about how long they would remain in teaching (Barclay, 2006, p. 6).

As the data show, the alternate route in New Jersey has not only added a large pool of teacher candidates to the teacher supply, it has also had a significant impact on the traditional teacher preparation route. Timing is the major difference between the traditional and alternate route in New Jersey. Teacher candidates in college-prepared programs take their coursework and practice teaching before taking over a classroom; individuals enrolled in the alternate route take their training while being the classroom teacher.

Revisions in New Jersey's Alternate Route. In 1992, in an effort to stem the tide of rising attrition rates of traditionally prepared teachers, the New Jersey State Board of Education required all beginning teachers to undergo the support and evaluation requirements of the Provisional Teacher Program. Since 1992, all beginning teachers in New Jersey are employed under a provisional certificate while being mentored.

In 2003, New Jersey changed its alternate route to include credit toward a master's degree for alternate route candidates enrolled through college-based programs. Also in 2003, the state authorized regional training centers and introduced a 20-hour preservice survival skills class that could be completed prior to employment.

California

Allan Bersin, California's secretary of education, acknowledged the significance of the alternative routes in California in the text of a speech he delivered at the Third Annual Conference of the National Center for Alternative Certification (NCAC) in February 2006. In his address, Bersin (2006) said,

> Alternative certification has . . . helped California address the dual challenge of quality and supply. Alternative routes have been a significant source of new teachers, as more than 30,000 individuals have earned their credential through these programs in the last decade.
>
> Alternative certification programs allow us to expand the talent pool of teachers in ways that we have not accomplished through more traditional routes to teaching.
>
> - Nearly half of those who have become teachers through alternative routes have been from ethnic and racial groups under-represented in our teaching workforce. That is twice the diversity of those currently teaching.
> - These routes have increased the number of males who have become elementary and special education teachers. Approximately 26% of the elementary and 34% of special education intern teachers are male.
> - Half of all newly credentialed math teachers in the state came through internship programs.
> - More than half of those who have come into teaching through alternative routes have come after pursuing another professional career. These routes build on prior experiences, utilize a learning by doing approach, and do not require individuals to forgo a salary while learning to teach.

- Growth in the number of participants in the programs and growth in the number of local education agencies offering these intern programs indicate that there is a demand for alternative to traditional teacher preparation programs. This not only helps address the supply issue, but also creates more choice for prospective teachers. I believe this choice results in improved quality of programs across the spectrum of teacher preparation programs– both traditional and alternative. (p. 2)

Production of Teachers Through California Intern Routes.   As shown in Table 4.6, the number of interns participating in California's intern programs rose, per year, from 1,238 in 1994–1995 to 8,429 in 2005–2006.

For the same years, the number of school districts involved increased from 150 to 842. California funded 29 intern programs with $2.0 million in 1994–1995. By 2005–2006, the state had supported 74 programs with $24.9 million in funding. Table 4.6 also shows the annual increases in the number of intern programs, interns, and districts served by funds from California.

Retention of Intern Teachers.   California's data show that teachers who enter through its intern programs have high retention rates. Eighty-five percent of interns are still teaching 5 years after they first became teachers, a record Secretary Bersin (2006) called "a remarkable achievement [that] helps to sustain the supply of highly qualified teachers" (p. 3).

Table 4.6   California Internship Program Participation and Funding Trends

Fiscal Year	Number of Funded Programs	Number of Interns Served	Number of Districts Involved	Funding (Millions)
1994–1995	29	1,238	150	$2.0
1995–1996	23	1,471	178	$2.0
1996–1997	23	1,888	186	$2.0
1997–1998	52	3,706	271	$4.5
1998–1999	58	4,340	330	$6.5
1999–2000	65	4,827	408	$11.0
2000–2001	75	5,649	465	$21.5
2001–2002	81	7,236	594	$31.8
2002–2003	79	7,505	762	$18.8
2003–2004	78	8,880	792	$22.2
2004–2005	72	8,341	842	$20.8
2005–2006	74	8,429	842	$24.9

Source: California Commission on Teacher Credentialing, 2006.

Furthermore, Bersin (2006) said, "If interns are well selected, are provided preparation that links theory and practice, and are supported and nurtured by programs that have high performance expectations, they will become successful teachers and they will stay" (p. 3). Table 4.7 shows retention data for California interns after 4 and 5 years of teaching.

California's alternative certification programs annually produce 30% of all newly credentialed teachers. All teacher preparation programs in California, traditional or alternative, are postbaccalaureate. The alternative certification (District Intern) programs are intended to alleviate shortages in the teacher labor force. To do so, the District Intern programs require candidates to be fully employed as teachers of record while concurrently participating in a teacher preparation program. The state mandates that candidates are provided with a mentor during the entire internship. In 1996, the state adopted and legislated funding ($2,500 per intern for the 2 to 3 years that an intern is enrolled in a program) for alternative teacher certification programs.

The alternative certification program may be district based, administered as a partnership between a university and a district or several districts, or be through the one distance learning intern program offered through the California State University systems: CalState Teach.

Revisions in California's Alternate Routes.   In 2002, recognizing the value of its intern programs in attracting and credentialing individuals in areas of need, state lawmakers included preparation for special education teachers through its District Intern program. In 2004–2005, California's internship programs produced a third of the 24,000 new teachers hired in the state (CCTC, 2006).

Study of District Intern Program Confirms Value of California's Alternate Routes.   Elaine Chin and John W. Young (2006) surveyed California's intern candidates (8,881 enrolled in 2004); of 6,367 who visited the Website, 4,239 (67%) completed the majority of survey questions on the interns' backgrounds. A subset of 1,862 (not demographically different from all interns) completed all questions. Thirty-eight alternative route to certification programs participated in the study published as *Beyond Demographics: Who Enters and Completes Alternative Teacher Credential Programs in California.*

A goal of the study, through surveys at the beginning of the program and near the end of the program (during the 2002 to 2004 academic years), was to develop a model that could predict program completion and the acquisition of a teaching credential by the interns. The authors found that the variable that had the strongest effect was school placement. Interns were more likely to finish *if they were in a hard-to-staff school*. Chin and Young (2006) speculate that the "higher completion rates may be a function of the experiences interns bring to their preparation program and the resilience that they may

Table 4.7   *California Retention Composite for Teaching Interns (1993–2005)*

Years of Service	5 Years as Teacher of Record			4 Years as Teacher of Record			3 Years as Teacher of Record			2 Years as Teacher of Record			1 Year as Teacher of Record		
	No. Admitted to Program	No. Still Teaching	% Still Teaching	No. Admitted to Program	No. Still Teaching	% Still Teaching	No. Admitted to Program	No. Still Teaching	% Still Teaching	No. Admitted to Program	No. Still Teaching	% Still Teaching	No. Admitted to Program	No. Still Teaching	% Still Teaching
1993–1998				2,367	1,674	70	1,810	1,340	74	2,555	2,306	93	2,798	2,288	82
1995–2000	694	533	77	993	847	85	1,522	1,379	86	2,419	2,257	93	4,827	4,713	98
1996–2001	1,062	692	65	1,793	1,171	65	2,011	1,552	76	2,940	2,360	86	3,251	3,195	98
1997–2002	1,774	1,434	89	2,188	1,863	85	2,478	2,127	86	2,687	2,492	93	3,143	3,043	98
1998–2003	2,573	2,184	85	3,199	2,769	87	3,886	3,392	87	5,003	4,436	89	5,319	5,068	95
1999–2004	3,097	2,587	84	3,716	3,223	87	4,406	3,982	90	5,117	4,638	91	5,979	5,749	96
2000–2005	3,576	3,041	85	4,232	3,733	88	4,870	4,328	89	5,922	5,390	91	5,203	4,968	96

Source: California Commission on Teacher Credentialing, 2006.

have developed from previous work in schools" (p. 21). From their survey data analysis, they found that "it is probably true that the intern population attracts men, second career seekers and people interested in becoming special education teachers at higher rates than are typically found in traditional programs" (p. 19).

Texas

In "Comparison of Preparation Routes in Texas," Karen S. Herbert (2004) wrote, "In addition to traditional undergraduate degree programs in education, teachers can be prepared and certified through alternative certification programs offered through education service centers, school districts, community colleges, and private entities, as well as through universities" (p. 5). Teachers "can also train," she said, "in university post-baccalaureate programs . . . created to provide alternative routes to certification for individuals for whom traditional programs may be too costly, time-consuming, or cumbersome" (p. 5). Herbert (2004) wrote that "the distinction between post-baccalaureate and alternative certification programs is often unclear" (p. 5). In fact, both programs:

- are intended to prepare individuals who already hold baccalaureate degrees
- share many design features, and
- may provide essentially the same experiences to teacher candidates (p. 5).

Production in Texas Through Its Alternate Routes.   In 1989, the Texas state legislature eliminated the requirement that teacher shortages be used as a prerequisite for the alternative certification programs. Texas has revised other provisions as well as regulations to expand its programs, and the results in Texas have been dramatic and the contrasts clear.

In 1989, traditional college campus–based programs in Texas prepared 96% of the 14,061 initially certified teachers. By 2003, of the 20,528 initially certified teachers, the proportion prepared through traditional undergraduate programs dropped to 46% while the percentage of initially certified alternate route teachers increased to 35%. The proportion prepared through postbaccalaureate programs stayed about the same as previous years at 19%.

A 2004 Texas report prepared for the Texas State Board of Educator Certification (SBEC) stated,

> The growth of alternative certification programs has been particularly strong. Not only are these programs on track to become the primary source of new teachers in Texas within the next ten years, but they have already become the primary source of minority teachers and male teachers. They also produce the majority of teachers in special education and bilingual education, as well as growing numbers of mathematics and science teachers. (Herbert, 2004)

Figure 4.3 Percentage of Initially Certified Teachers in Texas by Traditional and Nontraditional Certification Routes (1989–2003)

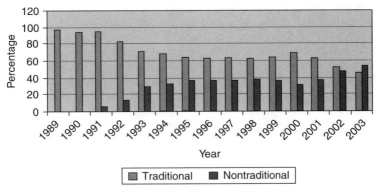

Source: Texas State Board of Educator Certification, 2006.

Data from the Texas SBEC show that in 2003, the number of new teachers in Texas from nontraditional (alternate route, postbaccalaureate, and experience-based) routes exceeded that of teachers from traditional undergraduate programs in the state, as shown in Figure 4.3.

Retention of Alternate Route Teachers in Texas. Retention rate data from Texas show that, whereas nearly all initially certified teachers from alternate route programs teach the following year, 10% to 11% of those prepared in traditional undergraduate programs and 14% to 15% from postbaccalaureate programs did not teach in the first few years after being certified. However, the retention rates after 3 years even out among these three sources of new teachers.

Florida

In 2001, the Florida legislature mandated the use of alternate routes to certification throughout the state, stipulating that by July 1, 2002, every school district in the state of Florida had to have an alternative route to teacher certification. Florida's mandate is a noteworthy development in the evolution of alternate routes. Florida's requirement that its 67 school district/counties (the boundaries are the same) must operate an alternate route program seems a milestone that might signal a future trend for other states as well, to help meet school staffing needs.

To carry out the mandate, in 2002–2003 Florida initiated statewide implementation of competency-based school district alternative certification programs that satisfied the professional preparation requirements of all teachers in the state. Among other provisions, the Florida law stated,

> The Department of Education shall develop and each school district must provide a cohesive competency-based professional preparation alternative certification program by which members of a school district's instructional staff may satisfy the mastery of professional preparation and education competence requirements specified in this subsection and rules of the State Board of Education. Participants must hold a state-issued temporary certificate. A school district shall provide a competency-based alternative certification preparation program developed by the Department of Education or developed by the district and approved by the Department of Education. (Florida Statutes, 2006)

During the first year of mandatory alternative certification in Florida (2002–2003), the Florida Department of Education (FLDOE) collected both quantitative and qualitative data to guide program effectiveness. By 2005, Florida State University, in collaboration with the FLDOE, had completed four evaluation reports, including the *Third Annual Progress Report* by Pam Flood and Sande Milton, which covered program and research findings only on state-approved district alternative certification programs.

The report found these characteristics of teachers in Florida's alternative certification programs:

- Over 50% reported that knowing about the alternative route to certification positively influenced their decision to enter the field of teaching.
- Half were older than 36 years of age, and nearly 60% were between 27 and 45.
- Florida alternative certification programs are not attracting more minorities or men.
- Over 50% had majored in business, the physical sciences, or the social sciences.
- Over 70% were teaching in middle and high schools.
- Over 30% reported that their mentors influenced their decision to stay in teaching.
- Most rated their training as positive or very positive (75%), and 90% reported that they would choose an alternative certification program again.
- Over 75% of mentor respondents reported that they were teaching while mentoring.
- Over 95% of the responding principals reported that alternative certification program teachers met their criteria for rehiring.

School Districts Call for Help. Florida experienced a phenomenon that had happened in other states, including New Jersey, Texas, and California: School districts, when given the authority to set up their own "grow your own teachers" programs, often replied, "Help." Many school districts say they are ill equipped to train teachers, don't have the resources, and don't particularly want to take on the task.

So, following in the footsteps of several states that turned to higher education to provide pedagogy and instructional support, the Florida legislature in 2004 established a new alternative route through Educator Preparation Institutes (EPIs). An accredited institution of higher education, including community colleges, may offer an EPI, approved by the state, for baccalaureate degree holders to participate in a field-based, competency-based alternate route. Also, in 2004, Florida allowed individuals who acquired the ABCTE Passport to obtain certification.

New York

New York provides an example of changes in how a state defines alternate routes over time. When the state approved a collaborative effort between colleges and local school partners, it opened the way for another innovative alternate route in New York City.

New York's history in the alternative teacher certification movement reflects the ambiguous nature of this and other states' approach to alternate routes. In 1990, when NCEI was collecting data for its annual guide about alternate routes, New York officials insisted that the state had had an alternate route "for 60 years." State officials reported that New York had created its Transcript Analysis option in the 1930s "to enable persons who had not completed a state-approved teacher education program to attain certification" (Feistritzer, 1990, p. 93).

The Transcript Analysis route to certification still exists in New York. Applicants submit an official form and transcripts of collegiate-level study for evaluation. If the applicant's study and experience meet requirements comparable to those completed by graduates of registered teacher preparation programs, the state issues the appropriate initial certificate. If there are deficiencies, the applicant is informed and must complete the missing requirements to get a certificate to teach. Regional Certification Offices conduct evaluations of transcripts and experiences, and the State Department of Education issues the certificates.

Also in 1990, New York reported having three additional "alternate routes" to teacher certification:

1. The "Internship Certificate," which state officials said had been "in effect for 27 years" (p. 72). This route basically "enables persons to teach during and as part of their program of study for a Master of Arts in Teaching"—a novel idea in the 1960s, but not so today.
2. The "Visiting Lecturer" route, which has been available since "about 1960" (p. 94). New York is not unique in having an entrée into teaching for individuals who have "unusual qualifications and expertise in

a specific subject area . . . not found in the teaching occupation." New York's Visiting Lecturer credential is valid for 1 year.

3. In 1987, New York instituted a "Temporary License," which the state later identified as an alternate route. This route was available "when no certified and qualified teacher is available after extensive and documented recruitment" (p. 45). In this route, applicants had to have a bachelor's degree and a request from a hiring school district.

These types of "alternate routes" were common in the 1980s. Individuals had to complete regular required coursework over an extended period of time. New York issued the temporary certificate for 1 year, renewable three times. At the end of the 3 years, the individual had to have fulfilled all requirements for the regular Provisional Certificate to teach in New York.

New York continued its three routes to certification just described, but chose, in 1991, for unspecified reasons to declassify them as alternative routes to teacher certification.

In 1991, New York certification officials reported to NCEI that the state was not implementing *any* alternative routes to teacher certification, and it was "not even considering alternative certification like they have in New Jersey, but never say never" (Feistritzer, 1991, p. 13).

Then, in July 2000, the New York State Board of Regents instituted the Alternative Teacher Certification—Transitional B route, which allows colleges to partner with local schools. This program features an accelerated introductory component, followed by paid employment. Extensive mentoring, coursework, and other supports from the college and school district complete the program requirements.

This alternate route to teacher certification opened the door for the creation of the highly publicized, highly studied New York City Teaching Fellows Program (Boyd et al., 2005). The authors of *How Changes in Entry Requirements Alter the Teacher Workforce and Affect Student Achievement* focused their study on pathways into teaching in New York City and the "effects of such programs on the teacher workforce and on student achievement," which is discussed in Chapter 7.

Kentucky

Kentucky's approach to alternate routes has been to create separate alternate routes for different populations of potential K–12 teachers. Kentucky enacted legislation for several separate alternate routes to teacher certification between 1984 and 2000. The state first approved the Adjunct Instructor Certification Option in 1984. This alternative route allowed entry into part-time K–12 teaching for persons with training or expertise in specialty area(s).

By 1990, legislation known as the Kentucky Education Reform Act of 1990, called for new alternative certification programs. The Kentucky legislature enacted alternative routes for teacher and administrator certification for "persons who have demonstrated exceptional work and/or educational experiences." The state designated the Education and Professional Standards Board (EPSB) as the state agency to establish the standards and procedures for alternative route options. The Local District Certification Option created as a result of the 1990 law was open for all subjects and grade levels, except special education.

Similar to alternate route entry requirements in other states, Kentucky requires that individuals must complete a bachelor's degree with a 2.5 grade-point average (or a 2.0 GPA with "exceptional life experience" related to teaching); pass written tests of knowledge in the specific teaching field (or must have completed a 30-hour major/minor, or have 5 years' experience in the field to be taught); and have been offered employment in a school district that has an alternative certification program approved by the state's Education Professional Standards Board (EPSB). These are Kentucky's seven alternate route options:

Option 1: Exceptional Work Experience Certification
Option 2: Local District Training Program Certification
Option 3: College Faculty Certification
Option 4: Adjunct Instructor Certification
Option 5: Veterans of the Armed Forces
Option 6: University-Based Alternative Route to Certification
Option 7: University Institute Alternative Route to Certification

Production of Teachers Through Kentucky's Alternate Routes.   Kentucky is aggressively using alternative routes to meet the state's needs for teachers. As shown in Table 4.8, most of the growth in alternatively certified teachers is through the state's university-based option 6.

Table 4.8   Teachers Certified Through Alternative Routes in Kentucky (2002–2003 Through 2005–2006)

Alternate Route	2002–2003	2003–2004	2004–2005	2005–2006
Option 2: Local District Training	9	9	11	14
Option 3: College Faculty	65	41	20	31
Option 4: Adjunct Instructor	83	91	34	89
Option 1: Exceptional Work Experience	39	26	18	33
Option 5: Veteran of the Armed Forces	29	29	21	21
Option 6: University Based	424	695	859	1,778
Option 7: University Institute[*]	0	0	0	0
Total Count	649	891	963	1,966

[*]Option 7 had its first program approved in May 2006.

Source: Kentucky Education Professional Standards Board, 2006.

These are but a few of the states' approaches to opening teaching to wider audiences of individuals who want to obtain certification to teach. Not only are the number of alternative routes made avaiable by states growing, the providers within states that are creating and implementing the state routes are growing even more rapidly. An analysis of alternate route program providers follows in Chapter 5.

5

※

How Do Providers Implement
State Alternate Routes?

Depending on a state's guidelines for its alternative route(s), there may be different providers implementing the state's routes. States specify eligible providers, such as school districts, regional service centers, individual schools, private companies, consortia, community colleges, as well as traditional 4-year colleges and universities.

Within each state, the eligible providers create programs to implement the alternate routes to certification. Upon successful completion of the state-approved alternative route program and recommendations from the provider, the state certifies individuals to teach in the state. In 2006, nearly all of the 50,000 participants were teachers of record in schools across the country while they were becoming certified. Providers implemented 125 state alternate routes through an estimated 485 alternate route programs.

Diverse Alternate Routes Require
Flexible Providers

State-Approved Providers Vary from State to State

New Jersey is a state that has one alternate route, which the New Jersey State Department of Education administers. The state's regulations legally refer to state-approved district training programs. Individual school districts are the direct providers of the selection, mentoring, performance evaluation, and certification elements of the New Jersey program. State regulations also give the districts ultimate authority over the noncredit formal instruction component. New Jersey colleges and universities may provide formal instruction in subject matter and pedagogy that the state deems is necessary to fulfill the

200 clock hours of instruction required. Growth in the number of service providers within New Jersey has been steady, as it has been elsewhere.

In the 1990s, New Jersey authorized nine service providers (seven colleges and universities and two district consortia) to train teacher candidates enrolled in the alternate route. By 2006, New Jersey had expanded its service providers, who were training approximately 3,000 alternate route participants, to 18 (13 colleges/universities and 5 district consortia).

Not surprisingly, large states like California and Texas have approved scores of providers for their alternate routes. Texas, in 2006, had 78 alternate route program providers encompassing every provider option, as shown in Table 5.1.

Table 5.1 shows that, in 1 year—from August 1, 2005 through July 31, 2006—78 alternate route program providers in Texas prepared 10,280 teachers. The numbers vary considerably, but iteAChTexas (I Teach Texas) produced 1,147 teachers, by far the most teachers of any of the other alternate route programs. It is the first private alternative certification program approved by the State Board for Educator Certification that is based on distance learning.

Fourteen Regional Education Service Centers trained nearly 30% (3,003) of alternate route teachers in Texas from August 1, 2005, through July 31, 2006. Fifteen other institutions prepared about half of all teachers trained through alternate route programs. At the other end of the continuum of alternate route providers in Texas, 9 institutions (private and specialized, for instance) had prepared fewer than 10 teachers each over the 1-year period, and 53 entities had prepared fewer than 100 teachers each.

The numbers of participants in different programs vary for a variety of reasons: the length of time the program has been available, the breadth of subject-matter preparation and certification areas, program entry requirements, program completion requirements, program cost, and access to the program. Overall, there is no correlation in the type of provider of an alternate route program and the number of participants in the program.

Texas is one of the few states that tracks alternate route providers and subsequently teachers prepared through alternate route programs by those providers. Most states are still struggling with creating data systems that will track needed information, spurred on recently because of federal reporting requirements.

Providers Report to NCAC Through a Data Template

In early 2004, two groups asked the National Center for Alternative Certification (NCAC)[1] for help. Researchers suggested that inconsistencies

---

[1] The National Center for Alternative Certification (NCAC) was established in September 2003 by the National Center for Education Information (NCEI) with a U.S. Department of Education grant of $2.25 million. NCAC is the nation's first clearinghouse for alternative routes to teaching and can be accessed at *www.teach-now.org*.

Table 5.1   Production of Teachers on Alternative Certificates in Texas by Educator Preparation Program for the Period 8/1/2005 Through 7/31/2006

Alternate Route Provider	Total
21st Century Leadership	5
A Career in Teaching–ACP	19
ACT Rio Grande Valley	346
ACT–Houston	851
ACT–San Antonio (Alt Cert for Teachers)	118
Alamo Community College District	36
Alief ISD	92
Alternative Cert for Teachers NOW!	17
Alternative–South Texas Educator Program	323
Austin Community College	29
Blinn College	49
Brookhaven College	21
College of the Mainland (Galveston County)	69
Collin County Community College	56
Cy-Fair College	96
Dallas Christian College	13
Dallas ISD	394
Education Career Alternatives Program	549
Houston Community College System	51
Houston ISD	474
Huston-Tillotson University	23
iteAChtexas.com	1,147
Kingwood College	291
Lamar State College–Orange	158
Lamar University	5
Laredo Community College	20
McLennan Community College	82
Montgomery College	18
Mountain View College	64
North Harris College	132
Pasadena ISD	98
Prairie View A&M University	49
Quality ACT: Alternative Certified Teachers	10
Region 01 Education Service Center	149
Region 02 Education Service Center	51
Region 03 Education Service Center	76
Region 04 Education Service Center	801
Region 06 Education Service Center	48
Region 07 Education Service Center	142
Region 09 Education Service Center	1
Region 10 Education Service Center	713

(Continued)

Table 5.1   Continued

Alternate Route Provider	Total
Region 11 Education Service Center	227
Region 12 Education Service Center	136
Region 13 Education Service Center	195
Region 14 Education Service Center	14
Region 18 Education Service Center	73
Region 19 Education Service Center	45
Region 20 Education Service Center	332
Richland College	36
San Antonio College Center for Ed Prep	41
San Jacinto College North	11
Schreiner University	2
South Texas Transition to Teaching ACP	2
State Board for Educator Certification	13
Steps to Teaching–ACP	28
Tarleton State University	131
TeacherBuilder.com	12
Teachers for the 21st Century	6
Texas–Alternative Certification Program	179
Texas A&M International University	34
Texas A&M University	31
Texas A&M University–Commerce	220
Texas A&M University–Kingsville	48
Texas A&M University–Texarkana	25
Texas Alternative Center for Teachers	4
Texas Teachers of Tomorrow	55
Texas Teaching Fellows	81
Tomball College	21
Training via E-Learning: An Alternative Cert Hybrid	13
Tyler Junior College	9
University of North Texas	55
University of Texas – Brownsville	46
University of Texas – El Paso	155
University of Texas – Pan American	144
Weatherford College	36
Web-Centric Alternative Certification Pg	5
West Texas A&M University	102
Western Governors University	27
Total	**10,280**

Source: Texas State Board of Educator Certification, data run and accessed, August 12, 2006, rpt_tchr_prod_counts_lvl2006812131431.

and varieties of alternate route programs compounded studies of alternate route programs. Program providers indicated that they would welcome a template that standardized information gathering and reporting.

By mid-2004, NCAC had developed and made available a template for program providers. Providers of alternate route programs responded by logging into a secure online site made available by NCAC and entering data and information about their programs. NCAC posts all information from alternate route program providers through the data template on its Website: www.teach-now.org.

By July 2006, 262 providers of alternate route programs had completed a template about their programs. An additional 223 alternate route program providers had supplied some information about their programs but had not completed the template as of the writing of this book.

An analysis of the data of the 262 providers that completed the template provides the basis for the analyses used throughout the rest of this chapter. NCAC's online template allows for an ongoing analysis of the data after being completed and submitted by providers. It is noteworthy that the percentages reported in this chapter have not significantly changed since we analyzed information from the first 80 templates completed by alternate route program providers.

Furthermore, when we compare our data with those collected by the states, we find no significant differences by who administers the program, basic requirements for entry and completion of the program, and length of programs.

Analyses of Selected NCAC Data Template Responses from Alternate Route Program Providers

Analysis of Program Provider Data

Despite some striking differences, such as the number of college courses candidates must take, the NCAC analyses reveal striking similarities in most programs, from entry requirements through program completion, even as the number of participants varies widely from program to program.

In all, the NCAC data template requests information on 44 items in four parts: contact information, information about the alternative teacher certification program features and requirements, information about the participants in the program, and employment and cost information about the program. Some provider responses included considerable specificity, others less so, but the information requests were standardized. The analysis includes some of the comments, especially those that fell within the "other" category, an option for several of the items.

Who Administers the Alternate Route Program?

The biggest difference among providers of alternate route programs is who administers the program. As shown in Figure 5.1, nearly half (46%) are administered by a college or university.

Community colleges—a fast-growing newcomer in this field—administer 6%. School districts, regional service centers, and schools administer about a fourth (24%) of alternate route programs. State agencies administer about 6%; various consortia, 4%; and "other" about 14%. The "other" category included mostly collaborations and a handful of private companies and online providers.

The fastest growth in alternate route programs is in college-administered programs. From the NCAC template data, 6 out of 10 college-administered alternate route programs were established since 2000. All of the community college–administered alternate route programs were started in the 2000s, as were 7 out of 10 school district–based alternate route programs. All of the alternate route programs administered by regional service centers reported they began before 2000.

Requirements and Program Features

To facilitate the analyses, NCAC combined responses into three groups by who administers the program. Program providers are grouped as follows:

1. College providers (colleges/universities/community colleges)
2. Local providers (school districts/regional service centers/schools)
3. Consortia and others

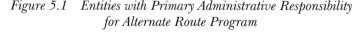

*Figure 5.1   Entities with Primary Administrative Responsibility
for Alternate Route Program*

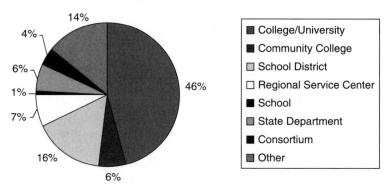

Source: National Center for Alternative Certification Data Template, August 1, 2006.

Because most responses included multiple options, the sample size (*n*) varies from item to item, but is not noted because the total answered remains close to 262, the number of respondents.

Entry Requirements.   Nearly all (99%) alternate route programs require at least a bachelor's degree from an accredited institution of higher education to enter the program. A few alternative route programs, such as some of those funded by the federal Transition to Teaching program, are for training paraprofessionals to become certified as teachers. Paraprofessionals are teacher aides and others who may be employed by the school district but who have not completed an undergraduate degree.

As shown in Figure 5.2, two thirds of alternate route programs require an interview to get into the program. Of other entry criteria, 64% require passage of a basic skills test, and 56% require that a candidate pass a subject-area test. Other entry requirements cited were specified number of credit hours in subject(s) to be taught and various test requirements, grade-point averages (ranging from 2.2 to 3.0), references, background checks, and, sometimes, prior work experience.

Figure 5.2   Specific Entry Requirements for Alternative Teacher Certification Programs

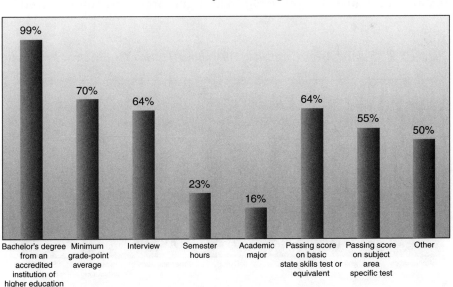

Source: National Center for Alternative Certification Data Template, August 1, 2006.

Grade Levels. More than 80% of noncollege-administered alternate route programs lead to certification at the pre-K, elementary, and middle school levels, whereas more than 80% of college-administered alternate route programs lead to certification to teach at the secondary level.

Subject Areas. Providers of alternate route programs differ considerably in subject-area preparation options. Because of the emphasis on reducing teacher shortages in mathematics and the sciences, nearly 9 out of 10 of all alternate route programs focus on preparing teachers to become certified in mathematics and the sciences. Figure 5.3 shows the breakdown from respondents by subject area of the preparation programs. A significantly higher proportion of the noncollege-administered programs prepare candidates for teaching special education and bilingual students, two other high-need teacher shortage areas.

Courses Required and Delivery Options. A major difference among alternate route programs is the number of college courses candidates are required to take for which they pay tuition at a college or university. For example, as shown in Figure 5.4, 38% of alternate route programs do not require participants to take *any* college semester hours for which they pay tuition at a college or university.

At the other end of the spectrum, 28% require participants to take 31 or more semester hours for which they pay college tuition. Not surprisingly, as shown in Figure 5.5, more alternate route programs administered by

Figure 5.3   Subject Areas Certified by Alternative Teacher Certification Programs

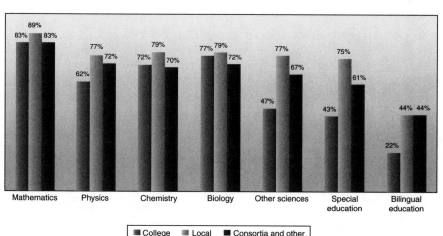

Source: National Center for Alternative Certification Data Template, August 1, 2006.

Figure 5.4   College Tuition-Paid Semester Hours Required in Alternate Route Programs

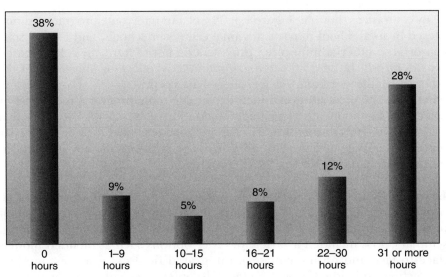

Source: National Center for Alternative Certification Data Template, August 1, 2006.

Figure 5.5   College Tuition-Paid Semester Hours Required in Alternate Route Programs by Who Administers the Program

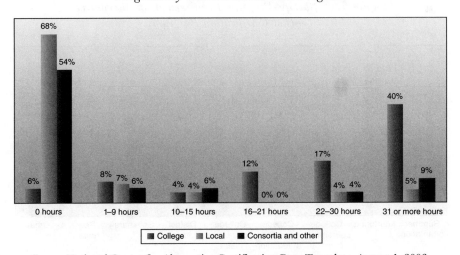

Source: National Center for Alternative Certification Data Template, August 1, 2006.

colleges, universities, and community colleges require participants to take courses for which participants pay tuition to a college than do other providers of alternate route programs.

By contrast, as shown in Figure 5.5, 68% of alternate route programs administered by local school districts, regional centers or schools, and 54% of state consortia or other-administered providers do not require *any* college-based courses for which the candidate pays tuition to a college or university. At the other end of the spectrum, 40% of college-based providers, 9% of consortia and others, and 5% of locally administered alternate route programs require 31 or more semester hours of college tuition-paid coursework. Of the programs that require candidates to complete 31 or more semester hours for which they pay tuition at a college or university, about a fourth of the candidates are enrolled in a master of arts in teaching (MAT) program.

Learning Components. As shown in Figure 5.6, 8 out of 10 (81%) of all providers of alternate route programs include mentoring as a component of their programs. More than half (54%) of program respondents offered seminars, 43% included a variety of other options such as blended models (face-to-face and online courses), integrated field experiences, module instruction, individual growth plans, teleconferences, and various mandatory training sessions. About a fifth (18%) included candidates reviewing each other's work (peer review) as part of the alternate route program.

As shown in Figure 5.7, mentoring is a component of 91% of locally administered programs, compared with 72% of those administered by colleges. Not

Figure 5.6   Specific Program Requirements of Alternative Teacher Certification Programs

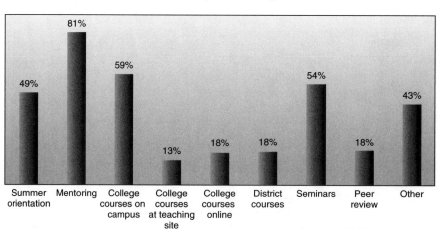

Source: National Center for Alternative Certification Data Template, August 1, 2006.

Figure 5.7   Specific Program Requirements of Alternative Teacher Certification Programs, by Provider Category

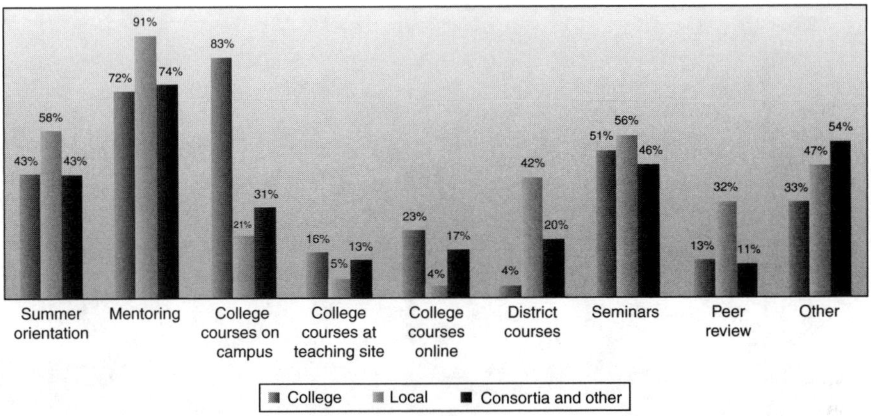

Source: National Center for Alternative Certification Data Template, August 1, 2006.

surprisingly, college courses on campus are a requirement in 83% of college-administered alternate routes and only 21% of those administered by school districts and other local entities.

Cohorts.   Regardless of which entity administers the alternative route program, 82% reported that the participants in their programs function as a cohort while in the program, (e.g., they meet together regularly, take courses/seminars together, and learn from each other).

Teaching While Learning.   Just as most alternate route programs require a baccalaureate degree to enter the program, program providers report that virtually all program participants teach with salary and benefits during their alternate route programs. Although most (79%) are full-time employees, some (21%) are employed part time.

Candidate Support.   As shown in Figure 5.8, alternate route program providers reported that while candidates are teaching, they received support most often (95%) from mentor teachers.

Program providers reported that beginning teachers received support from others as well: from school principals, 74%; from college personnel, 69%; and from state agency personnel, 11%.

Forty-three percent of alternate route program providers listed "other" support personnel for candidates in their programs, including peer coaches, retired administrators, district personnel, itinerant teacher support specialists, other members of the cohort, and retired teachers.

Figure 5.8   Types of Support a Participant Receives During Alternative Teacher Certification Programs

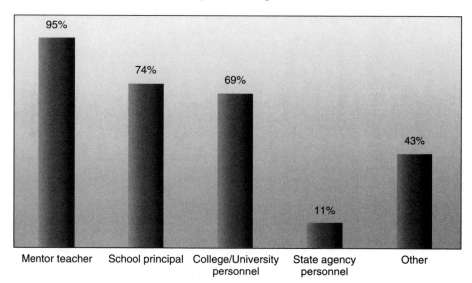

Source: National Center for Alternative Certification Data Template, August 1, 2006.

As shown in Figure 5.9, more local and regional providers of alternative route programs include mentoring components in their programs than do college providers. Not surprisingly, 96% of college-administered program providers, compared with 26% of locally administered program providers, report that participants in their programs received support from college/university personnel.

Candidate Assessments.   The most commonly used assessment to evaluate a candidate for certification is direct classroom observation, reported by 93% of alternate route program providers and shown in Figure 5.10.

Portfolios and written examinations are used more often as part of candidate assessment than essays and videos. Most program administrators use several of these assessments in their programs to evaluate candidates.

Respondents identified a number of other assessments used by program administrators, including Web-based assessment, activities through learning teams, presentations, case study assignments, journals, completion of online modules, principal evaluations, and teacher and student work samples.

Criteria for Certification.   Virtually all (99%) alternate route program providers use completion of the program as the primary criterion to recommend candidates for certification, as shown in Figure 5.11.

Figure 5.9   Types of Support a Participant Receives During Alternative Teacher Certification Programs, by Provider Category

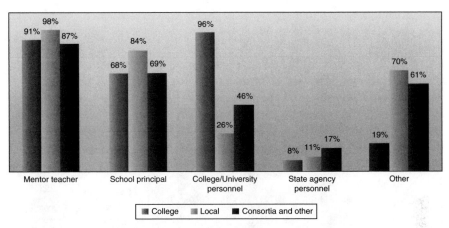

Source: National Center for Alternative Certification Data Template, August 1, 2006.

Figure 5.10   Assessments Used in Alternative Teacher Certification Programs to Evaluate a Participant for Certification

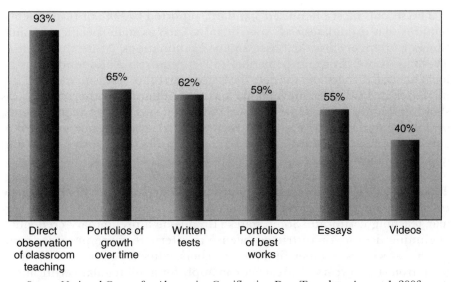

Source: National Center for Alternative Certification Data Template, August 1, 2006.

Figure 5.11   Criteria Used to Determine Successful Completion of Alternative Teacher Certification Programs

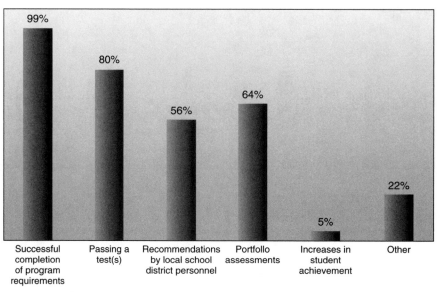

Source: National Center for Alternative Certification Data Template, August 1, 2006.

The second most often used standard, reported by 80% of respondents, requires that candidates pass specific tests, such as state-specific examinations or other professional assessment examinations. More than half of alternate route program providers (56%) require recommendations by local school district personnel; 64% use portfolio assessments, 5% use increases in student achievement, and 22% identified other criteria, as shown in Figure 5.11. "Other" criteria included specific test requirements, oral presentation before an oral review board, competency evaluation, and recommendations from school administrators, field supervisors, and university mentors.

Type of Certificate Received.   Upon successful completion of an alternate route program, providers reported that 85% of completers receive a full regular teaching certificate. Some states (15%) issue a preliminary credential, beginning license, or restricted license to alternate route program completers, as well as to other first-time teachers. After a period of time, most often from 1 to 5 years, the teacher can apply for a full regular certificate.

Program Completion Time.   The length of time a candidate has to complete the program has little correlation to the entity that administers the program, as shown in Figure 5.12.

Figure 5.12   Length of Time Expected to Complete Alternative Teacher Certification Programs Requirements

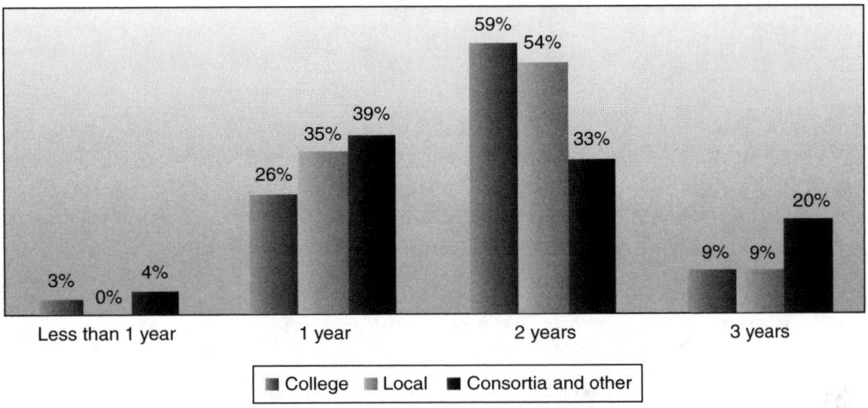

Source: National Center for Alternative Certification Data Template, August 1, 2006.

The time in which a candidate is expected to complete an alternate route program varies from less than 1 year to 3 years. Slightly more than half (54%) of program providers indicated that their candidates are expected to finish the program requirements in 2 years. About a third (32%) of the programs expect candidates to complete the program in 1 year, 3% in less than 1 year, and the remaining programs extend completion to 3 years. The greatest range in how much time it takes to get certified through an alternate route are in programs administered by states, consortia, and other entities. A third of these providers' programs last 1 year or less; 20% require 3 years to complete.

Program Costs.   Several factors affect the cost of an alternate route program to the candidate. For example, the number of required college courses and the price per credit hour may add significantly to cost, depending on the institution. In some cases, however, the individual may qualify for certification and have earned an advanced degree such as an MAT. Various fees, such as application fees, testing or assessment fees, and preservice fees, may add to the cost. The time required to complete the program may also affect the final cost.

Programs or providers might offer full or partial scholarships. State or federal funds may assist with the candidate's costs, or other financial incentives may be available to encourage program participation. As shown in Figure 5.13, as a result of a variety of factors, program costs for participants range from no cost to $18,000 or more. Excluding housing costs, the cost to a participant is most often from $3,000 to $6,000.

Figure 5.13   *Approximate Cost to Participant to Complete Alternative Teacher Certification Programs (Excluding Housing Costs)*

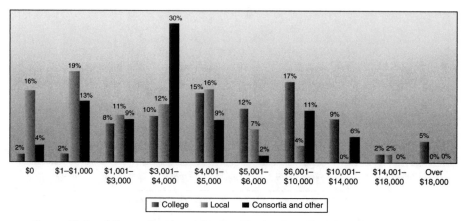

Source: National Center for Alternative Certification Data Template, August 1, 2006.

The Bottom Line

There are many types and modes of delivery of alternate routes at the program level within states and across the nation. Individuals who already have a baccalaureate degree and want to be a K–12 teacher have a wide variety of alternative pathways and alternate route providers from which to choose.

6

✿

Who Are Alternate Route
Teachers?

*T*wenty years ago the alternative certification movement for teachers was in its fledgling stage. The idea that high-quality teachers could be recruited from outside established education channels was regarded as avant-garde if not downright radical.

Experience in states all over the country has proven that educated individuals from a wide variety of occupations, including the military, can and do make excellent teachers. Teachers entering through alternate routes have become an important part of our education system. As they impart their knowledge and experience to a generation of students, they provide a vital source of talent and energy to classrooms across America. After two decades, we are beginning to learn more about them as a group and as individuals within the ranks of the 3.7 million elementary and secondary school teachers.

As discussed throughout this book, not only are alternate routes and alternate route programs increasing, but teachers also are coming into the profession through alternative routes to teacher certification programs in ever-increasing numbers as shown in Figure 6.1.

Profile of Alternate Route Teachers

In response to its annual state collection effort regarding alternative routes to teacher certification, state data submitted to the National Center for Education Information (NCEI) indicated that states issued teaching certificates to approximately 50,000 individuals who had entered teaching through alternate route programs in 2004–2005. State data further indicate that these individuals made up about a third of all new teachers hired that year (Feistritzer, 2006).

*Figure 6.1 Numbers of Teachers Certified Through
Alternate Routes (1985–2005)*

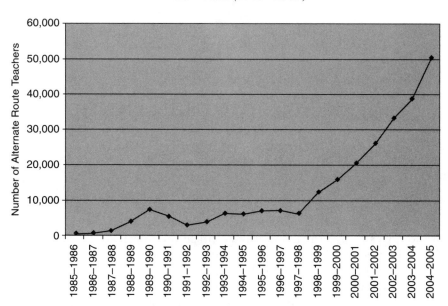

Source: Data submitted by state licensing offices to the National Center
for Education Information, (2006).

Data submitted by the states to NCEI over the years show that individuals who have participated in alternate route programs share many common characteristics. State data, as well as research from independent researchers, show similar demographic profiles, the subjects these individuals teach, the mobility of these teachers, and the prior career background of teachers prepared through alternate route programs. Teachers entering the profession through alternate routes are older, more diverse, and more willing to teach wherever the jobs are and in high-demand subjects than are traditionally trained teachers.

The single most critical question regarding alternate routes to teaching is *Would the individuals entering teaching through these routes have become teachers if the alternate routes were not available?* To get an answer to this question, as well as many others, NCEI conducted a survey of individuals who had participated in an alternate route program.

NCEI Conducted a National Survey of Alternate Route Teachers

In 2004–2005, NCEI conducted a national survey of individuals entering teaching through alternative routes to teacher certification. In an effort to have the survey reflect a national sample, NCEI identified populations that reflect the diversity and complexity of alternate route programs at large. NCEI sampled 7,567 individuals entering teaching through alternate routes in Texas, Florida, the Troops to Teachers program, the Milwaukee Teacher Education Center program, and the New York City Teaching Fellows program. NCEI used a paper survey for the sample, except those in Florida, who completed the survey online.

By March 12, 2005, 2,647 usable surveys were completed representing a 35% response rate. NCEI compared the responses from the first 1,582 questionnaires completed to the responses when all 2,647 questionnaires were completed. On no item was there ever more than a 1% difference.

NCEI also compared response data from the survey with data kept by the states regarding basic demographics and found no significant differences. Comparisons between NCEI survey responses and data maintained by the sample sources in Texas, Florida, New York City Teaching Fellows, and Troops to Teachers showed that the NCEI sample was, indeed, reflective of each of these respective populations.

Profile of Alternate Route Teachers was the result of an analysis of the 2,647 usable questionnaire survey responses received (Feistritzer, 2005a). Some of the findings as published are discussed here. Figure 6.2 shows one of the most significant findings.

Findings from Profile of Alternate Route Teachers

Half of Participants Would Not Have Become Teachers Without an Alternate Route.   Nearly half (47%) of those entering teaching through alternative routes responded that they would not have become a teacher if an alternate route to certification had not been available, and 25% of survey

Figure 6.2   Would You Have Become a Teacher if an Alternate Route to Certification Had Not Been Available?

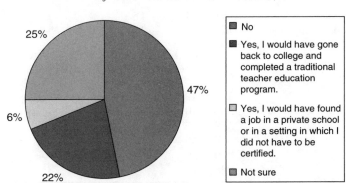

Source: National Center for Education Information, *Profile of Alternate Route Teachers*, (2005).

respondents said they were not sure, as shown in Figure 6.2. An additional 6% reported they would have found a job in a private school or in a setting in which they would not have to be certified to teach. Twenty-two percent said they would have gone back to college and completed a traditional teacher education program.

Furthermore, more than half (54%) of individuals entering teaching from a professional occupation said they would not have become teachers if an alternate route had not been available as shown in Table 6.1. Less than 20% of career switcher professionals and those coming from noneducation jobs indicated that they would have gone back to college and completed a traditional program to become a teacher.

Table 6.1   Would You Have Become a Teacher if an Alternate Route to Certification Had Not Been Available?

| | | | **Alternate Route Teachers** | | |
		No %	Yes, I would have completed a traditional teacher education program %	Yes, I would have found a job in a private school or in a setting in which I did not have to be certified %	Not sure %
All Respondents		**47**	**22**	**6**	**25**
By Prior Main Activity Before Alternate Route					
Professionals	1,021	54	18	4	24
Other noneducation job	176	48	17	5	31
Students	290	46	19	11	25
Teacher-related job	567	35	30	9	26
By Age					
18–24	425	49	17	9	25
25–29	500	40	24	4	32
30–39	589	46	20	7	27
40–49	676	50	24	6	20
50–59	239	56	18	4	22
60+	25	76	4	8	12

Source: National Center for Education Information, *Profile of Alternate Route Teachers* (2005).

Most Participants Came from Outside of Education.   As discussed in Chapter 1, until recently, the nation has focused on high school students who went to college and completed a state-approved college teacher education program for its supply of new teachers (USDoE, 1993, p. 1). The fact that states created alternative routes to teacher certification to expand the pool of potential teachers to include nontraditional populations, such as midcareer switchers and retirees, is reflected by those to whom the programs appeal.

Recall that in 2004–2005, school districts had hired about 150,000 new teachers, and approximately 50,000 had been hired through alternate route programs that year. Results of the 2004–2005 NCEI survey of alternate route teachers reflect the variety of occupations held by survey respondents prior to enrolling in an alternate route program as shown in Figure 6.3.

Figure 6.3 shows that nearly half (47%) of the people entering teaching through alternate routes were working in a noneducation job the year before they began an alternate route to teacher certification program. Forty percent were working in a professional occupation outside the field of education. Twelve percent were students, and 9% of the NCEI sample had been in the military the year before they began an alternate route program. Of those occupied in "other" jobs, 2% were caring for family members, 2% were unemployed and seeking work, and 1% were retired.

Some Participants Had Been in Education-Related Jobs.   Of the 22% who had been working in an education field before entering an alternate route program,

- 17% were working in a teaching job, for example,
  - As a substitute teacher (10%)
  - Teaching subject(s) for which they needed to obtain certification to meet the *No Child Left Behind* requirements (3%)

Figure 6.3   Activity 1 Year Prior to Beginning Alternate Route Program

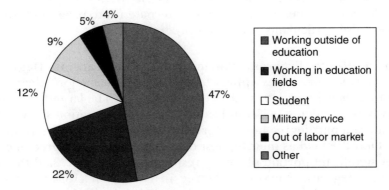

Source: National Center for Education Information, *Profile of Alternate Route Teachers* (2005).

- Teaching in a private school (2%)
- Teaching in a college or university (1%)
- Teaching in a preschool (1%)
- 5% were working in a position in the field of education, but not as a teacher.

Practicing Teachers.   Interestingly, about a third (35%) of the NCEI survey respondents who reported that they had been in a teaching job right before beginning an alternate route program said that they would *not* have entered a traditional teacher education program if the alternate route program had not been available.

There may be several reasons why practicing teachers are enrolling in alternate route programs. One significant reason is likely because the *No Child Left Behind* act requires that all teachers become highly qualified by the end of the 2006–2007 school year, which includes certification as well as mastery of subject matter to be taught. Most alternate routes require that the candidate demonstrate mastery in the subjects to be taught, a key element in the federal government's highly qualified teacher requirement.

In addition, individuals who may have taught for a while, stopped teaching, and are returning to teaching may enroll in an alternate route program to become certified for the first time, to reinstate their credentials, or to become certified in another subject area, such as special education.

Some Alternate Route Participants Had Been Students.   Also as shown in Table 6.1, 46% of the 12% of respondents in the NCEI survey who reported they had been students the year before entering an alternate route program said, too, that they would not have become teachers without an alternative route. The Teach For America (TFA) recruits are most often recent college graduates whom TFA places in schools in states that have alternate route programs. Four percent of the individuals in the NCEI survey who reported they were students before entering an alternate route program indicated they were also participants in the TFA program.

Alternate Route Program Participants Held Various Degrees.
Alternate route programs appeal to those with a bachelor's degree in a field other than education, as shown in Figure 6.4. The largest proportion of survey respondents (57%) indicated that a noneducation BA was their highest academic degree held before enrolling in an alternate route program. Only 3% held as their highest degree a bachelor's degree in education. A significant portion of survey respondents, however, said they held advanced degrees: a master's degree in education (19%), a master's degree in a field other than education (18%), and other professional degrees.

Figure 6.4   Highest Degree Earned

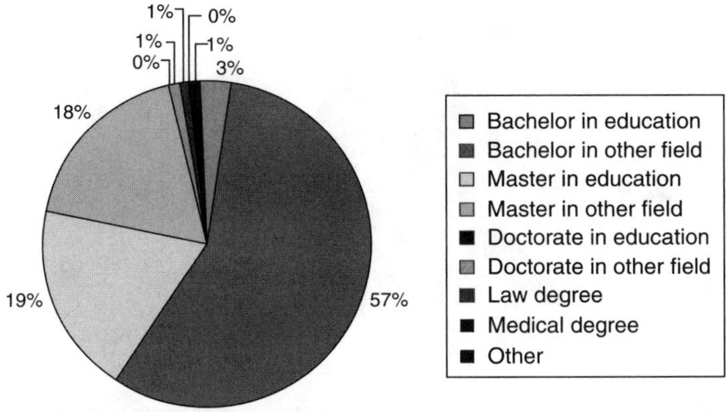

Source: National Center for Education Information, *Profile of Alternate Route Teachers* (2005).

Fifty-nine percent of women, compared to 49% of men, held, as their highest academic degree, a bachelor's degree in a field other than education.

How Age Affects Entry into an Alternate Route Program.   The breakout data in Table 6.1 also indicates that the older one is, the less inclined one is to enter teaching without using an alternate route. Nearly 6 out of 10 (59%) of those surveyed who were in their 50s or older when they entered an alternate route said they would not have become a teacher if an alternate route had not been available. Half (50%) of those in their 40s responded similarly.

As shown in Figure 6.5, nearly two thirds (63%) of alternate route teachers surveyed reported they had been 30 years of age or older at the time they entered an alternate route program. Thirty-nine percent entered a program at age 40 or older, and 11% began an alternate route program when they were 50 years or older.

Why Do Participants Choose an Alternate Route Program?

Alternate routes appeal to older adults and individuals concerned about employment and costs related to the program. Not surprisingly, respondents to the 2004 NCEI survey ranked several variables as very important to them in choosing an alternate route to teacher certification, as shown in Figure 6.6.

About 3 out of 4 (76%) of survey respondents indicated that receiving a teacher's salary and benefits and being able to teach while getting certified ranked highest among the reasons why they chose an alternate route to teacher certification. More than half of respondents (57%) considered out-of-pocket costs very important to them. Costs are related to the time it takes

Figure 6.5   Age When Began an Alternate Route Program

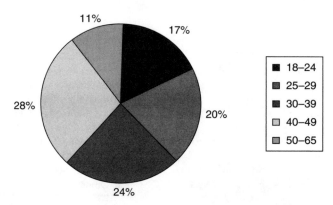

Source: National Center for Education Information, *Profile of Alternate Route Teachers* (2005).

Figure 6.6   Very Important Reasons in Choosing an Alternate Route Program

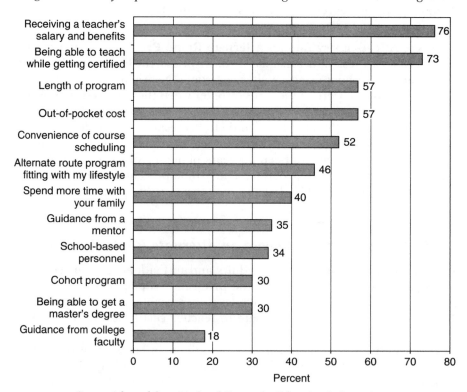

Source: Adapted from National Center for Education Information,
Profile of Alternate Route Teachers (2005).

to complete an alternate route program. Most alternate route participants complete a program within 2 years. The length of the program was an important consideration to 57% of survey respondents.

Variables that ranked among the least important were guidance from college faculty, the option of being able to get a master's degree, and being able to go through the program in a cohort. Mentoring, considered by many to be a very important component of any teacher preparation program, elicited favorable responses from 35% of survey respondents. They agreed that having guidance from a mentor had been a very important reason to them in choosing an alternate route to teaching.

Alternate Routes Appeal to Men and Minorities. The appeal to men and ethnic minorities are two issues that proponents of alternate route programs suggest are valuable characteristics of alternate routes. Data in Table 6.2 bear this out: More than half (52%) of men, compared with 45% of women, who were certified through alternate route programs said they would not have become a teacher if an alternate route had not been available.

Table 6.2 Would You Have Become a Teacher if an Alternate Route to Certification Had Not Been Available? (by Gender and by Race)

		Alternate Route Teachers			
		No %	Yes, I would have completed a traditional teacher education program %	Yes, I would have found a job in a private school or in a setting in which I did not have to be certified %	Not sure %
All Respondents		**47**	**22**	**6**	**25**
By Gender					
Male	888	52	21	5	23
Female	1,526	45	22	7	26
By Race					
Black or African American	298	43	26	5	26
Hispanic or Latino	342	53	23	5	19
White	1,611	48	21	6	25
Other	129	43	17	9	31

Source: National Center for Education Information, *Profile of Alternate Route Teachers* (2005).

Figure 6.7   Percentage of Teachers Who Are Men (by Source)

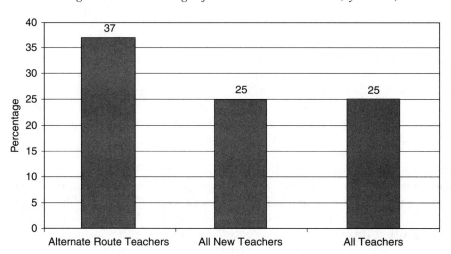

Source: Alternate route teacher data from the National Center for Education Information, *Profile of Alternate Route Teachers* (2005). Data for all new teachers and for all teachers are from the National Center for Education Statistics, *Schools and Staffing Surveys*, 2003–2004.

Similarly, more than half (53%) of individuals who identified themselves as Hispanic said they would not have become a teacher if an alternate route had not been available. In addition, 43% of African Americans indicated they would not have become teachers without the availability of an alternate route. In 2005, 37% of the respondents to the NCEI survey were men, as shown in Figure 6.7.

When compared to the U.S. Department of Education Schools and Staffing Survey of 2003–2004, 25% of all teachers and 25% of all new teachers were men. This 12% increase of male teachers prepared through alternate certification programs is another reason cited by proponents as a value of alternate certification programs. These statistics have remained close to those percentages since the late 1980s.

Figure 6.8 shows that 67% of survey respondent teachers prepared and certified through alternate route programs were white. Again, this is considerably different from the statistics concerning traditional teacher preparation programs. The U.S. Department of Education, through NCES, reported that 83% of BA recipients who went on to teach in 2003–2004 were white (USDoE, 2005b, p. 4).

Geographic Areas Where Alternate Route Teachers Teach.   Participants in alternate routes are teaching in geographic areas where the demand for teachers is greatest—in large cities, as shown in Figure 6.9. Half of participants in

Figure 6.8 Alternate Route Teachers (by Race)

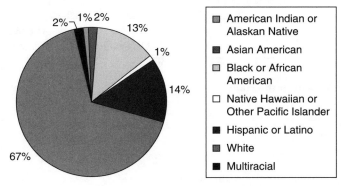

Source: National Center for Education Information, *Profile of Alternate Route Teachers* (2005).

alternate route programs, compared with 28% of all teachers, teach in large cities. Sixteen percent teach in a medium-size city (50,000–249,999), 10% in a suburban area outside a central city, 10% in a small city, 8% in a rural area (less than 10,000), and 6% teach in a small town (10,000–19,999).

Mobility of Alternate Route Teachers. Teachers who entered teaching though alternate routes also reflected a higher degree of mobility than did teachers in the overall teaching force. Not only do alternate route teachers already teach in high-demand communities, they also are more willing to move if the demand for teachers warrants such a move, as shown in Table 6.3.

Figure 6.9 What Type of Community Do You Teach In?

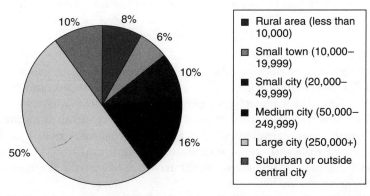

Source: National Center for Education Information, *Profile of Alternate Route Teachers* (2005).

Table 6.3   How Likely Would You Be to Move from Where You Live to Where the Demand for Teachers Is Greatest?

	All Teachers	Alternate Route Teachers
	%	%
To a rural area within the state		
Very likely	10	9
Somewhat likely	18	22
Somewhat unlikely	12	16
Very unlikely	56	46
Not sure	4	7
To a large metropolitan city within the state		
Very likely	6	12
Somewhat likely	12	24
Somewhat unlikely	13	17
Very unlikely	64	40
Not sure	5	7
To a rural area out of state		
Very likely	4	6
Somewhat likely	12	16
Somewhat unlikely	13	15
Very unlikely	67	56
Not sure	5	8
To a large metropolitan city out of state		
Very likely	3	10
Somewhat likely	10	21
Somewhat unlikely	11	15
Very unlikely	73	47
Not sure	4	8

Source: Alternate route data from National Center for Education Information, *Profile of Alternate Route Teachers*, (2005). Data for all teachers from National Center for Education Information, *Profile of Teachers in the U.S.* (2005).

Thirty-six percent of alternate route teachers said that it was very likely or somewhat likely that they would move to a large metropolitan area within the state if demand for teachers were great; 31% said it was very likely or somewhat likely that they would move to a rural area within the state.

Thirty-one percent indicated they would be very or somewhat likely to move to a metropolitan area out of state, and 22% said they would be very or somewhat likely to move to a rural area out of state if the demand for teachers warranted such a move.

Mobility of teachers prepared through alternate routes may be a partial explanation of the survey findings that nearly two thirds (62%) of alternate route teachers were *not* teaching within 150 miles of where they were born, whereas 64% of all *public school teachers* were teaching within 150 miles of where *they* were born.[1]

Alternate Routes Appeal to Career Changers.   Changing careers is becoming a common occurrence, and participants in alternate route programs are no exception. Again from the 2004–2005 NCEI survey, more than half (57%) of those entering teaching through alternate routes reported having made two or more career changes in their lives. Only 9% entered alternate route programs without having had a previous career.

Alternate Route Teachers Teach Subjects and Grade Levels Where Demand Is Greatest.   Teachers who had gone through an alternate route program reported teaching subjects where the demand for teachers was greatest: in mathematics, the sciences, and special education. For example, 20% of alternate route teachers were teaching mathematics in 2005, whereas 7% of all teachers were teaching mathematics. In the sciences, including biology, geology, physics, and chemistry, alternate route teachers exceed all teachers by a significant percentage (28% to 18%). Similarly, 44% of alternate route teachers were teaching special education classes.

From survey results in 2004–2005 and as shown in Figure 6.10, of those who had entered teaching through alternate route programs, 40% were teaching pre-K and elementary grades; the 60% who were teaching in junior and senior high grades were evenly divided between the two upper-grade levels.

Figure 6.10   Current Grade Level Alternate Route Teachers Teach

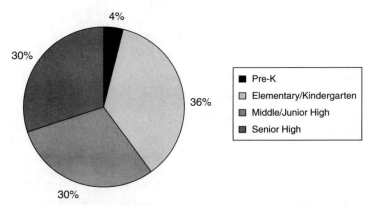

Source: National Center for Education Information, *Profile of Alternate Route Teachers* (2005).

---

[1] NCEI survey of public school teachers conducted in 2005.

Reasons Why Alternate Route Teachers Teach. The "desire to work with young people" and the "value and significance of education in society" are far and away the top two reasons individuals enter teaching, according to 2004 NCEI survey results of all teachers and of teachers who entered teaching through alternate route programs, as shown in Figure 6.11.

Respondents shared other similar concerns in comparable percentages, with two exceptions. A higher percentage of teachers prepared through alternate routes (23%) considered the "influence of a teacher in school" a more important reason to teach than did all other teachers (8%). Because alternate route teachers often come into teaching from other careers, "wanting

Figure 6.11   Reasons for Teaching

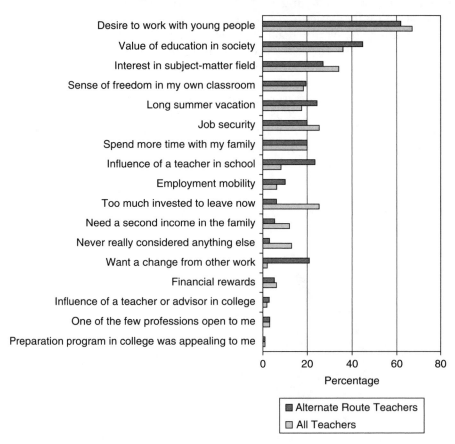

Source: Alternate route data from National Center for Education Information, *Profile of Alternate Route Teachers*, (2005). Data for all teachers from National Center for Education Information, *Profile of Teachers in the U.S.* (2005).

a change from other work" might be a partial explanation of why alternate route teachers (21%) identified this as a much stronger reason for teaching than did all other teachers (2%).

Alternate Route Participants Take Fewer Education Courses.   For decades, the number of semester hours or courses in education taken in college by teacher candidates was a hallmark of teacher preparation. More recently, however, participants in alternate route programs are likely to take fewer, if any, education courses and fewer courses still on a college campus. Thirty-nine percent of alternate route participants said they took *no* credit hours in college education courses.

This statistic mirrors the data from alternate route program providers as discussed in Chapter 5. Thirty-eight percent of providers do not require any college-based education courses in their programs.

For the 61% of alternate route teachers who reported they *did* take education courses during their alternate route programs, the number of credit hours in education courses they took varied widely—from 34% who reported they took 1 to 12 semester credit hours, to 25% who reported taking 31 to 50 semester hours of education courses. An additional 18% said they did not remember how many credit hours in education courses they took.

As a result, when the survey responses of those who reported taking education courses were compared to those who say they did not take education courses in their alternate route program, some very interesting findings emerge:

- Individuals entering teaching from other careers are evenly split in whether or not they were in alternate route programs that required taking college education courses.
- Former teachers are less likely to have taken education courses during their alternate route program.
- Length of the program, being able to teach while getting certified, guidance from a mentor, the program fitting one's lifestyle, and spending more time with one's family were the most important variables in choosing an alternate route for those who did not take education courses as part of their program.
- Forty-three percent of those who say they did not take college education courses indicated they did take off-campus courses in methodology/pedagogy, 71% indicated they took school-based courses/seminars in education, and 21% took online education courses.
- Sixty-eight percent of those who reported they did not take college education courses during their alternate route program, compared to 58% of those who said they did, reported they expected to be teaching K–12 levels 5 years from now.

What Is Valuable in Developing Competence to Teach? NCEI surveys of K–12 teachers in 1996 and in 2005 showed that teachers in general rank their own experiences as a teacher and working with colleagues/other teachers the highest in developing competence to teach (Feistritzer, 1996, p. 59; 2005b, p. 32). It is no different for alternate route teachers, as shown in Figure 6.12.

One's own teaching experiences and working with other teachers/ colleagues were perceived as most valuable in developing competence to teach by all the teacher groups surveyed. Least valuable to all of them were college of education faculty.

Figure 6.12   "Very Valuable" in Developing Competence to Teach

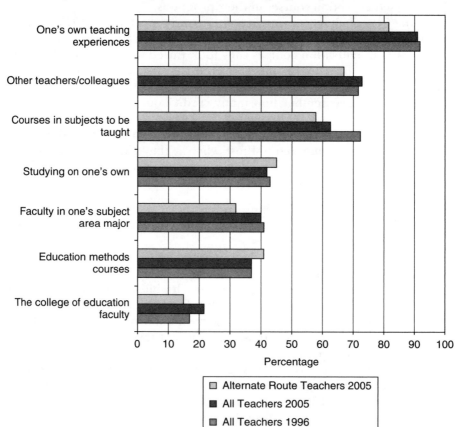

Source: Alternate route data from National Center for Education Information, *Profile of Alternate Route Teachers*, (2005). Data for all teachers from National Center for Education Information, *Profile of Teachers in the U.S.* (1996, 2005).

Table 6.4   Comparison of Alternate Route Teacher Satisfaction with That of Public School Teachers over Time (Percentage Very or Somewhat Satisfied)

Aspects of Teaching	Alternate Route Teachers	All Public School Teachers			
	2005	2005	1996	1990	1986
	%	%	%	%	%
Relationship with students	95	93	93	N/A	N/A
Relationship with other teachers	94	94	93	93	95
Overall job satisfaction	89	83	83	83	84
Relationship with parents of students	82	84	84	83	85
Relationship with principal	78	85	79	80	83
Present curriculum	72	78	75	74	78
General working conditions	72	81	71	69	73
Present textbooks	58	63	58	67	71
Salary	44	46	50	45	45

Source: Alternate route teacher data from National Center for Education Information, *Profile of Alternate Route Teachers*, (2005). Data for all teachers from National Center for Education Information, *Profile of Teachers in the U.S.*, (1986, 1990, 1996, and 2005).

Satisfaction by Alternate Route Participants.   At the end of the day, all teachers—regardless of how they enter teaching—seem quite satisfied with several aspects of their jobs, as shown in Table 6.4. Alternate route teachers report a slightly higher level of satisfaction with their jobs overall than do public school teachers in general. However, teachers in general seem more satisfied with their principals than do alternate route teachers.

Alternate Route Teachers Strongly Recommend Alternate Route Programs.   As shown in Figure 6.13, a high percentage (82%) of those entering teaching through alternate routes say they would recommend an alternate route to teacher certification to others interested in becoming teachers. An additional 15% say maybe. Only 3% would not recommend an alternate route to others.

Data leave little doubt that participants in alternate route programs are satisfied with the alternate route they selected, as well as the majority of the components of the programs. Few could seriously suggest that the teaching force could not be more ethnically diverse, that more men are not needed in school classrooms, and that mobility of teachers is not important. All of these areas and more are enhanced by alternate route programs and the participants in the programs as discussed in this chapter.

Figure 6.13   *Would You Recommend an Alternate Route to Teacher Certification to Others Interested in Becoming a Teacher?*

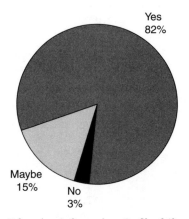

Source: National Center for Education Information, *Profile of Alternate Route Teachers*, (2005).

Furthermore, data also show that the profiles of the participants in alternative routes to teacher certification provide us with important information. Not only have we learned about who chooses to become a teacher by taking an alternate route to the traditional campus-based college teacher education program route but also about why they made the choices they did and what they value in the experience.

The alternative routes to teacher certification movement is not just producing more teachers, but more teachers who come from many walks of life, who make a deliberate choice to teach and, as defined by the U.S. Department of Education in its HQT Guidance, are "highly qualified" (USDoE, 2005a, p. 5). In part, this is happening because alternate routes exist to meet the demands for the teachers needed.

7

What Does the Research Say About Alternate Routes?

*M*ost of the research conducted concerning alternative routes to teacher certification shows that alternate routes do what they are designed to do: bring people into teaching who would not otherwise have become teachers. The research also indicates that the route one goes through does not seem to matter all that much as far as effective teaching goes. Experience and effective mentoring seem to be the most important variables for becoming a competent teacher.

Different Studies Yield Similar Results

Since the 1980s when the alternate route movement began, several studies have focused on comparing teachers who came through alternative routes to teachers who prepared to teach through traditional routes. Examples of this research show:

- In an early study of the first district-based alternate route in the country—Houston Independent School District—student achievement scores were similar for students taught by alternate route teachers and other first-year teachers (Goebel, 1986).
- Hawk and Schmidt (1989) compared teachers who had been certified through traditional programs with those certified through alternate routes in terms of classroom performance. They found that alternatively certified teachers were superior on some outcomes; traditionally certified teachers were better on other outcomes.
- A Texas study found that grade-point averages of alternate route candidates were higher than those of traditionally prepared candidates or teachers on emergency certificates. However, the researchers found

no differences among the three groups in classroom performance. (Brown et al., 1989)
- A study of the New Jersey alternate route found that "although the New Jersey alternate-route teachers had lower grade point averages than their college-based counterparts, they came from more selective colleges and also scored higher on NTE tests." (Natriello & Zumwalt, 1992, p. 76)
- A series of studies designed to determine the effectiveness of alternative programs compared traditionally certified teachers with alternatively certified teachers in Georgia on both teacher performance and student achievement measures. The researchers concluded that, basically, the two groups of teachers were equally effective. (Miller, McKenna, & McKenna, 1998)
- A study of North Carolina teachers showed that students of teachers with probationary or emergency certificates performed no worse than those students taught by fully certified teachers, leading the authors to state, "Although certification is pervasive, there is little rigorous evidence that it is systematically related to student achievement." (Goldhaber & Brewer, 2000, p. 141)

A growing body of research shows that after a couple of years' experience, differences in teacher performance measures and/or student achievement disappear regardless of what kind of route a teacher comes into teaching through, as indicated by the studies just referenced.

An ongoing scientifically designed study shows similar results. *How Changes in Entry Requirements Alter the Teacher Workforce and Affect Student Achievement* reported findings from this study being conducted by Donald Boyd and colleagues. The researchers focused their study on pathways into teaching in New York City and the "effects of such programs on the teacher workforce and on student achievement" (p. 1). The study's basic findings indicate that, after 2 years, the small differences among the groups at the beginning of teaching disappear (Boyd et al., 2005).

Compilations of Research on Alternate Routes

As studies have became more frequent, one of the challenges has been to compile and analyze the results of the published studies, similar to that developed by Adelman, Michie, and Bogart in 1986. Of Adelman's 58 citations, only two dealt with some aspect of alternative certification in the titles, as discussed previously in Chapter 2.

The compilation report, *Teacher Preparation Research: Current Knowledge, Gaps, and Recommendations*, which "found

14 papers[1] reporting on 11 studies that shed light on issues of alternative certification" (p. 26). The U.S. Department of Education, Office of Educational Research and Improvement supported the report, which Wilson, Floden, and Mundy (2001) prepared for the Center for the Study of Teaching and Policy in collaboration with Michigan State University. The resulting report was intended to "provide directions" to improve teacher preparation nationally (p. i).

Three of the studies reviewed in *Teacher Preparation Research* compared graduates of alternate routes to traditionally prepared first-year teachers in New Hampshire, Georgia, and California. Stoddart conducted an analysis of one program: the Los Angeles Unified School District Intern Program. Three other studies compared and evaluated alternative routes in Dallas and Houston (Houston, Marshall, & McDavid, 1993; Hutton & Lutz, 1989; Williamson, 1990). An interpretive study involved three case studies of new teachers who had no prior preparation (Grossman, 1989). One study compared alternate route teachers' knowledge and beliefs with a national sample of graduates from teacher preparation programs (McDiarmid & Wilson, 1991). Goldhaber and Brewer used the National Educational Longitudinal Survey 1988 to look at student effects with teachers who held standard certification or other forms of certification.

---

[1]Goldhaber and Brewer, 2000; Grossman, 1989; Guyton, Fox, and Sisk, 1991; W. Robert Houston, Faith Marshall, and Teddy McDavid, "Problems of Traditionally Prepared and Alternatively Certified First-Year Teachers," (*Education and Urban Society*, 1993, Volume 26, pp. 78–89); Jerry B. Hutton, Frank W. Lutz, and James L. Williamson, "Characteristics, Attitudes, and Performance of Alternative Certification Interns" (*Educational Research Quarterly*, 1990, Volume 14, pp. 38–48); James Jelmberg, "College-Based Teacher Education Versus State-Sponsored Alternative Programs" (*Journal of Teacher Education*, Volume 47, 1996, pp. 60–66); Frank W. Lutz and Jerry B. Hutton, "Alternative Teacher Certification: Its Policy Implications for Classroom and Personnel Practice" (*Educational Evaluation and Policy Analysis*, 1989, Volume 11, pp. 237–254); McDiarmid and Wilson, 1991; John W. Miller, Michael C. McKenna, and Beverly A. McKenna, "A Comparison of Alternatively and Traditionally Prepared Teachers" (*Journal of Teacher Education*, 1998, Volume 49, pp. 165–176); Ruth A. Sandlin, Beverly L. Young, and Belinda D. Karge, "Regularly and Alternatively Credentialed Beginning Teachers: Comparison and Contrast of Their Development (*Action in Teacher Education*, 1992–1993, Volume 14, pp. 16–23); Jianping Shen, "Has Alternative Certification Policy Materialized Its Promise? A Comparison Between Traditionally and Alternatively Certified Teachers in Public Schools" (*Educational Evaluation and Policy Analysis*, 1997, Volume 19, pp. 276–283); Jianping Shen, "Alternative Certification, Minority Teachers, And Urban Education" (*Education and Urban Society*, 1998a, Volume 31, pp. 30–41); Jianping Shen, "The Impact of Alternative Certification on the Elementary and Secondary Public Teaching Force" (*Journal of Research and Development in Education*, 1998b, Volume 31(1), pp. 9–16); Trish Stoddart, "Los Angeles Unified School District Intern Program: Recruiting and Preparing Teachers for an Urban Context" (*Peabody Journal of Education*, 1990, Volume 67, pp. 84–122).

Wilson et al. (2001) reported that the research they reviewed supported "several important results" (p. 27), although not all of the 14 studies supported each of these findings:

- Alternative routes are attracting a more diverse pool of perspective teachers in terms of age and ethnicity.
- Alternative routes have a mixed record for attracting the "best and brightest."
- There are higher percentages of alternatively certified teachers teaching in urban settings or teaching minority children.
- Evaluations of the performance of alternate route and traditionally prepared teachers produce mixed results.
- Teachers who have come through high-quality alternative routes and teachers traditionally certified show some similarities.

Wilson et al. (2001) singled out the Stoddart study as providing several of the features that may be important to a high-quality alternative certification program, including the following:

- High entrance standards
- Extensive mentoring and supervision
- Extensive pedagogical training in instruction, management, curriculum, and working with diverse students
- Frequent and substantial evaluation
- Practice in lesson planning and teaching prior to taking on full responsibility as a teacher
- High exit standards

As discussed throughout this book, these are the characteristics of most alternative routes to teacher certification currently being implemented and classified as A through E by NCEI. By their very design, compilations include the same previously reviewed research along with considering contemporary research and occasionally new issues.

By the time Birkeland and Peske (2004) compiled their *Literature Review of Research on Alternative Certification* for the National Education Association (NEA), they cited 90 studies, almost all of which were published from the late 1990s through 2004. The works cited dealt with research on attrition of teachers, findings from a single alternative route program to national studies, comparisons of teacher preparation programs to the problems of underqualified teachers in urban schools, and a host of other issues.

Similarly, Brannan and Reichardt (n.d.) of Mid-continent Research for Education and Learning (McRel) developed a review of selected literature about alternative teacher education for the Western Interstate Commission for Higher Education after the new millennium began. A particularly useful addition to this review is a glossary of terms related to alternative teacher education.

Reaching back to the Adelman study in 1986 and from there to research produced in 2004, Zeichner and Conklin (2005) reviewed 38 studies that met their criteria for inclusion in a chapter in *Studying Teacher Education: The Report of the AERA Panel on Research and Teacher Education*. In addition to providing narratives about the studies, the authors also summarized the focus of the study, the context of the research, the research design, and also the findings.

The Education Commission of the States (ECS) (2003) produced a report on teaching quality. The report included a review of the research, which found that alternative route programs graduate high percentages of effective new teachers with average or higher-than-average rates of teacher retention. ECS reviewed 15 studies that met its criteria for inclusion in the research report as having effective alternative route preparation programs.

As alternative preparation programs expand, some are developed for specific purposes, such as specialized subject-matter courses in science and mathematics or other subjects. For example, Rosenberg and Sindelar (2005) reviewed research on alternative routes to certification in special education. In "The Proliferation of Alternative Routes to Certification in Special Education: A Critical Review of the Literature," the authors reiterated the persistent shortages of qualified special educators. Through a careful search of existing studies, Rosenberg and Sindelar included studies that reported "empirical data on program outcomes" (p. 120). The authors reviewed six program evaluation studies and four comparative studies, concluding that additional reliable and valid research is needed "to strengthen our understanding of effective preparation" of special educators (p. 125).

AERA Conclusions Were Similar to Others' Findings

In 2005, the American Educational Research Association (AERA) released *Studying Teacher Education: The Report of the AERA Panel on Research and Teacher Education*. Work on this project began in 1999. Cochran-Smith and Zeichner (2005) were appointed as the panel's cochairs and coeditors.

The compendium's findings regarding alternative routes included the following points:

- The studies provided some evidence that alternatively certified teachers may be "more willing than traditionally certified teachers to teach in low-SES urban schools, but these data may reflect more where teachers can get jobs than actual teacher preferences." (p. 663)
- "There were no differences between alternatively and traditionally certified teachers in terms of teacher efficacy or in teaching competence as measured by classroom observations." (p. 663)
- The research showed "very little difference between alternatively and traditionally certified teachers". (p. 670)

- "The studies of the alternative certification programs in Houston, Dallas, and Milwaukee school districts indicate inconclusive results" (p. 674). Anticipated retention was higher in Milwaukee in alternative programs. In Houston there were no significant differences between traditionally certified and alternatively certified teachers' "perception of the problems they faced in the classroom," at the end of the first academic year. (p. 674)
- The studies that "compared the impact of multiple teacher education programs on various dimensions of teacher quality have suggested that alternatively certified teachers may in some circumstances have higher expectations for the learning of students of color living in poverty than teachers who have been traditionally certified." (p. 689)

SRI Finds Variations Within Training Pathways and Importance of School Context

According to Daniel C. Fallon (2006), chair of the Education Division of the Carnegie Corporation of New York, "provided a grant to SRI International, carried out by Daniel C. Humphrey and Marjorie Wechsler (2005). SRI's conclusion was that there was greater variation in training and outcome within pathways than between them" (p. 1).

The two authors of *Insights into Alternative Certification: Initial Findings from a National Study* found "teacher development in alternative certification to be a function of the interaction between the program as implemented, the school context in which participants are placed, and the participants' backgrounds and previous teaching experiences" (p. 4).

From their study of six alternate route programs and their participants, Humphrey and Wechsler also found that "Alternative certification program participants are a diverse group of individuals who defy generalization," and there is "a great deal of variation between and within alternative certification programs" (p. 4).

Two Significant Studies of Alternate Routes Are Ongoing

How Changes in Entry Requirements Alter the Teacher Workforce and Affect Student Achievement is an ongoing study in New York. As noted earlier in this chapter, Boyd and colleagues (2005) are conducting an elaborate study on pathways into teaching in New York City and the "effects of such programs on the teacher workforce and on student achievement" (p. 1). The authors used data on students and teachers in grades 3 through 8 in

New York City. Boyd et al. (2005) identified three distinct pathways and divided teachers in the study into six groups "as defined by their pathway into their *first* job in New York City" (p. 6).

The distinct pathways were identified as:

1. Traditional university-based programs, both at the graduate and undergraduate level
2. Transcript review, a process of individual evaluation
3. Alternative routes (prior to being issued a Transitional B certificate (good for 3 years) to teach, a candidate must complete preservice training and pass two examinations)

The authors reviewed student demographic and test score data for approximately 65,000 to 80,000 students in grades 3 through 8 in New York City schools. They constructed sets of data to identify value added score increases by the pathways to teaching of the classroom teachers in the study. They write, "For this purpose a student was considered to have value added information in cases where we had a score in a given subject (English Language Arts or math) for the current year and a score for the same subject in the immediately preceding year for the immediately preceding grade" (p. 9). The authors did not include scores of those who had either skipped a grade or were repeating a grade.

To enrich their data on teachers, the authors used a crosswalk file provided by the New York City Department of Education. Variables included teacher experience, teacher demographics, ranking of college selectivity of undergraduates, teacher test score performance, initial pathway into teaching, and whether or not the teacher had completed a college-recommended teacher preparation program (p. 10).

Using various controls and models, including teacher and student characteristics and school work environments, the authors reached several conclusions. About teacher experience models, the authors write,

> Teaching Fellows start out performing worse, but gain more over the first year than do other teachers. By their second year, their students are doing as well as students of College Recommended teachers. Teach For America members also appear to make substantial gains during their first year but this coefficient is never statistically different from a College Recommended teacher. For Elementary English Language Arts (ELA) results, Teaching Fellows and TFA members have more trouble improving their students' reading achievement initially than do temporary license teachers or College Recommended teachers, and, unlike the situation for math, these teachers do not make differentially large gains in student achievement by their second year. By their third year differences are not statistically significant (p. 18).

Among other findings, the authors also conclude that alternative routes into teaching that reduce both the tuition and the time costs of preservice preparation attracted many new teachers, most of whom replaced temporarily licensed teachers. Alternative route teachers have stronger measurable qualifications than teachers entering through any other pathway. In recent years, Teaching Fellows have been working in difficult-to-staff subject areas, "such as middle and high school mathematics and science and special education—subjects that attract very few traditionally prepared applicants" (p. 7).

Differences in attrition rates across pathways are statistically significant and meaningful, according to the authors. "For example, 9.6 percent of Teaching Fellows are predicted to leave teaching after the first year, substantially less than the attrition of College Recommended teachers" (p. 22). After 2 years, however, the attrition rates are comparable, and in years 3 and 4, Teaching Fellows exceed the attrition rates of College Recommended teachers (p. 23).

Based on the state and federal requirements to have a qualified teacher in every classroom, the authors write, "we believe that different pathways bring different strengths to teaching. These differences in pathways provide a means to discuss potential improvements in how all pathways prepare teachers" (p. 25).

The Evaluation of Teacher Preparation Models is also an ongoing study. Sponsored by the U.S. Department of Education's Institute of Education Sciences, the purpose of the evaluation is "to rigorously test whether the extent or content of teacher preparation programs are related to teacher practice or to the effectiveness of teachers, as measured by student academic achievement" (p. 12).

In September 2005 at a forum hosted by Learning Point Associates, Paul Decker, vice president of Human Services Research at Mathematica Policy Research, described the 4-year study under way (2003–2007) for $6.7 million. Decker reported that there is little research as to the effectiveness of different teacher training strategies within the variations of teacher preparation through alternative certification and traditional certification programs. Because some alternative certification programs require substantially less education coursework than traditional certification programs, the variations can be examined to learn whether the form of teacher training is associated with differences in teacher performance.

The study will evaluate the existing variation in teacher preparation to address questions in three specific areas: (1) professional preparation and support, (2) classroom practices, and (3) student performance.

Data collection will occur during the 2004–2005 and 2005–2006 school years. Data will include pre-and poststandardized tests for students, student demographic characteristics, ATC or SAT scores of each sampled teacher, context interviews with program and school staff, and four classroom observations of each sampled teacher. Measuring classroom practice will provide data on an important link between teacher preparation and student achievement. A key hypothesis of the study is that differences in teacher preparation will lead to differences in classroom practice that ultimately will affect student achievement.

Sharing Research

National Association for Alternative Certification

In addition to the resources just described, a variety of professional journals and publications include research findings. An early venue that permitted providers of alternate route programs to share developments—and setbacks—through their research was the annual meeting of the National Association for Alternative Certification (NAAC) begun in 1990. First organized in Houston, Texas, as a state association, the group eventually expanded to become the National Association for Alternative Certification. The annual NAAC national conference provided speakers and panelists a forum for their research and also networking opportunities.

National Center for Alternative Certification

Established by the National Center for Education Information (NCEI) in September 2003, the National Center for Alternative Certification (NCAC) is a comprehensive clearinghouse for information about alternative routes to certification in the United States. With a 3-year grant of $2.25 million from the U.S. Department of Education, NCEI developed a major interactive Website (www.teach-now.org), continually updated, and designed to provide information pertaining to alternative routes to certification in every state and the District of Columbia. NCAC disseminates the latest research information, data, and reports about alternate routes to teaching through its Website and annual conference. In 2007, NCAC and NAAC will host a joint conference in lieu of the separate conferences held previously.

Despite the dearth of scientifically based research, researchers have produced hundreds of studies—and even more commentaries—about alternative teacher certification. The debates are no longer about whether teacher preparation through alternate routes is a viable option. Credible research now assists policymakers and practitioners alike to support effective programs and improve those not up to par in producing effective teachers. Even so, concerns still exist, some of which are discussed in the next and final chapter about the trends and emerging issues of alternate routes.

8

✿

Where Will Alternate Routes
Go from Here?

*I*t was not until the state of New Jersey grabbed national headlines in 1983 with its out-of-the-box solution that significant changes began to emerge to help solve teacher quality and quantity issues. New Jersey, followed by other states, has created alternative routes to teacher certification specifically to attract and transition liberal arts graduates into elementary and secondary teaching without going through a college-based teacher education program.

After the alternative teacher certification movement was born, the nation took notice. As documented in this book, the growth and development of alternative routes to teaching are huge. The impact of this movement on the teaching profession and all of education is profound.

Why Alternative Routes Work

We take the position that alternative routes are just that, alternative routes. There is no one route, no one way, no best way. High-quality alternative routes to teacher certification opened the floodgates, as it were, to a grand experiment in the who, what, when, where, and how of becoming a teacher and getting credentialed to teach, as has been described throughout this book.

Alternate routes work because they

- Offer efficient and cost-effective means of producing the teachers the nation needs.
- Recruit widely from qualified individuals who already have a baccalaureate degree.
- Select participants carefully to benefit students and to improve teacher retention rates.

- Are flexible programs that exist to train individuals to meet the subject-matter demands in the schools where vacancies exist.
- Provide extensive, ongoing support through experienced and effective mentors.
- Are continuously improved to meet the needs of participants, schools, and state and federal requirements.

Alternative routes, so far, have escaped the lure of institutional rigidity; however, there are those calling for precise definitions and standardization. Some take the position that any avenue that even remotely looks like a traditional teacher education program cannot possibly be called an alternate route. Still others attempt to grade alternate routes, using an A-B-C-D-F approach, based on self-established criteria for judging.

There are also those rigidly in the camp of professional only or craft only, when discussing teacher preparation. Arthur Levine (2006) wrote,

> Teacher education is the Dodge City of the education world. Like the fabled Wild West Town, it is unruly and chaotic. Anything goes and the chaos is increasing as traditional programs vie with nontraditional programs, undergraduate programs compete with graduate programs, increased regulation is juxtaposed against deregulation, universities struggle with new teacher education providers, and teachers are alternatively educated for a profession and a craft. (p. 3)

Despite the objections of some, mentors and school principals who work with alternate route candidates report over and over that these individuals are better prepared for teaching than teachers coming out of traditional college-based programs, as documented throughout this book. From their beginning, alternate routes to teaching have been creative solutions to issues relating to teacher quality and quantity. They continue to be, and given the new evidence as states comply with requirements in *No Child Left Behind*, alternate routes are likely to expand and grow.

Going Forward

Data from state reports and research show that all 50 states and the District of Columbia now have some type of alternative route to teacher certification available. Of the 125 routes identified by the states, about a third have emerged since 2000. With the development of more alternate routes, the states have approved nearly 500 program providers to implement these alternative routes in their states. Providers include school districts, regional service centers, individual schools, private companies, consortia, and community colleges as well as traditional 4-year colleges and universities. Alternative routes are now producing about a third of all new teachers being hired.

By 2006, institutions of higher education (IHEs) provided administrative services for nearly half (46%) of all alternate route programs in their states.

And nearly all of the 50,000 certified through alternate routes in 2004–2005 were teachers of record in schools across the country while getting certified, indicating that teachers were receiving on-the-job training and receiving the salary and benefits of a beginning teacher, even through some IHE programs.

Providers of alternate route programs recognize the potential pool of teachers among graduates who have a latent interest in teaching, a characteristic long recognized by the states as they developed alternatives to the traditional college-based teacher preparation program. Partnerships and collaborations between IHEs and school districts are likely to continue to play a role in alternate route preparation programs.

New to the marketplace of alternate route program providers are community colleges that may very well play an increasing role in attracting mature adults from all walks of life into teaching through alternate routes.

Credible research conducted at the national, regional, and state levels increasingly shows "very little difference between alternatively and traditionally certified teachers" (AERA). What has become increasingly significant is identification of those characteristics of teachers—however prepared—that increase student achievement. Recently, researchers have focused on the value added to student achievement by effective teaching from highly qualified teachers. By eventually isolating the qualities that contribute most to increasing student achievement, such research becomes increasingly valuable to all teacher preparation programs.

No Child Left Behind assumes that a teacher's knowledge of the subject matter to be taught is a significant part of teacher quality. Having all teachers highly qualified is a national challenge and the responsibility of states and school districts everywhere.

Looking Ahead at Alternate Routes

Federal Requirements for Highly Qualified Teachers Could Play a Significant Role

The use of alternate routes in the states could increase dramatically if the revised plans each state submitted to the U.S. Department of Education in July 2006 were any indication. When no state had met the highly qualified teacher (HQT) requirements for newly hired teachers by the end of the 2005–2006 school year, the U.S. Department of Education extended the deadline. States were given another year, but the department required that all states submit a "Revised Plan" by July 7, 2006, stating how they would meet the HQT requirements by the end of the 2006–2007 school year.

An analysis of the plans submitted by the 50 states and District of Columbia illustrates just how important alternate routes have become in American education, as shown in Table 8.1; their significance can hardly be overestimated.

Table 8.1 States That Specifically State in Their Revised Plans to the U.S. Department of Education That Alternate Routes Will Be Used in Meeting the Highly Qualified Teacher (HQT) Requirements, July 7, 2006

State	Revise or Expand Existing Alternate Routes	Encourage use of Existing Alternate Routes	Create NEW Alternate Routes Specifically to Meet HQT Requirements	Does not Specifically Mention Alternate Routes, but Describes Similar Programs	Lists Other "Alternative" Programs, such as Teach For America and Troops to Teachers
Alabama		ARs for career changers in hard-to-staff schools; financial assistance for undergraduates to go into Master's levels ARs		"Additional Teaching Field Approach" to get out-of-field teachers HQ through passage of Praxis II	Troops to Teachers
Alaska			Standards-based AR in Anchorage for special education; working on ARs for other high need areas		
Arizona			Transition to Teaching used to create an AR		Troops to Teachers; other programs similar to ARs
Arkansas			Non-Traditional Licensure Program		Troops to Teachers; Teach For America
California	X	X	X		NBPTS; Troops; several others

(Continued)

155

Table 8.1 Continued

State	Revise or Expand Existing Alternate Routes	Encourage use of Existing Alternate Routes	Create NEW Alternate Routes Specifically to Meet HQT Requirements	Does not Specifically Mention Alternate Routes, but Describes Similar Programs	Lists Other "Alternative" Programs, such as Teach For America and Troops to Teachers
Colorado				X	
Connecticut	Durational Shortage Area Permits, includes Praxis II	X	New AR for special education		Teach For America
Delaware		X			
District of Columbia				X	TFA and TNTP
Florida				X	
Georgia	Expand and support high quality ARs; development of online courses for GA TAPP AR	GA TAPP, PSC test-based option			
Hawaii		Increase use of ARs			
Idaho		PACE AR	Three new state ARs go in effect July 1, 2006		ABCTE
Illinois					Grow Your Own (GYO) – enable paraprofessionals and parents to become

156

State		
Indiana		certified teachers; Troops to Teachers; Teach For America; STEP and others
Iowa		Troops to Teachers
Kansas	X	Online course
Kentucky	Transition to Teaching Alternate Route	
	X	
	Increased focus on ARs to increase number of highly qualified educators and to attract non-traditional candidates	
Louisiana	3 new ARs with focus on content mastery	Foreign teachers program
Maine	MARC created specifically as solution to meeting HQT requirements	
Maryland	Expand ARs as solution to HQT; cites 7 ARs, including Troops to Teachers and Teach For America	Efforts to help people pass Praxis
Massachusetts	MINT	New teachers and those seeking additional licensure must take MTEL (subject test); foreign teachers program
Michigan	State funding to Wayne State for development of ARs in critical shortage areas	Troops to Teachers
Minnesota	License Through Portfolio AR	non-HQT can take appropriate Praxis II subject test; since 1999 all new teachers have to pass Praxis II tests

157

(Continued)

Table 8.1 Continued

State	Revise or Expand Existing Alternate Routes	Encourage use of Existing Alternate Routes	Create NEW Alternate Routes Specifically to Meet HQT Requirements	Does not Specifically Mention Alternate Routes, but Describes Similar Programs	Lists Other "Alternative" Programs, such as Teach For America and Troops to Teachers
Mississippi					
Missouri	Expand the MS Alternative Path			X	Transition to Teaching; test requirement since 1985
Montana					
Nebraska		Transitional Teacher Certification which has significantly lessened the number of teachers who are teaching out of field		X	
Nevada		Conditional Endorsement	Grow Your Own AR in Clark County		several; Praxis test help;
New Hampshire		Modified AR IV to require a B.A	X		test option for out-of-state; ABCTE in selected subjects
New Jersey		X			
New Mexico				X	Transition to Teaching
New York	Continue to encourage ARs and recommend changes where needed	Encourage development of ARs to attract 2nd career people; strengthen programs such as NYCTF			Incentives for retired teachers to come back into teaching

(Continued)

State				
North Carolina	Expansion of Lateral Entry AR to create an accelerated route for individuals who have 5 or more years of relevant experience	Lateral Entry AR		
North Dakota			X	test option for out-of-field teachers; retired teacher provision
Ohio		Emphasis on AR as solutions to meeting HQT requirements	X	
Oklahoma				
Oregon				Troops to Teachers
Pennsylvania	Continue to encourage districts to use ARs to attract mid-career professional and top of the class graduates to teaching	Alternative Accelerated Certification Program for Teachers Teaching on Emergency Permits proposed – will be issued an Intern Certificate		Transition to Teaching; Troops toTeachers; Teach For America; The New Teacher Project; ABCTE; ACT Program
Rhode Island				
South Carolina	PACE	Restricted AR allows teachers already fully certified to add other areas to their credentials	X	Troops to Teachers; re-hire retired teachers program

Table 8.1 Continued

State	Revise or Expand Existing Alternate Routes	Encourage use of Existing Alternate Routes	Create NEW Alternate Routes Specifically to Meet HQT Requirements	Does not Specifically Mention Alternate Routes, but Describes Similar Programs	Lists Other "Alternative" Programs, such as Teach For America and Troops to Teachers
South Dakota		Renewed interest in AR programs			Troops to Teachers; Teach For America
Tennessee				X	
Texas	X	X	X		Troops; TFA; TNTP; others
Utah				X	
Vermont				X	
Virginia		Encourage use of Career Switcher AR			
Washington	Expand ARs; increase number of AR completers		Grow Your Own program		
West Virginia	Elaborate ARs created for non-HQT teachers; school districts require that all non-HQT enroll in an AR				
Wisconsin				X	
Wyoming				X	

Source: NCEI. Basic data from Highly Qualified Teachers Revised State Plans Submitted to the U.S. Department of Education, July 7, 2006. Retrieved July 24–25, 2006, from http://www.ed.gov/programs/teacherqual/hqtplans/index.html.

As shown in Table 8.1, 36 states mention alternative routes to teacher certification as a way the state plans to ensure that every teacher in its state is or becomes highly qualified. Two states that have not utilized alternative routes to certification in the past—Maine and West Virginia—have explicitly created alternative routes to meet HQT requirements. An additional 11 states have added alternative routes to those already established to meet the HQT requirement. For example,

- Alabama has created the "Additional Teaching Field Approach" alternate route to get out-of-field teachers highly qualified through Praxis II, a test to measure general and subject-specific knowledge and teaching skills.
- Connecticut has created a new alternate route for certifying special education teachers.
- Idaho created three new alternate routes scheduled to go into effect on July 1, 2006.
- Louisiana designed three new alternate routes focused on content mastery as a prerequisite for program entry. Louisiana characterized the new programs as a "streamlined approach to certification." The programs are designed to attract noneducation college graduates with in-depth content knowledge who are able to achieve full certification in a short period of time.
- Nevada's plan includes a provision for a Grow Your Own alternate route in Clark County, where the demand for HQTs is greatest in the state. The new program will target "candidates who have licenses in social studies and who would be willing to prepare for positions in elementary, English, math, and bilingual education," among other high-need subject areas. In the 2005–2006 school year, more than 76% of the 3,047 newly hired teachers were hired from outside Nevada.

Ten states—Connecticut, Georgia, Kentucky, Maryland, Mississippi, New Hampshire, New Jersey, North Carolina, Texas, and Washington—indicate that each intends to expand existing alternate routes to enroll more teachers to meet the HQT requirement. Twenty-one states plan to actively encourage the use of their states' alternative routes as a solution to get all of their teachers highly qualified by the 2006–2007 deadline.

Several states are allowing their teachers who do not meet the HQT requirement of mastery of subjects taught to take the appropriate Praxis II test(s) or other content test. Three states—Idaho, New Hampshire, and Pennsylvania—mention in their revised plans that they allow use of the American Board for Certification of Teacher Excellence (ABCTE) Passport to Teaching test to meet the HQT standard. This test-only option could become another very popular alternate route if states accept this credential or one of their own as Texas and California have done.

The states give a variety of reasons why they are turning to alternative routes to teacher certification to ensure that all of their teachers meet the HQT requirements. Nebraska noted that its "Transitional Teacher Certification alternate route has significantly lessened the number of teachers who are teaching out of field." New York, citing the success of the New York City Teaching Fellows Program (NYCTF) and other routes throughout the state, plans to encourage more development of alternate routes to attract second career people and to strengthen programs such as the NYCTF. South Carolina noted that restricted use of its alternate route allows teachers already fully certified to add other subject areas to their credentials.

Data show that 17% of participants in alternate route programs surveyed by NCEI in 2005 had prior teaching experience. Of those, 3% specifically reported that they had participated in an alternate route to meet the HQT requirement. The number of teachers in alternate route programs who will use alternate routes to meet the HQT requirements is expected to rise significantly.

Role of Community Colleges

As mentioned before, the likely increased role of community colleges could have a significant impact on alternate routes. In 2001, Florida lawmakers involved community colleges in teacher preparation programs to help meet the demand for teachers fueled in part by the increase in student enrollment throughout the state. "There's a group of people that would like to be teachers, and they aren't the people who would go to traditional programs," said Don Sullivan, the former state senator who introduced the law and now serves as St. Petersburg College's vice president for innovation and program development. "If you really want to solve the need for teachers in Florida, you're going to have to bring education out into the communities" (Blair, 2003, p. 22). Most baccalaureate programs offered at community colleges in Florida are in teacher education.

Like proponents in Florida, advocates elsewhere say community colleges can generate huge new pools of educators, many of whom are members of minority groups. *Education Week* cited a report by Recruiting New Teachers, [1] a nonprofit group in Belmont, Massachusetts, that estimated that such colleges could provide more than 25% of the estimated 2.4 million new teachers needed over the next decade.

Maryland was the first state to offer an associate of arts degree in teaching, an AAT degree that allows prospective teachers to take community college class credits that correspond to the first 2 years of a teacher education program (ECS, 2004, pp. 4–5). According to ECS, Maryland's 22 4-year colleges offering teacher education programs produced only 2,550 teacher

---

[1]"Report Touts Community Colleges as Source of Teachers," October 30, 2002.

candidates; 1,585, or 62%, became teachers, but the state needed about 8,900 new teachers for the 2002–2003 school year (ECS, 2004, p. 5). To encourage a smooth transition for the AAT degree holders, the Maryland Higher Education Commission developed a plan to ensure "a fully articulated transfer to any of the 22 four-year public and independent institutions offering education programs in the state" (ECS, 2004, p. 5).

California has developed similar partnerships. In Texas, community colleges offer an alternative certification program for people who have already earned bachelor's degrees. As indicated by the state plans to meet the HQT requirements by the end of 2006–2007, several states intend to include their community colleges and alternate routes as a winning combination.

Reciprocity Issues

Despite reciprocity agreements, most states do not accept a teacher's certificate or license in the receiving state without requiring additional courses or other steps before the state issues a license. Because alternate route programs vary considerably in entrance requirements, program completion requirements, and exit requirements, states have become wary of teachers prepared through routes about which they are not familiar.

The National Association of State Directors of Teacher Education and Certification (NASDTEC) is taking an active role in getting states to recognize each other's teaching certificates. All state directors of teacher education and certification are members of NASDTEC, which is in the process of sorting out the reciprocity issues as a partner in a federal grant under way in Maryland. Through the Enhancing Troops to Teachers Mobility grant, funded by the U.S. Department of Education, Maryland intends to identify positive strategies to overcome existing barriers to reciprocity, especially as those issues relate to retiring military personnel.

Clarification of reciprocity issues as they relate to alternative routes to teacher certification will go a long way toward helping all highly qualified teachers, such as those who are relocating and want to continue to teach.

Like the Passport to Teaching certification developed by ABCTE, which must be accepted state to state, other test and portfolio options for certification also provide challenges to reciprocity issues. For example, teacher certification by the National Board for Professional Teaching Standards (NBPTS), which was intended to be a universally accepted accreditation of excellence, had been accepted by 10 states of the 38 that responded to a NASDTEC survey in 2000 (Islas, 2001, pp.11–12).

States could benefit from recognizing teachers who have successfully met the rigorous requirements of these new options as being fully certified and licensed. A variety of data show that individuals who desire to teach frequently have degrees beyond the bachelor's degree and several years of experience in other careers. These attributes would be beneficial in meeting the test-out options of the recent alternate routes to teacher certification.

Potential Teachers

The market for teaching is huge. Numerous individuals from all over the world contact organizations and Websites looking for information on how to become a teacher. Visitors to www.teach-now.org, the Website of the National Center for Alternative Certification, have been invited to complete a voluntary online informal survey. Interestingly, their responses mirrored the profile of teachers in alternate routes presented in charts, graphs and tables in Chapter 5. Of the first 2,000 respondents,

- Ninety percent were very interested in becoming a teacher.
- Eighty-two percent expect to be teaching K–12 five years from now.
- Fifty-two percent earned their bachelor's degree from 2 to 15 years ago; thirty percent longer than 15 years ago.

Many of the responses were nearly identical to those received by the National Center for Education Information (NCEI) in previous surveys of alternate route teachers and analyses cited throughout the preceding chapters. For example,

- Fifty percent of online respondents are between the ages of 30 and 50.
- Sixty-seven percent are women; thirty-three percent are men.
- Thirty-three percent identified themselves as ethnic minorities.

Not surprisingly, respondents are engaged in dozens of occupations and professions, many in the sciences, health care, marketing, and communications. And

- Sixty-four percent wish to use an alternative route to teacher certification, especially because being employed and paid as a teacher is an option and the 1- to 2-year time frame is important as well.

Alternate routes exist for these individuals "who want to teach" and "to make a difference in someone's life." State authorities have long recognized this pool of potential teachers; alternate routes can make it happen for them.

Conclusions

It cannot be said often enough: Teachers matter. Effective teachers matter more to students. The national challenge is for the states to achieve highly qualified teachers in every classroom. Expanded collaboration among the stakeholders that allow the states continued creativity to meet the need for highly qualified teachers in every classroom can help achieve the HQT goal and make dreams come true for those wanting to teach. In addition to meeting the social needs expressed by those interested in teaching (and those who also teach), alternative routes are efficient and effective ways of meeting the demands of the education marketplace. Disclosure and accountability are essential to alternate routes, and variety and choices help account for their continued growth, success, and innovation.

The once sharp lines between alternative and traditional routes to teaching continue to disappear as more educators concur that new pathways to teaching are needed. We agree with Dan Fallon (2006) of the Carnegie Corporation who said,

> The fields of teaching and learning, and pathways into teaching have undergone rapid changes in just the past decade and promise to continue to be volatile for the foreseeable future. The changes are being driven by underlying forces in the economy, of course, but also by new and better research with sophisticated new technologies and a generation of new researchers approaching old problems without old preconceptions.
>
> At the same time, accumulating evidence is pointing toward the value and importance of clinical training for prospective teachers, implying that whatever methods are used, supervised apprentice teaching is essential to salutary outcomes. Finally, the regulatory environment is bound to become more (not less) restrictive and complicated because of inevitable and inexorable accountability pressures being driven by the new economy.
>
> In short, it seems to make little sense to speak of "alternative" certification. The right frame of reference is pathways into teaching. There can be different kinds of pathways, suited to the differing life circumstances of prospective teachers. All pathways should be held to a high professional standard, governed at least by a threshold condition that the teachers emerging from each pathway can be shown to be associated with substantial appropriate learning by pupils in their classrooms. (personal communication, 2006)

It is our hope that this grand experiment of creating new pathways to teaching that meet the needs of students and the needs of emerging populations of individuals from all stages of life will continue to play a vital role in American education.

Appendix

Supplemental Information
New Jersey

The information provided about each of the state alternate route(s) is from *Alternative Teacher Certification: A State-by-State Analysis* 2006, published by the National Center for Education Information.

Description of New Jersey's Alternate Route to Teacher Certification

Title: Provisional Teacher Program—Alternate Route	
History:	Adopted by the State Board of Education in Sept. 1984. New licensing regulations approved by the State Board of Education in January 2004 have expanded areas in which an alternate route is available to include special education, bi-lingual/bi-cultural, and English as a Second Language.
Motivation:	The Provisional Teacher Program—Alternate Route is intended to enhance both the quantity and quality of teaching candidates.
Grade Levels and/or Subject Areas Covered:	All.
Who Operates:	LEAs, supported by district consortia and colleges of education that are providing formal instruction, with coordination and authority provided by the State Department of Education.
Requirements to Enter:	To be eligible for employment in the Provisional Teacher Program, applicants must present completion of the following: 1. Bachelor's degree from an accredited institution.

2. For secondary candidates: a major in the subject teaching field (e.g., English, mathematics). For elementary and pre-school through grade three candidates: a major in the liberal arts or sciences. Details about additional eligibility requirements for vocational, ESL, bi-lingual/bi-cultural, and special education certificates of eligibility are available on the New Jersey Department of Education website at: nj.gov/njded/educators/license.

3. Test requirement—Applicants for certification in a subject teaching field must pass the appropriate Praxis II Subject Assessment/NTE Programs Specialty Area tests. Applicants for certification in elementary education must pass the Elementary Ed: Content Knowledge Test. Candidates in the following subject teaching fields available through the Alternate Route are exempt at this time from the test requirement: foreign languages other than French, German, and Spanish; health education; psychology; English as a second language, bi-lingual/bi-cultural, pre-school through grade three, special education, military science, and vocational education.

4. Cumulative grade point average (GPA) requirement of 2.5 or higher on a 4.0 scale. Candidates graduating on or after Sept. 1, 2004, will be required to hold a GPA of 2.75 or higher.

Upon completion of the above requirements, a candidate receives a Certificate of Eligibility, which provides the opportunity to seek employment through the Provisional Teacher Program.

When offered employment, applicants are advised of documents required before a provisional license can be issued. A provisional license is required to legalize employment during the 34-week Provisional Teacher Program.

Program Description: Provisional teachers attend a program of formal instruction that takes place concurrently with employment during the first year. This instruction supplements a program of on-the-job mentoring, support, and evaluation, aimed at developing and documenting the teacher's instructional competency. In 2003–2004, the Department began piloting a 20 hour pre-service experience for holders of Certificates of Eligibility. Also, several alternate route MAT programs were approved to provide formal instruction programs that lead to a graduate degree.

Mentoring is arranged by the local district and provided by an experienced mentor teacher. Other professionals, as determined by the district, may also participate.

After successful completion of the program, provisional teachers are eligible to be recommended for standard licensure in the teaching area(s) listed in the Certificate of Eligibility. Certificates are issued in subject teaching fields (N–12), elementary education (K–5), Preschool through Grade Three (P–3) and special education.

Number of Credit Hours to Complete:

Formal instruction requirements vary depending on the certificate sought:

For candidates with an elementary or N–12 CA: 200 hours at a Regional Training Center or alternate route MAT program;

For candidates with a preschool through grade three CE: 13–17 credits at colleges or universities offering the specialized alternate route P–3 pedagogy;

For candidates with a special education, EDL, or bi-lingual/bi-cultural CE: 200 hours of formal instruction at a regional training center of alternate route MAT program *and* completion of an approved college or university program.

Who Evaluates:

Evaluations are conducted by the school principal or administrative designee. The teacher is evaluated on at least three occasions during the initial year. The first two evaluations are used to aid the teacher's development.

The third and final evaluation is conducted after the provisional teacher has completd 34 weeks of full-time teaching. This last evaluation will contain the principal's recommendation regarding licensure. Recommendations for standard licensure are made by the principal (on forms provided by the New Jersey Department of Education), and are submitted for final action to the State Board of Examiners.

Length of Time:

34 weeks of full-time employment. The length of the Program is extended for part-time novice teachers and for those whose formal instruction includes regional training and an approved college or university program.

California

Description of California's District Alternate Route

Title: District Intern Certificate

History:	Legislation passed in 1983 originally authorized the program for secondary school teachers only; the first interns were in place in 1984. The law was changed in 1987 to expand the program to include bilingual and elementary teachers and again in 2002 to include special education teachers.
Motivation:	Teacher supply and demand, but available in all grades and subject areas.
Grade Levels and/or Subject Areas Covered:	Originally for secondary only; later expanded to include bilingual and elementary and then special education teachers.
Who Operates:	LEA.
Requirements to Enter:	A bachelor's degree.
	A passing score on the CBEST basic skills test.
	Subject matter competence demonstrated by completing an approved program of study (secondary only), or passing appropriate subject area portions of the state-approved subject matter exam.
	Bilingual classroom teachers must pass oral language component of state exam.
	Knowledge of U.S. Constitution.
	Character fitness (fingerprints).
Program Description:	The school district must employ persons to provide guidance and assistance. Each intern must be supported by at least one mentor or other designated support person.
	The school district must develop a professional development plan for intern—including training (120 clock hours or equivalent pre-service component including child development and methods of teaching), and ongoing teacher preparation, support and assistance, and annual performance evaluation.
	The intern will be eligible for a preliminary credential with the school district's recommendation, based on a performance assessment of successful teaching.

Number of Credit Hours to Complete:	120 clock hours of professional development training and a professional development program (approximately 360 additional clock hours). Special education has an additional 120 clock hour requirement.
Who Evaluates:	LEA evaluates candidates; state evaluates LEA programs.
Length of Time:	The Intern Credential is valid for two years of teaching and may be extended.
Other:	14 percent of the state's Intern teachers are teaching as district interns. Of these, about 60 percent are in Los Angeles Unified School District.
	Four county offices of education have developed consortium programs for multiple districts in their respective service areas. There are four urban single district programs. $25 million has been allocated in the state's budget act for alternative certification (both University and District Intern and Pre-intern programs). One charter school has begun a district intern program. More than 8,400 Interns (both University and District) are teaching in 760 districts through 74 funded programs.
	The retention rate of participating District Interns is approximately 91 percent after 3 years in the classroom and 83 percent after 5 years.
	Interns receive full beginning teacher's salary and benefits.
	The total number of District Interns in classrooms in 2004–05 was 1,202.
	2003 Legislative deleted the 2 year service requirement and instead requires all programs to meet same standards and performance requirements as all teacher preparation programs in California.

California's Early Completion Intern Option

Title: Early Completion Intern Option	
History:	Legislation passed and signed by the governor in 2001.
Motivation:	Provides fast-track options for:
	a) Private school teachers who want to become public school teachers;
	b) Well-qualified individuals who can demonstrate that pedagogical preparation or supervised field experience is unnecessary for them through passage of the Foundations in Teaching exam.

Grade Levels and/or
Subject Areas Covered: Multiple and Single Subject (K–12) teachers. Exams currently available in Multiple Subject, and in four single subject areas: Math, Science, English and Social Studies.

Who Operates: District and University Internship Programs

Requirements to Enter: **Early Completion Internship**

1. Baccalaureate degree

2. Subject matter content proficiency (exam or coursework)

3. Character fitness (fingerprints).

4. Written assessment of teaching knowledge and subject matter pedagogy in the areas of:

    a. Special needs students and learning differences

    b. English learners

    c. Classroom management

    d. Subject matter pedagogy

    e. Assessment of pupil progress

Program Description: Individuals who complete the prerequisites—including the Foundations in Teaching exam—may enter the Early Completion Option if they are offered a teaching position and are accepted into the internship program.

Once admitted into the Early Completion Internship Option, a candidate completes the California Teaching Performance Assessment or other authorized assessment of classroom performance. The candidate's performance is demonstrated with his or her students in the classroom. If the candidate passes all sections or elements of the performance assessment and other district requirements, he or she is eligible for a preliminary credential. Candidates must also demonstrate knowledge of reading and computer technology.

If the candidate does not pass all sections of the performance assessment, he or she continues in the intern program and receives an individualized program of study, based on the assessment results and any district or intern program requirements. Early Completion Option interns, as well as all interns, must pass the Teaching Performance Assessment at the end of the internship to be recommended for a preliminary credential. Candidates for a multiple-subject

	credential must also pass the Reading Instruction Competency Assessment for credential recommendation.
Number of Credit Hours to Complete:	No set number of credit hours. Completion is determined by the candidate successfully passing the teaching foundations exam and performance assessment.
Who Evaluates:	California Commission on Teacher Credentialing and participating internship program and districts.
Length of Time:	No time limit, but could be completed in as little as one semester.
Other:	In addition to the Early Completion Option, the statute also allows private school teachers to achieve California credentials, and has an option for challenging the induction portion of teacher preparation.
	The private school option allows teachers with six years of full-time teaching experience in a regionally accredited private school and two years of rigorous performance evaluations to seek a preliminary credential. The evaluations must address the effectiveness areas in the California Standards for Teacher Profession.
	Private school teachers with three years of successful teaching and two years of successful evaluations under the same conditions as above may waive teacher preparation fieldwork.
	Private school applicants also must demonstrate knowledge of basic skills, reading, the U.S. Constitution, and subject matter, and have fingerprint clearance.
	The statute also requires development of a fast track method to complete the formative assessment of teaching performance portion of the professional clear teaching credential.
	In August 2004 a special administration of the qualifying pedagogy (Teaching Foundations Exam) was offered in order to set a passing score for the exams. Sufficient persons took the exam to set passing scores in the multiple subject, English and Mathematics.
	In 2004–2005 there were approximately 100 persons who completed certification through the Early Completion Option.

California's University Intern Credential

Title: University Intern Credential	
History:	Authorized by legislation in 1967, but issuance of the first such credentials dates back to the early 1950s.
Motivation:	In practice, its use is targeted at subject area shortages, although this is not required by law.
Grade Levels and/or Subject Areas Covered:	The state's fastest-growing route, especially in special education, but available for all types of credentials.
Who Operates:	IHE and LEA (must be collaborative programs).
Requirements to Enter:	A bachelor's degree.
	A passing score on the CBEST basic skills test.
	Subject matter competence demonstrated by completing an approved program of study (secondary only), or passing appropriate subject area portions of the state-approved subject matter exam.
	Knowledge of U.S. Constitution.
	The teacher's union for the local school district hiring the intern must sign-off on the application.
	Character fitness (fingerprints).
Program Description:	Professional education courses in methods must be completed or formed during the time the individual is employed as an intern teacher.
	The individual must demonstrate subject matter competencies through an approved program or equivalent exam. For elementary teachers, this means competencies in the seven subjects taught in elementary schools by exam; for secondary teachers, this means competency in the subject area to be taught, at the level equivalent to a major. The college may require completion of courses it deems necessary to achieve these competencies.
	Admission requirements must take into account the accelerated responsibilities of interns. Applicants should have a high degree of maturity and previous experience with children.
	Pre-service training must be provided to ensure a minimum level of knowledge in the 13 Teaching Performance Expectations. Programs emphasize blending theory and practice and frequently include professors and experienced teachers on the program's faculty.
	The local school district must designate someone to provide support and evaluation for the intern. The university must also provide supervisors.

Number of Credit Hours to Complete:	Coursework as required by the IHE to meet competencies (approximately 36 semester units usually spread over 2 years). Programs may be 1 to 2 years long with instruction dispersed throughout the prior summer through the end of the program.
Who Evaluates:	Individuals are evaluated by the IHE.
	IHE programs are subject to periodic review by the state.
Length of Time:	The intern may teach two years with the credential, which may be extended.
Other:	University Internships are offered in elementary, secondary, administrative, pupil personnel, special education and bilingual credential programs. There are more than 180 intern programs available at California colleges and universities.
	This program is operated on 21 campuses of the California State University System, 7 campuses of the University of California System, and 31 campuses of independent colleges and universities. A program operated by the California State University system (CalState Teach) provides a program throughout the state using distance learning, internet technology, and on-site support and assessment.
	Interns receive full beginning teacher's salary and benefits.
	$25 million has been allocated in the state's budget for alternative certification. Approximately 7,139 interns were in university internships in 2004–2005.

Texas

Description of Texas Alternate Route

Title: Alternative Teacher Certification	
History:	First implemented in 1985 with single program in the Houston school district. The state currently has 67 programs, including 21 programs in community colleges and 8 programs conducted by private entities.
Motivation:	Originally to alleviate shortages, but state legislation passed in 1989 eliminated that requirement.

Grade Levels and/or
Subject Areas Covered: The alternative preparation programs are approved to offer teacher preparation in all grade levels and content areas offered by the State of Texas. In addition, alternative preparation programs are currently available for administrators to include principal, superintendent, educational diagnostician, master teacher, school counselor, and school librarian.

Who Operates: Typically, each program involves a combination of three entities—LEA, IHE, and regional education service center. Development of each certification area includes practitioners from the field. Recently, community colleges and private for-profit companies have created programs in partnership with LEAs.

Requirements to Enter: The individual must:

Hold a bachelor's degree.

Demonstrate acceptable college level skills in reading, oral and written communication, critical thinking, and mathematics as determined by the program.

Complete screening activities to determine appropriateness for the certification sought.

If seeking a Bilingual Education/English as a second language (ESL) certificate, must give evidence of oral and written language proficiency before being assigned to a bilingual education classroom.

Program Description: All programs may be jointly created through a collaborative process involving the local school districts, colleges, and education service center. Participants from these entities develop the curricula, based on the State's standards that are necessary to prepare teachers for the target certificate. The curricula cover the same State standards that would be included in traditional undergraduate programs, as well as any unique local needs. Instruction is delivered by the partners most suited to the task, either in coursework or in contact hours, and includes a one-year paid internship or a one semester non-paid clinical teaching experience.

During the one-year internship, the intern holds a one-year probationary certificate and receives close support and assistance on a regular basis from a certified mentor teacher who is teaching either in the same or in a related subject area.

Since the intern is on a probationary certificate, he or she receives the full financial benefits of a classroom teacher (i.e., salary and benefits).

	Provisions are made for the intern to observe the teaching of the mentor teacher, and for the mentor teacher to observe the intern.
	The intern must complete any training in teaching methods and classroom management prescribed by the state, either during the pre-assignment training or during the internship year.
	The internship leads to a standard teaching certificate, identical to that received by a graduate of a traditional undergraduate teacher preparation program.
Number of Credit Hours to Complete:	Individual certificate programs require varying-amounts of additional coursework to meet unique competency requirements of each certificate.
Who Evaluates:	The school principal, ACP program supervisor, or ACP director.
Length of Time:	Probationary certificate is valid for one year. It may be renewed annually for up to two additional years.

REFERENCES

Adelman, N. E. (1986). *An exploratory study of teacher alternative certification and retraining programs.* Washington, DC: Policy Studies Associates, Inc.

American Association of Colleges for Teacher Education [AACTE]. (1985). Alternative certification: A position statement of AACTE. *Journal of Teacher Education.* 36(3), 24.

American Board for Certification of Teacher Excellence [ABCTE]. (2006). Retrieved June 21, 2006, from http://www.abcte.org/

American Federation of Teachers [AFT]. (2004). Resolution. Retrieved June 19, 2006, from http://www.aft.org/about/resolutions/2004/alt_certif.htm

Angus, D. L. (2001). *Professionalism and the public good: A brief history of teacher certification.* Washington, DC: Thomas B. Fordham Foundation.

Ashton, P. (Ed.). (1991). Alternative approaches to teacher education. *Journal of Teacher Education* 42(2), 82.

Ballou, D., & Podgursky, M. (2000). Gaining control of professional licensing and advancement. In T. Loveless (Ed.), *Conflicting Missions? Teachers Unions and Educational Reform.* Washington, DC: Brookings Institution Press.

Barclay, R. (2006). *Alternate route program evaluation: Phase I report.* Trenton, NJ: The College of New Jersey.

Bersin, A. D. (2006, February). *Meeting the challenges of reform.* Paper presented at the meeting of the Center for Alternative Certification, San Diego, CA.

Birkeland, S. E., & Peske, H. G. (2004). Literature review of research on alternative certification. Unpublished paper retrieved from www.teach-now.org

Blair, J. (2003). Community colleges offering 4-year teaching programs. *Education Week* 22(33), 1, 22–23.

Bliss, T. (1990). Alternate certification in Connecticut: Implications for the improvement of teaching. *Peabody Journal of Education* 67(3), 35–54.

Boyd, D., Grossman, P., Lankford, H., Loeb, S., & Wyckoff, J. (2005). *How changes in entry requirements alter the teacher workforce and affect student achievement.* Unpublished manuscript.

Boyer, E. L. (1984). *Report of panel on the preparation of beginning teachers.* Paper submitted to the New Jersey State Department of Education, Trenton.

Brannan, L., & Reichardt, R. (n.d.). *Alternative teacher education: A review of selected literature.* Aurora, CO: Mid-continent Research for Education and Learning.

Brown, D., Edington, E., Spencer, D. & Tinafero, J. (1989). A comparison of alternative certification, traditionally trained, and emergency permit teachers. *Teacher Education and Practice, 5*(2), 21–23.

Bush, G. (1992). *The American Presidency Project: George Bush statement on signing the Higher Education Amendments of 1992.* Accessed August 9, 2006, from http://www.presidency.ucsb.edu/ws/print.php?pid=21259

California Commission on Teacher Credentialing [CCTC]. 2006. *Teacher Supply in California: A Report to the Legislature.* Eighth Annual Report 2004–2005. Report 06–01.

Carnegie Forum on Education and the Economy Task Force on Teaching as a Profession. (1986). *A Nation Prepared: Teachers for the 21st Century.* Washington, DC: Author.

Chin, E., & Young, J. W. (2006, April). *Beyond demographics: Who enters and completes alternative teacher credential programs in California?* Paper presented at the annual meeting of the American Educational Research Association (AERA), San Francisco, CA.

Clifford, G. J., & Guthrie, J. W. (1988). *Ed School: A brief or professional education.* Chicago: University of Chicago Press.

Cochran-Smith, M., & Zeichner, K. (Eds.). (2005). *Studying teacher education: The report of the AERA panel on research and teacher education.* Mahwah, NJ: Erlbaum.

Cohen-Vogel, L. (2005). Federal role in teacher quality: "Redefinition" or policy alignment? *Educational Policy 19*(1), 18–43.

Coleman, J. S., & Campbell, E. Q. (1966). *Equality of educational opportunity.* Washington, DC: U.S. Government Printing Office.

Cooperman, S., & Klagholz, L. (1985). New Jersey's Alternate Route to Certification. *Phi Delta Kappan, 66,* 691–695.

Cornett, L. M. (1990a). Alternative certification: State policies in the SREB states. *Peabody Journal of Education, 67*(3), 55–83.

Cornett, L. M. (1990b). Teaching and knowledge: Policy issues posed by alternative certification for teachers. *Peabody Journal of Education, 67*(3), 123–154.

Dill, V. S. (1994, Winter). Teacher education in Texas: A new paradigm. *The Educational Forum, 58,* 147–153.

Dill, V. S., & Stafford, D. (1996). *Alternative teacher certification: history, handbook and how-to.* Houston, TX: The Haberman Foundation.

Dougherty, P. H. (1988, February 25). Advertising; public service promotes teaching. *New York Times.*

Earley, P. M. (1998). *Teacher quality enhancement grants for states and partnerships: HEA Title II.* American Association of Colleges for Teacher Education (AACTE) Issue Paper. Washington, DC.

Earley, P. M., & Schneider, E. (1996). Federal policy and teacher education. In J. Sikula, T. Buttery, & E. Guyton (Eds.), *Handbook of research on teacher education.* (2nd ed.). New York: Simon & Schuster.

Education Commission of the States [ECS]. (2004). Seamless pipeline from two-year to four-year institutions of teacher training. Policy Brief by Gina Shkodriani. Denver, CO.

ERIC Digest. (1986). *Alternative certification for teachers.* SP027271. American Association of Colleges for Teacher Education, pp. 1–3.

Fallon, D. C. (2006, October 5). Chair, Education Division, Carnegie Corporation of New York. Commentary in a letter to Emily Feistritzer.

Feistritzer, C. E. (1984). *The making of a teacher: A report on teacher education and certification.* Washington, DC: National Center for Education Information.

Feistritzer, C. E. (1990). *Alternative teacher certification: A state-by-state analysis* 1990. Washington, DC: National Center for Education Information.

Feistritzer, C. E. (1991). Alternative Teacher Certification: *Alternative Teacher Certification: A State-by-State Analysis 1991.* Washington, DC: National Center for Education Information.

Feistritzer, C. E. (1996). *Profile of teachers in the U.S.* Washington, DC: National Center for Education Information.

Feistritzer, C. E. (1999). *The making of a teacher: A report on teacher preparation in the U.S.* Washington, DC: National Center for Education Information.

Feistritzer, C. E. (2005a). *Profile of alternate route teachers.* Washington, DC: National Center for Education Information.

Feistritzer, C. E. (2005b). *Profile of teachers in the U.S. 2005.* Washington, DC: National Center for Education Information.

Feistritzer, C. E. (2005c). *Profile of Troops to Teachers.* Washington, DC: National Center for Education Information.

Feistritzer, C. E. (2006). *Alternative teacher certification: A state-by-state analysis 2006.* Washington, DC: National Center for Education Information.

Feistritzer, E., & Chester, D. (1991). *Alternative teacher certification: A state-by-state analysis.* Washington, DC: National Center for Education Information.

Fenstermacher, G. D. (1990). The place of alternative certification in the education of teachers. *Peabody Journal of Education, 67*(3), 155–185.

Finn, C. E., Jr. (1991). *We must take charge: Our schools and our future.* New York: The Free Press.

Flood, P., and Milton, S. (2005). *Alternative certification in Florida: Third annual progress report.* Tallahassee, FL: The Florida State University, College of Education, Department of Educational Leadership and Policy Studies.

Florida Statutes. (2006). *Florida Statutes, Chapter 1012.56.* Retrieved August 15, 2006, from http://www.flsenate.gov/Statutes/index.cfm?App_mode=Display_Statute& URL=Ch1012/ch1012.htm

Fullan, M., Galluzzo, G., Morris, P., & Watson, N. (1998). *The rise & stall of teacher education reform.* Washington, DC: American Association of Colleges for Teacher Education.

Goebel, S. (1986). *Alternative certification program final report* [Minutes]. Austin: Texas Education Agency State Board of Education.

Goldhaber, D. D., & Brewer, D. J. (2000). Does teacher certification matter? High school teacher certification status and student achievement. *Educational Evaluation and Policy Analysis, 22*(2), 129–145.

Goodlad, J. I. (1990). *Teachers for our nation's schools.* San Francisco: Jossey-Bass.

Haberman, M. (1986). Alternative teacher certification programs. *Action in Teacher Education, 8*(2), iii, 13–18.

Haberman, M. (1988). Proposals for recruiting minority teachers: Promising practices and attractive detours. *Journal of Teacher Education, 39* (4): 38–44.

Hawk, P. P., & Schmidt, M. W. (1989). Teacher preparation: A comparison of traditional and alternative programs. *Journal of Teacher Education, 36*(3), 13–15.

Herbert, K. S. (2004 April). *Production and retention of beginning teachers from 1999 to 2003: A comparison of preparation routes.* (Rev. ed.). Preliminary report Issued to the State Board for Educator Certification.

Holmes Group. (1986). *Tomorrow's teachers: A report of the Holmes Group.* East Lansing, MI: Author.

Holmes Group. (1990). *Tomorrow's schools: Principles for the design of professional development schools: Executive summary.* East Lansing, MI: Author.

Holmes Group. (1995). *Tomorrow's schools of education: A report of the Holmes Group.* East Lansing, MI: Author.

Humphrey, D. C., & Wechsler, M. E. (2005). Insights into alternative certification: Initial findings from a national study. *Teachers College Record, 107* (11).

Hunt, J. B., Jr. (2003). Unrecognized progress. *Education Next 3*(2), 24–27.

Islas, R. M. (2001). *License reciprocity: Eliminating the barriers to teaching in the mid-Atlantic region.* Paper prepared for the Mid-Atlantic Regional Teachers Project, Baltimore, Maryland.

Keegan, L. G. (2003). Help wanted. *Education Next, 3* (2), 29–31.

Kennedy, M. M. (1999). *Learning to teach writing: Does teacher education make a difference?* New York: Teachers College Press.

Kentucky Education Professional Standards Board. (2006). Database retrieved July 17, 2006 from http://kyepsb.net/certification/

Kerchner, C. T. (1984). Shortages and gluts of public school teachers: There must be a policy problem here somewhere. *Public Administration Review, 44*(4), 292–298.

Klagholz, L. (2000). *Growing better teachers in the Garden State.* Washington, D.C: The Thomas B. Fordham Foundation.

Klagholz, L. (2006). Correspondence with Emily Feistritzer, October 16.

Leenhouts, T. (2006, February). *Transition to Teaching program.* PowerPoint presentation at the 2006 National Center for Alternative Certification, San Diego, CA. Retrieved August 1, 2006, from www.teach-now.org

Levine, A. (2006). *Educating School Teachers.* Retrieved October 27, 2006, from http://www.edschools.org/pdf/Educating_Teachers_Exec_Summ.pdf

Lutz, F. W., & Hutton, J. B. (1989). Alternative teacher certification: Its policy implications for classroom and personnel practice. *Educational Evaluation and Policy Analysis, 11*(3), 237–254.

Mabry, M. (1990, July 16). The new teacher corps. *Newsweek.*

Mathematica Policy Research, Inc. (2005, September). *The evaluation of teacher preparation models.* Paper presented by Paul T. Decker at the "Alternative Teacher Certification: A Forum for Highlighting Rigorous Research," Washington, DC.

McDiarmid, G. W. & Wilson, S. (1991). An exploration of the subject matter knowledge of alternate route teachers: Can we assume they know their subject? *Journal of Teacher Education, 42*(2), 93–103.

McKibbin, M. D. (2001, Winter). One size does not fit all: Reflections on alternative routes to teacher preparation in California. *Teacher Education Quarterly,* pp. 133–149.

McKibbin, M. D., & Ray, L. (1994). A guide for alternative certification program improvement. *The Educational Forum, 58*(2), 201–208.

Miller, J. W., McKenna, M. C., & McKenna, B. A. (1998). A comparison of alternatively and traditionally prepared teachers. *Journal of Teacher Education, 49*(3), 165–176.

National Commission on Excellence in Education [NCEE]. (1983). *A Nation at Risk: The Imperative for Educational Reform.* Washington, DC: U.S. Government Printing

Office. Retrieved May 10, 2006, from http://www.ed.gov/pubs/NatAtRisk/recomm.html

National Council for Accreditation of Teacher Education. (2005). *High quality alternate routes that ease financial barriers to teaching.* Retrieved May 31, 2006 from http://www.ncate.org/public/alternateRoute.asp?ch=41

National Education Association. (1987). *Status of the American public school teacher: 1985–86.* Washington, DC: U.S. Department of Education, NCES 93–424, by Mary R. Rollefson.

National Education Association [NEA]. (2003). *Meeting the challenges of recruitment & retention.* Washington, DC: Author.

National Education Association. (2005). *NEA Handbook.* Resolution D. Washington, DC: Author. Retrieved June 19, 2006, from http://www.nea.org/handbook/images/resolutions.pdf

Natriello, G., & Zumwalt, K. (1992). Challenges to an alternative route for teacher education. In A. Lieberman (Ed.), *The 91st yearbook of the Society for the Study of Education* (Part 1, pp. 59–78). Chicago: University of Chicago Press.

Natriello, G., & Zumwalt, K. (1993). New teachers for urban schools? The contribution of the provisional teacher program in New Jersey. *Education and Urban Society, 26*(1), 49–62.

Oliver, B., & McKibbin, M. (1985). Teacher trainees: Alternative credentialing in California. *Journal of Teacher Education, 36*(3), 20–23.

Ravitch, D. (1983). *The troubled crusade: American education, 1945–1980.* New York: Basic Books.

Ravitch, D. (1985). *The Schools we deserve: Reflections on the educational crises of our times.* New York: Basic Books.

Ravitch, D. (2003). The Test of Time. *Education Next, 3*(2), 33–38.

Reagan, R. (1983). Remarks at the National Forum on Excellence in Education, Indianapolis, IN. Retrieved October 24, 2006, from http://www.presidency.ucsb.edu/ws/print.php?pid=40844

Rosenberg, M. S., & Sindelar, P. T. (2005). The proliferation of alternative routes to certification in special education: A critical review of the literature. *Journal of Special Education. 39(2),* 117.

Roth, R. A. (1986). Alternate and alternative certification: Purposes, assumptions, implications. *Action in Teacher Education, 8*(2), 1–6.

Rotherham, A. (1999). *Toward performance-based federal education funding: Reauthorization of the Elementary and Secondary Education Act.* Washington, DC: Progressive Policy Institute.

Sawyer, J. (1993, September 13). Troops for teachers gains support; Senate's action called 'a dream come true.' *St. Louis Post-Dispatch.*

Scannell, D. P. (1994). *Report to the American Council on Education Presidents' Task Force on Teacher Education: Models of Teacher Education.* Washington, DC: American Council on Education.

Serial No. 106–37. (1999). *Developing and maintaining a high-quality teacher force hearing.* Washington, DC: House of Representatives, Committee on Education and the Workforce.

Smith, G. P. (1988). Tomorrow's white teachers: A response to the Holmes Group. *Journal of Negro Education 57*(2), 178–194.

Spring, J. (2002). *American education* (10th ed.). New York: McGraw-Hill.

Steffensen, J. (1994). Certification: The past as prelude. *The Educational Forum, 58* (2), 126–131.

Stoddart, T. (1990). Los Angeles Unified School District Intern Program: Recruiting and preparing teachers for an urban context. *Peabody Journal of Education, 67* (3): 84–122.

Stoddart, T., & Floden, R. E. (1995). *Traditional and alternative routes to teacher certification: Issues, assumptions, and misconceptions.* Issue Paper 95–2. East Lansing, MI: National Center for Research on Teacher Learning.

Stutz, T. (2005, December 11). Teacher shortage quick fix fails. *Dallas Morning News.*

Teach For America [TFA]. (2005). *Equity within reach: Insights from the front lines of America's achievement gap.* New York: Author.

Texas State Board for Educator Certification. (2006). Database retrieved August 12, 2006, from www.sbec.state.tx.us/downloads/rpt_tchr_prod-countslvl2006812131431

Texas Statutes. (2006). Retrieved August 5, 2006, from http://tlo2.tlc.state.tx.us/statutes/statutes.html

Transition to Teaching: Retrieved September 6, 2006, from http://www.ed.gov/programs/ transitionteach/index.html

Urban, W, & Wagoner, J. (2000). *American education: A history.* New York: McGraw-Hill.

U.S. Department of Education [USDoE]. (1993). NCES 93–424. *Teacher supply in the United States; Sources of newly hired teachers in public and private schools,* by Mary R. Rollefson.

U.S. Department of Education. (1995). NCES 1995–348. *Teacher supply in the United States: sources of newly hired teachers in public and private schools, 1987–88 to 1993–94,* by Stephen P. Broughman and Mary R. Rollefson.

U.S. Department of Education. (2000). NCES 2000–152. *Progress through the teacher pipeline:* 1992–93 *college graduates and elementary/secondary school teaching as of 1997.*

U.S. Department of Education. (2000/01). NCES. *Baccalaureate and beyond longitudinal study.* Retrieved August 12, 2006, from http://nces.ed.gov/surveys/b&b/

U.S. Department of Education. (2002a). NCES 2000–130. *Digest of education Statistics* 2001, by Thomas D. Snyder. Production Manager, Charlene M. Hoffman. Washington, DC: Author.

U.S. Department of Education. (2002b). Office of Postsecondary Education, Office of Policy Planning and Innovation. *Meeting the highly qualified teachers challenge: The secretary's annual report on teacher quality.* Washington, DC: Author.

U.S. Department of Education. (2003). Office of Postsecondary Education, Office of Policy Planning and Innovation. *Meeting the highly qualified teachers challenge: The secretary's second annual report on teacher quality.* Washington, DC: Author.

U.S. Department of Education. (2004a). NCES. *Digest of education statistics* 2004. Retrieved from http://nces.ed.gov/programs/digest/d04/

U.S. Department of Education. (2004b). Office of Innovation and Improvement. *Innovations in education: Alternative routes to teacher certification.* Washington, DC: Author.

U.S. Department of Education. (2004c). Office of Postsecondary Education, Office of Policy Planning and Innovation. *Meeting the highly qualified teachers challenge: The secretary's third annual report on teacher quality.* Washington, DC: Author.

U.S. Department of Education. (2005a). ESEA. Office of Elementary and Secondary Education. *Highly qualified teachers: Improving teacher quality state grants.* ESEA Title II, Part A. Non-regulatory Guidance. Revised August 3, 2005.

U.S. Department of Education. (2005b). NCES. *Digest of education statistics.* Retrieved August 8, 2006, from http://nces.ed.gov/programs/digest/

U.S. Department of Education. (2005c). Office of Postsecondary Education, Office of Policy Planning and Innovation. *Meeting the highly qualified teachers challenge: The secretary's fourth annual report on teacher quality.* Washington, DC: Author.

U.S. Department of Education. (2006a). Fiscal year 2007 president's budget [1–21 pp.]. Retrieved March 21, 2006, from http://www.ed.gov/about/overview/budget/budget07/summary/appendix4.pdf

U.S. Department of Education. (2006b). NCES 2005–074. *Projections of education statistics to 2015,* by William J. Hussar. Washington, DC: Author.

U.S. Department of Education. (2006c). NCES. *Characteristics of schools, districts, teachers, principals, and school libraries in the United States.* 2003–04 schools and staffing survey. Revised April 2006. Retrieved August 11, 2006 from http://www.federalgrantswire.com/teacher_quality_enhancement_grants.html.

U.S. Department of Education. (2006d). Office of Postsecondary Education, Office of Policy Planning and Innovation. *Meeting the highly qualified teachers challenge: The secretary's annual report on teacher quality.* Washington, DC: Author.

U.S. Department of Education. (2006e). Office of the Secretary, Office of Public Affairs. *A guide to education and No Child Left Behind.* Washington, DC: Author. Retrieved May 27, 2006, from http://www.ed.gov/nclb/overview/intro/guide/guide.pdf

U.S. Department of Education. (2006f). Teacher quality enhancement grants. Retrieved June 5, 2006, from http://www.federalgrantswire.com/teacher_quality_enhancement_grants.html.

U. S. Government Accountability Office [GAO]. (2006). *Troops-to-Teachers: Program brings more men and minorities to the teaching workforce, but education could improve management to enhance results.* GAO-06–265. Washington, DC: Author.

Van Tassel, P. (1983, December 4). State to Name Panel to Explore Teacher Quality. *The New York Times.*

Van Tassel, P. (1984, March 18). Boyer Report Gets Raves and Caveats. *The New York Times.*

Wilson, S. M., Floden, R. E., & Ferrini-Mundy, J. (2001). *Teacher preparation research: Current knowledge, gaps, and recommendations.* Seattle, WA: Center for the Study of Teaching and Policy in collaboration with Michigan State University.

Wong, M. J., & Osguthorpe, R. T. (1993). The continuing domination of the four-year teacher education program: A national survey. *Journal of Teacher Education, 44* (1), 64–70.

Zeichner, K., & Conklin, H. (2005). Teacher education programs. In M. Cochran-Smith and K. Zeichner (Eds.), *Studying Teacher Education: The Report of the AERA Panel on Research and Teacher Education.* Mahwah, NJ: Erlbaum.

Zumwalt, K. (1991). Alternate routes to teaching: Three alternative approaches. *Journal of Teacher Education, 42,* 83–92.

Zumwalt, K. (1996). Simple Answers: Alternative Teacher Certification. *Educational Researcher, 25*(8), 40–42.

INDEX

A

AACTE (American Association of Colleges for Teacher Education). *See* American Association of Colleges for Teacher Education

ABCTE (American Board for Certification of Teacher Excellence). *See* American Board for Certification of Teacher Excellence

Accountability, 70–71, 72–73, 76. *See also* U.S. Government Accountability Office (GAO)

Acronyms, for alternative routes, 3

Adelman, Nancy E., 40, 48, 50–53, 144

Adjunct Instruction Certification Option (Kentucky), 106

Age, affect of, 131

Alabama, 95, 161

Alaska, 89

Alternate Certification in Connecticut (Bliss), 53–54

Alternate route programs
administration of, 114
analysis of, 63–64
characteristics of, 7–8, 87
choosing, 131–133
completion time for, 122–123, 131, 133, 168
defined, 2–6, 50
in each state, 4, 88–91
effectiveness of, 75, 152–153
emergence of, 36–37
entry requirements for, 115
high quality, 84–85, 146
innovation in, 80–81
market demand for, 8–9, 11, 54–55

NCEI analysis of, 61–62
opposition to, 37–38, 55–56, 153
providers for, 109–110, 114–115
questions about, 2
reasons for, 6
regional differences in, 92–94
role of, 26
skills of participants in, 52–53
subject areas of, 116
support for, 56–57, 81–82
teacher's view of, 141–142
variations in, 58–61

Alternate Teacher Certification (NCEI), 89–91

Alternative teacher certification
defined, 59–60
as deregulation of teacher preparation, 57–58
early programs in, 50–52
individuals attracted by, 60
use of term, 7

Alternative Teacher Certification: A State-by State Analysis (Feistritzer), 61–62, 63–64

Alternative Teacher Certification (NCEI), 4

"Alternative Teacher Certification Programs" (Haberman), 44

Alternative *vs.* alternate, defined, 3

American Association of Colleges for Teacher Education (AACTE), 29, 38, 39, 49, 71, 73

American Board for Certification of Teacher Excellence (ABCTE), 81, 85–86, 161

American Educational Research Association (AERA), 147–148, 154

American Federation of Teachers (AFT), 33, 84–85
American Institutes for Research, 79
Angus, D. L., 27, 28, 29
Ashton, P., 58
Association of Teacher Educators, 43

B

Baccalaureate and Beyond Longitudinal Studies (USDoE), 9
Bachelor's degrees, number of, 10–11
Ballou, Dale, 57–58
Barclay, R., 97
Beginning Teacher Support and Assessment Program (BTSA), 75
Bell, Terrell, 32–33
Berliner, David, 37
Bersin, Allan D., 98–99, 100
Beyond Demographics: Who Enters and Completes Alternative Credential Programs in California (Chin and Young), 100
Birkeland, S. E., 146
Blair, J., 162
Bliss, T., 53–54, 58
Bogart, Joanne, 48, 144
Boyd, Donald, 106, 144, 148–149
Boyer, Ernest L., 37, 38
Boyer Topics, 38
Brannan, L., 146
Branscomb, Lewis M., 47
Brewer, D. J., 144, 145
Broughman, S. P., 13
Brown, D., 143–144
Brown, Frank, 37
Bush, George H. W., 35, 69–70, 77–78, 87
Bush, George W., 72

C

California
  alternate route programs, 92, 95, 98–102, 169–174
  assessment in, 75
  certification in, 34, 81, 161
  creation of alternate routes, 40–41
  District Intern program, 100–102, 169–170

Early Completion Intern Option, 170–172
  providers for alternate routes, 110
  retention of teachers in, 99–100
  teacher graduates in, 82
  teacher training in, 96, 99, 163
  Teaching Foundations Examination, 86
  University Intern Credential, 173–174
California Commission on Teacher Credentialing (CCTC), 40–41, 100, 101
CalState Teach, 100
Campbell, Alan K., 47
Campbell, Ernest Q., 30
Candidates
  assessment of, 120–121
  costs to, 123–124, 149–150 (*See also* Federal government, grants to teachers)
  support for, 119–121
Career changers, 80, 137
Carnegie Forum on Education and the Economy, 45, 46–48, 50
Certification
  competency-based, 103–104
  criteria for, 120, 122
  emergency, 6, 7, 39, 40, 63
  history of, 27–29
  Master Teacher, 85
  on state report cards, 72–73
  types received, 122
Certification directors, pressure on, 60–61
Chester, D., 62
Chin, Elaine, 100, 102
Civil Rights Act, 29–30
Classification of alternate routes, 62–63
Clifford, G. J., 45
Clinton, Bill, 35, 71, 74
Cochran-Smith, M., 147
Cohen-Vogel, L., 31
Cohorts, 119
Coleman, James. S., 30
Coleman Report (*Equality of Educational Opportunity*), 30

Colleges
  in alternate route programs, 114,
    116–118
  support for candidates, 120
  teacher, 28, 58
Commission to Study Teacher
  Preparation Programs in
  New Jersey Colleges, 35
Committee on Education and the
  Workforce, 74
Community colleges, role of, 162–163
Competency approach, 42–43
*Conflicting Missions: Teachers
  Unions and Educational Reform*
  (Ballou and Podgursky), 57–58
Conklin, H., 147
Connecticut, alternate route of,
  53–54, 161
Connecticut Education Enhancement
  Act, 53
Cooperman, Saul, 36–37, 39
Core academic subjects, 77
Cornett, Lynn M., 42, 59–60
Cost, to candidates, 123–124, 149–150.
  See also Federal government,
  grants to teachers

D

Darling-Hammond, Linda, 55–56, 58
Data, aggregation of, 30
Decker, Paul, 150
Defense Activity for Non-Traditional
  Education Support (DANTES), 68
Delayed entrants, 13, 16
Deregulation of teaching, 75–76
Dill, V. S., 42, 54
Disclosure requirements in HEA,
  70–71, 73
Distance learning, intern program, 100
District-based model, 42–43
District Intern program (California),
  100–102
Dougherty, P. H., 9
Drill sergeants, as teachers, 68

E

Earley, Penelope M., 31, 71, 73
Economic Opportunity Act, 30

Education
  approved programs, 28
  expense of, 40, 131, 133
  inequalities in, 30
  for teachers, 28–29, 34, 51
Education and Professional Standards
  Board (EPSB), Kentucky, 107
Education Commission of the States
  (ECS), 35, 147, 162–163
Education Professions Development
  Act, 31–32
Educator Preparation Institutes (EPIs)
  (Florida), 104–105
Elementary and Secondary
  Education Act. *See* No Child
  Left Behind Act
Enrollment projections, 93
Epps, Edgar, 37
Equality of Educational Opportunity
  (Coleman and Campbell), 30
ERIC Digest, 49
Ethnic minorities
  alternate route teachers, 98, 102, 104
  in classroom evaluations, 54–55
  recruitment for teaching, 48, 54–55,
    56, 133–134
  shortage in teaching, 42
  from Troops to Teachers, 69
*Evaluation of American Board Teacher
  Certification* (Glazerman and
  Tuttle), 85
Evaluation of Teacher Preparation Models
  (USDoE), 150
*Exploratory Study of Teacher Alternative
  Certification and Retraining
  Programs, An* (Adelman), 50

F

Fallon, Daniel C., 148, 164
Federal government
  and alternate routes, 69–70
  grants to teachers, 77–79, 81–82
  requirements of, 154
  role of in education, 29–32
Feistritzer, C. Emily, 3–4, 12, 37, 54,
    58, 59, 61–62, 68, 69, 75, 91,
    105, 106, 125, 127, 140
Fenstermacher, Gary D., 57

Ferrini-Mundy, J., 144–145
Finn, Chester E., 56–57
Floden, R. E., 57, 144–145
Flood, Pam, 104
Florida
alternate route programs, 92, 95,
103–105
Educator Preparation Institutes
(EPIs), 104–105
teacher training in, 162
Florida Statutes, 104
Fullan, M., 45, 46
Fully prepared, defined, 55
Futrell, Mary Hatwood, 47, 48

G
Gardner, David P., 32–33
Gardner, John W., 47
Georgia
alternate routes in, 95, 161
certification in, 81
teacher graduates in, 82
Giamatti, A. Bartlett, 32–33
Glazerman, Steven, 85
Goals 2000: Educate America
Act, 35
Goebel, S., 143
Goldhaber, D. D., 144, 145
Goodlad, J. I., 45
Gottlieb, Jay, 37
Great Society, 29–30
Grossman, 145
Grow Your Own route, Nevada, 161
"Growing Better Teachers in the
Garden State" (Klagholz), 39
Guthrie, J. W., 45

H
Haberman, Martin, 43–45
Hamburg, David A., 47
Hawk, P. P., 143
Hazlett, J. S., 51
Hechinger, Fred M., 47
Herbert, Karen. S., 102
Higher Education Act (HEA), 30–31,
68, 69–73, 74–75
Higher Education Facilities
Act, 29

Highly qualified teachers (HQTs)
from alternate routes, 142, 162
defined, 76
requirements for, 72, 76–77, 130,
154, 155–160
waivers for, 82–83
Holmes, Henry W., 45
Holmes Group, 45–46
Holton, Gerald, 32–33
Honig, Bill, 47
Houston, W. R., 145
Houston Alternative Certification
Program, 52
Houston Independent School District
(HISD), 42, 143
How Changes in Entry Requirements Alter
the Teacher Workforce And Affect
Student Achievement (Boyd), 106,
144, 148–149
Humphrey, D. C., 148
Hunt, James. B., Jr., 35, 47
Hutton, J. B., 55, 145

I
Idaho, 161
Illinois, alternate route programs in,
92–93
Incentives, for student performance, 48
Indiana, 89, 91
Inner cities, teachers in, 69
Insights into Alternative Certification
(Humphrey and Wechsler), 148
Institutions of higher education (IHE),
52, 153–154
Integrated Postsecondary Education Data
System, "Completions Survey"
(IPEDS-C), 9
Internships, 99, 100–102, 105
Islas, R. M., 163
iteAChTexas (I Teach Texas), 110

J
Johnson, Lyndon B., 29, 31
Journal of Negro Education, 54

K
Kanstoroom, Marci, 75–76
Katz, Vera, 47

Kean, Tom, 34, 35, 36–37, 47
Keegan, L. G., 33
Kennedy, John F., 31
Kennedy, M. M., 58
Kentucky
    alternate routes in, 95, 106–108, 161
    production of teachers in, 107
Kentucky Education Professional
    Standards Board, 107
Kerchner, Charles T., 40, 41
Klagholz, Leo, 35, 36, 38, 39, 60,
    63–64, 87
Kopp, Wendy, 65

L

Lanier, Judith E., 45, 47
Lapointe, Archie, 37
Leenhouts, Thelma, 78–79
Levine, Arthur, 58, 153
Lezotte, Lawrence, 37
Liberal arts, 36
Licenses
    defined, 3
    emergency, 44, 59
    requirements for, 58–59, 60
    temporary, 106
*Literature Review of Research on
    Alternative Certification* (Birkeland
    and Peske), 146
Local educational agencies (LEAs),
    52, 77, 166
Los Angeles Unified School District
    (LAUSD), 40–41, 52
Louisiana, alternate routes in,
    95, 161
Lutz, F. W., 55, 145

M

Mabry, M., 65
MacDonald, Robert H., 68
Maddox, Kathryn, 37
Madrid, Arturo, 47
Maine, 91
Malcolm, Shirley M., 47
Males, in teaching, 98, 102, 104,
    133–134
Marshall, F., 145
Maryland, 161, 162–163

Master of arts in teaching (MAT),
    61, 81, 98, 123
McDavid, T., 145
McDiarmid, G. W., 145
McKenna, B. A., 144
McKenna, M. C., 144
McKeon, Howard P., 74
McKibbin, M. D., 40, 41, 54
Mentors and mentoring
    established teachers for, 35, 92, 104
    importance of, 118–119
    use of in alternate routes, 62, 84–85
Michie, Joan, 48, 144
Military Career Transition
    Program, 68
Miller, J. W., 144
Milton, Sande, 104
Misassignment, 20, 44, 74
Mississippi, 161
Mobility, of teachers, 135–137
Montana, 91
Moore, M, 76

N

Nation at Risk, A (NCEE), 33–35
*Nation Prepared: Teachers for the 21st
    Century* (CFEE), 46–48
National Association for Alternative
    Certification, 151
National Association of State Directors
    of Teacher Education and
    Certification (NASDTEC), 29, 163
National Board for Professional
    Teaching Standards (NBPTS),
    48, 163
National Center for Alternative
    Certification (NCAC), 98, 110,
    113, 117–124, 151, 164
National Center for Education
    Information (NCEI), 3–4, 17–18,
    61–64, 75, 125–126, 155–160, 164
National Center for Education
    Statistics, The (NCES), 93–94
National Commission on Excellence in
    Education (NCEE), 28, 32–33, 34
National Council for Accreditation
    of Teacher Education (NCATE),
    29, 57–58

National Defense Education Act
(NDEA), 29
National Education Association (NEA),
12–13, 29, 33, 57, 84
National Governors Association
(NGA), 35
Natriello, G., 54, 144
Nebraska, 91, 162
Nevada, 91, 161
New Hampshire, 161
New Jersey
alternate route programs, 35–40, 92,
95–98, 161, 166–168
and emergency licenses, 59
new teachers in, 97
production of teachers in, 37, 95–96
Provisional Teacher Program,
38–40, 52, 96–98, 166–168
revisions in alternate route, 98
school districts in, 109–110
in teacher certification, 3–4, 6–7,
34–35, 87, 152
teachers in, 82, 144
undergraduate education programs
in, 36
New Jersey Department of
Education, 97
New Jersey State Board of Higher
Education, 36
New York
alternate route programs, 92,
105–106
Alternative Teacher Certification—
Transitional B, 106
teacher graduates in, 82
Transcript Analysis in, 105
New York City, pathways to teaching,
148–149, 162
New York City Teaching Fellows
Program, 162
No Child Left Behind Act
authorization of, 30
funding of, 72, 74
and market forces for teachers,
8, 153
reauthorization of, 76–79
requirements of, 76–79, 130
Non-Regulatory Guidance (USDoE), 83

Normal schools, 28
North Carolina, 144, 161
North Dakota, 89, 91

O
Ohio, 92–93
Oliver, B., 40
Osguthorpe, R. T., 46

P
Paige, Rod, 76, 80, 81, 87
Panel on Preparation of Teachers
(New Jersey), 37
Participants, in alternate route
programs, 52–53
Passport to Teaching (ABCTE),
81, 85–86, 105, 161, 163
Peace Corps, 31, 65
Pedagogy, instruction in, 39–40,
55, 139
Peer review, 118
Pennsylvania, 92–93, 161
Peske, H. G., 146
Podgursky, Mike, 57–58
Practice teaching, 35–36, 39–40
Practicing teachers, 130
Professional development school
(PDS), 46
Professional occupations, teachers
from, 127–128
Profile of Alternate Route Teachers
(NCEI), 127–142
Program names, 59–61
Program providers, state-approved,
109–113
Projections of Education Statistics to 2015
(NCES), 93–94
"Proliferation of Alternative Routes
to Certification in Special
Education, The" (Rosenberg
and Sindelar), 147
Provisional Teacher Program, New
Jersey, 38–40, 52, 96–98, 166–168
Public school system, 18–26

Q
Qualifications, "special," 63
Quality, quantifying, 84

R

Ravitch, Diane, 9, 32, 33
Ray, L., 54
Reagan, R., 34
Reciprocity, 163
Reichardt, R., 146
Report cards, state, 72–73
Requirements, academic, 33–34
Reserve pool, 53
Retraining, 50
Rhode Island, 89, 91
Rise and Stall of Teacher Education Reform, The (Fullan), 46
Rollefson, Mary, 12, 13
Rosenberg, M. S., 147
Rosenshine, Barak, 37
Roth, Robert A., 43
Rotherham, Andrew, 74

S

Salaries, 48, 53
SASS (Schools and Staffing Survey), 13, 26
Sawyer, J., 67, 68
Scannell, D. P., 31
Schmidt, M. W., 143
Schneider, E., 31
Scholarships, 123
Scholastic Aptitude Test (SAT), 32, 35
School districts
  alternate route programs of, 104–105, 118
  numbers of, 18–19
  responsibility of, 44
  size and enrollment of, 20, 21
  training by, 49
Schools
  distribution of, 25–26
  flexibility in, 54, 77
  high-need, 66–67
  measuring performance of, 74
  size and enrollment of, 20, 22–23
  by state, 24–25
  urban, 147
Schools and Staffing Survey (SASS), 13, 26
Seaborg, Glenn, T, 32–33

Secretary's Annual Report on Teacher Quality (USDoE), 80–81
Serial No. 106-37, 75, 76
Shanker, Albert, 47
Sindelar, P. T., 147
Smith, G. P., 54
South Carolina, 95, 162
Southern Regional Education Board (SREB), 51, 59–60
Special education, 147
Spellings, Magaret, 80, 82–83
Spring, Joel, 33
SRI International, 148
Stafford, D., 42
Standards
  of educational performance, 27–29, 34, 48
State educational agencies (SEAs), 52, 77
States, 72–73, 155–160. *See also* individual states
Steffensen, J., 31
Stoddart, T., 40–41, 57, 146
Student aid, 70–71
Studies, on alternate routes, 143, 144–147
Studying Teacher Education (Zeichner and Conklin), 147–148
Stutz, T., 86
Supplemental instruction, 76
Surveys
  of alternate route teachers, 126–127
  of potential teachers, 164
  responses to, 127

T

Task Force on Education for Economic Growth, 35
Teach For America (TFA)
  in alternate route programs, 63, 149
  described, 65–67
  influence of, 87, 130
  in Nebraska, 91
  opportunities from, 67
Teacher Centers Program, 31–32
Teacher Corps, 31–32, 65
Teacher Education and Professional Standards (TEPS), 29

Teacher experience models, 149
Teacher preparation, variations
    in, 58
Teacher Preparation Research (Wilson,
    Floden and Mundy), 144–145
Teacher quality
    improving, 77
    in K-12 education, 74–76
Teacher Quality Enhancement
    Grants, 71–72
Teacher Trainee Program (LAUSD),
    40–41
Teachers
    alternate route, 125–126, 127–128
    background of, 15, 126, 129–131
    degrees of, 10, 11, 130–131
    demand for, 7, 12–17, 26, 44, 47,
        82, 137
    designations for, 13–14
    efficacy of, 147
    emergency, 44
    evaluation of, 72–73, 168
    experienced, 13
    hierarchy of, 45
    highly qualified (*See* Highly
        qualified teachers (HQTs))
    new, 12–13, 17
    potential, 1, 164
    as professionals, 47
    provisional, 38
    quality of, 71–72, 75
    recruitment of, 66, 125
    retention of, 96–100, 103, 147,
        148, 150
    returning, 16
    rural, 134–135, 136
    source of, 16
    training of, 45–46, 48
    urban, 44–45, 134–135, 136
Teaching
    developing competence in,
        140–141
    out-of-field (misassignment),
        20, 44, 74
    reasons for, 138–139
    satisfaction with, 141
    while learning, 119
Teaching Fellows, 149–150, 162

Temporary Licenses, New York, 106
TEPS (Teacher Education and
    Professional Standards), 29
Tests
    SAT, 32, 35
    scores of, 33, 150
Texas
    alternate route programs, 41–43,
        92, 95, 102–103, 161, 174–176
    certification in, 34, 81, 161
    emergency licenses in, 44
    iteAChTexas (I Teach Texas), 110
    providers for alternate routes, 110
    retention of teachers, 103
    studies of alternate routes in,
        143–144
    teacher graduates in, 82, 96,
        102–103, 111–112, 127
    teacher training in, 163
    Temporary Teacher Certificate, 86
Texas State Board for Educator
    Certification, 111–112
Texas Statutes, 42
TFA (Teach For America). *See* Teach
    For America
Third Annual Progress Report (Flood
    and Milton), 104
Title I, 76–77, 83
Title II
    assessment of teachers in, 72–73
    compliance with, 80
    and flexibility, 77
    purposes of, 71–72, 78
    reports, 81–84
Title V, part D, 69–73
Training
    of teachers, 49
    for TFA participants, 66
Transcript analysis, 62–63, 105
Transition to Teaching, 77, 79,
    89, 91
Transitional Teacher Certification
    route, Nebraska, 162
Troops to Teachers, 63, 67–69,
    87, 163
    in Nebraska, 91
Troubled Crusade, The (Ravitch), 32
Tuttle, Christina, 85

U

Unions
American Federation of Teachers
(AFT), 33, 84–85
National Education Association
(NEA), 12–13, 29, 33, 57, 84
role of, 57, 84–85
Urban, Wayne, 33
U.S. Department of Education, 48–53
U.S. Department of Education
(USDoE), 8, 9, 11, 12–13, 16, 18,
19, 21–26, 30, 71–72, 76, 78,
81–82, 83–84, 129, 134
U.S. Government Accountability
Office (GAO), 68, 77

V

Van Tassel, P., 37, 38
Virginia, alternate routes in, 95

Visiting Lecturers, New York, 105–106
Vocational Education Act, 29

W

Wagoner, Jennings, 33
Washington, 161
Wechsler, M. E., 148
Williamson, 145
Wilson, S. M., 58, 144–145, 146
Wirtz, Willard, 32
Wirtz panes, 32
Wong, M. J., 46

Y

Young, Beverly, 75
Young, John W., 100, 102

Z

Zeichner, K., 147
Zumwalt, Karen, 54, 58, 59, 144